CHRISTOPHER'S TALKS TO CATHOLIC PARENTS

By the same author :

CHRISTOPHER'S TALKS TO THE LITTLE ONES
CHRISTOPHER'S TALKS TO CATHOLIC CHILDREN (TWO BOOKS)

CHRISTOPHER'S TALKS TO CATHOLIC PARENTS

BY
DAVID L. GREENSTOCK

With an Introduction by
CHARLES BURNS, M.R.C.S., L.R.C.P., D.P.M.

968
LONDON
BURNS OATES

NIHIL OBSTAT : GEORGIVS SMITH, S.T.D.,PH.D.
CENSOR DEPVTATVS
IMPRIMATVR : E. MORROGH BERNARD
VICARIVS GENERALIS
WESTMONASTERII : DIE XVII NOVEMBRIS MCML

MADE AND PRINTED IN GREAT BRITAIN BY
CHARLES BIRCHALL AND SONS, LTD.,
LONDON AND LIVERPOOL
FOR BURNS OATES AND WASHBOURNE, LTD.,
28 ASHLEY PLACE, LONDON, S.W.I.

First published 1951

TO
THE HOLY FAMILY

MODEL FOR CATHOLIC PARENTS AND CHILDREN

this book is respectfully dedicated

INTRODUCTION

by CHARLES BURNS, M.R.C.S., L.R.C.P., D.P.M.

I T MAY SEEM STRANGE THAT HERE IS A BOOK ON HOW TO BRING up children, including babies, by a Catholic priest. We may wonder how he has acquired the necessary knowledge or what prompted him to do it, but this is not really our business. We are concerned with the question of what we can learn from it and how much of it we can put to good effect. Fr. Greenstock presumably wrote it because he felt that it was very much needed; and he was quite right. Such a book as this cannot tell us all there is to know about the subject any more than we can hope to bring up our children perfectly, for the simple reason that both the author and ourselves are human beings.

Our reaction may be: Why bother to tell us what we already know in a rough and ready way? We have all been ' brought up,' we have learnt from the faults as well as the virtues of our parents; we Catholic parents especially have our traditions—of responsibility, authority, moral training and so forth—and we don't want anything which smacks of new-fangled psychological ideas. This, however, would not be the reaction of many intelligent parents nowadays; they tend, if anything, to be too anxious about their capacity for bringing up children, not only with regard to physical matters such as calories and vitamins, but even more with regard to such questions as discipline, freedom, and education generally.

For this attitude, it may be said, psychologists are largely to blame, but whether you consider psychology a good or bad thing, you cannot escape from it: we are all psychologists nowadays.

If you have glanced at the book you will note however that the author hardly mentions the word psychology and uses none of its technical terms, and may conclude that he is only using his

vii

commonsense knowledge and traditional ideas. I maintain, however, that the teachings of modern child psychology are implicit in what he says, and without them the book would probably not have been written at all.

It is both as a psychologist and as the father of four that I commend this book to Catholic parents. I have not consciously played the part of psychological parent with my children—probably I have often been most unpsychological—and in any case the mother is the more important of the two! But in twenty years as a psychiatrist I have seen all too much of the effects of wrong upbringing and faulty attitudes. Of one thing we can be certain: that the core of most neurotic attitudes and problems in behaviour is to be found in the lack of affection, or the wrong kind of love, in the earliest years of a child's life. It might almost be said: you can do what you like with your children so long as you love them. " Love, and do what you will."

It must be the right kind of love: not possessive, selfish, demanding or sentimental, but deep and spontaneous. Understanding, warmth, tolerance, security, order: these are some of the elements in that love which is a condition of healthy growth. The marks of wrong parental attitudes are: harshness, excessive control, rigidity, possessiveness, intolerance, fussiness, weakness, and over-anxiety. To be relaxed in mind and body in your dealings with your children is a golden rule.

One of the commonest faults of parents in my experience is to make too high a demand on a child for its age; to expect it to conform too quickly to adult standards; to be irritable and discouraging because it doesn't.

With regard to the earliest years the trend in child psychology has been right away from the kind of thing that was considered ' scientific ' about twenty or thirty years ago (and still is in some quarters); one of these is feeding strictly by calories and clocks, rather than what this particular baby needs, and the other is over-strict habit training.

Now one of the main aspects of Father Greenstock's teaching where I feel inclined to differ is with this matter of habit training, and giving the baby just so much of everything as *we* think is for its own good. I think that if I am to sponsor this book with sincerity, it is right that I should mention a disagreement of this kind which is one of stress or emphasis rather than of principle.

I felt that, in reading what he has written about this early period, parents might conclude that they must be very strict with their babies if disorders later are to be avoided, whereas I think that he starts children on the path of self-denial rather too early —which may lead to an even more grasping nature! Also parents might gain the impression that, given the proper 'training' of character, progress should be in a continuous line, whereas there are many ups and downs, many phases of slight or serious difficulty or upset, which will mostly pass off with patience and forbearance.

Father Greenstock may feel that the pendulum has swung too far towards tolerance and excessive giving-in to the demands of babies and children, but I feel that there is still too little in many quarters, though in others there is foolish indulgence and spoiling. A tolerance based on a real understanding of the ways of early childhood, together with a great deal of patience and elasticity, though not inconsistency, in the matter of training, will avoid useless clashes of wills with consequent strains for both. We will agree, I feel sure, that is is very hard to achieve a golden mean.

I have dwelt at this length on matters affecting the earliest years because these are so crucial, and I would urge above all that parents should be natural, spontaneous, and *happy* with their babies: which most of them are, thank God!

I might also disagree with Father Greenstock in using " original sin " as a reason for smacking, not necessarily about smacking as such, but rather because original sin is a doctrine so easily misunderstood!

I must however say a few words about the rest of the book, since I have already taken up too much time and space on " quiet homes and first beginnings."

Father Greenstock has many wise things to say about adolescence—that other difficult period. The years between toddling and adolescence seem almost simple in comparison, though they are just as important.

The subject of sex has been handled at length, and with such care that it might almost strike too much awe into the parent, trembling at the idea of these talks with son or daughter. It will not be so difficult for the next generation, we hope, to talk to their children on the matter as it seems to be for ourselves— the products still of too much prudery.

Where the author, writing as a priest, has the advantage, is that he can achieve a blend of the natural and the supernatural. Avoiding the mistake of thinking that merely by stressing the supernatural you can cover up the mistakes and deficiencies of the natural, he can pass easily and smoothly from the one realm to the other, and show us how the spiritual can irradiate the humble necessary actions and duties of everyday life; how religion can give us a sense of tranquillity, order, and purpose, in our dealings with our children.

In this book, so wise and so practical, Catholic parents will find just what they are needing in the way of guidance, from the simplest material details to the undiscovered ends of the Spirit.

FOREWORD

Dear Parents,

As you can see, this book is dedicated to the Holy Family, your Model as parents. That Family must be your standard because the world needs saints, not merely in the priesthood or in religious orders whether of men or women, but also in the workshops, the docks, the factories and, most of all, in the family. Yours is a wonderful dignity and vocation, but it is also a great responsibility. When your marriage is blessed with children God is putting into your care souls which are destined to reach heaven ; but they can only do that with your constant help and guidance. The present state of civilization makes your task a difficult one, because God's standards are not those of the world. Your task is to bring up your children in such a way that they will be good Catholics in a world which has, for the most part, forgotten Christ and His teaching and knows little or nothing of His Church. Our generation has seen many books about education, but it has also seen a deplorable relaxation of even the most fundamental moral standards. The reason is not difficult to find. The world has forgotten the sublime dignity of man and the fact that there can be no true education which is not wholly directed towards eternity rather than the material things of this world. Never allow any consideration to make you forget that your primary obligation is to train souls for the Kingdom of God. That is why St. John Chrysostom says :—
" What greater task is there than training the mind and forming the habits of the young ? "

This book has been written to help you in that task; but you must remember that no book can succeed unless it has behind it your effort and your whole-hearted co-operation, together with prayer and good example. Experience has shown that, no matter how good the education in any particular Catholic school may be, it can never take the place of the training which the children receive in their homes. For that reason it would be impossible to over-estimate the importance of your task, and for good or evil the impression you make on your children's characters will be a lasting one. Think often on those words of Christ, " Whosoever shall receive one such child as this in My name, receiveth Me ".

In conclusion, I would like to express my grateful thanks to those parents who have written to me so kindly about the other books in this series. Their encouragement has been of great help to me, and I hope that this book, which is the reply to requests from many of them, will prove of some use to all Catholic parents in their responsible task of teaching their children to love God.

Yours in Christ,

CHRISTOPHER.

Feast of St. George,   Colegio de Ingleses,
April 23rd, 1950.   Valladolid.

CONTENTS

CONTENTS

CHAPTER ONE

THE PARENTAL OBLIGATIONS

THE FUNDAMENTAL OBLIGATIONS OF GOOD CATHOLIC PARENTS can be summed up in one simple sentence: they are expected to bring into the world and to educate, not merely good citizens of the civil State, but mainly good citizens of the Kingdom of God, the Church. Life is a very complex thing, and just because it is complex we have to make quite sure that the more important elements in it occupy the first place. This does not mean that other secondary things should be neglected entirely, but merely that, where there is a question of choice between them and the other more important thing, then they will take a second place. Consequently, although your primary obligation will be to see after the religious education of your children this need not imply any neglect of their secular training. As we shall soon see, the very opposite is the truth, because education is one whole, implying the formation of a complete character, which will be able to stand firm against any possible combination of adverse circumstances, with definite principles of self-government which will be applied no matter what the particular trials which the person concerned may have to face.

The most important thing in life is our eternal salvation, which has to be won by our own efforts aided by the grace of God. Those efforts will be directed mainly against three evils which are outlined for us simply but very accurately in the Catechism, namely, the world, the flesh and the devil. Most of us have to live a Catholic life in the world with all its difficulties, and our eternal salvation will depend on our ability to live that life in harmony with those great principles laid down for us by Christ, our Master and our Example. Even some Catholics make the great mistake of thinking that religion is something which is separate from life as such. They think of it as a part of life which cannot be expected to exercise its influence at every moment of the day. The contrary is, of course, the truth. Religion is necessarily identified with life under all its aspects, running through it as a golden thread runs through a piece of tapestry, forming the whole and directing it to its final end which is the beatific vision of God in heaven. Your obligation, then, in general terms, is to prepare your children to take up this fight for God in the world and to win it.

We shall lay special emphasis in the course of this book on the importance of the home and the family life in education. Perhaps, at the very outset, it will be as well to clarify our notion of the importance of the family life in order to avoid repetition later on. It is no exaggeration to say that the home life of the child is the one single factor in education which can either make or break a character and which can secure eternal salvation. This is true, not merely in the field of religious education as such, but also in that of secular training through all its branches. Notice, we have said that it is the one *single* factor; by which we intend to convey the idea that it is the element in education which controls and governs all the others. If the home and family life is as it should be, then other factors which undoubtedly have a great influence on the child's education will be welded into a coherent whole. On the other hand, if there is something missing in that home life, then those other factors, however important and even necessary they may be, will never supply that lack entirely. For that reason Pope Pius XI, speaking of the conditions which influence the child during his period of formation, says:

" The first natural and necessary element in this environment, as regards education, is the family, and this precisely because so ordained by the Creator Himself. Accordingly, that education, as a rule, will be more effective and lasting which is received in a well-ordered and well-disciplined family; and more efficacious in proportion to the clear and constant example set, first by the parents, and then by other members of the household."*

* *Christian Education of Youth*, C.T.S. trans., pp. 33-34.

This clear statement has even more force today than it had when first written. The whole tendency of our modern society is to belittle the obligations of the parents and to propagate the false notion that either the State or the school can do all that the parents did formerly, and do it ever so much better than they could. Now, this is a very dangerous doctrine, and one which the Church has always resisted and will always resist to the very limit of her power. She has always laid stress on the fact, through her Popes and theologians, that the family has the prior right in this matter of education and that no power on earth can take away that right lawfully. Thus, Pope Pius XI, in the same Encyclical, says:

" . . . The mission of education regards, above all, primarily the Church and the family, and this by natural and divine law . . . therefore it cannot be slighted, cannot be evaded, cannot be supplanted."

This natural right on the part of the parents gives rise to a corresponding obligation on the part of the Civil authority to see to it that parents have full and perfect liberty under the moral law in this matter of education and that they have every opportunity to fulfil this obligation in a fitting manner. Only when individual parents fail completely in their duty may the State intervene to remove their children from their care and supply what is lacking in those families by taking on itself the duty of the children's education.

The very basis of the present fight for our Catholic schools turns on this point that we, as parents and as Catholics, have a right to educate our children in their own religion. That right comes from the natural and the divine law and cannot be surrendered. A further point which has not been sufficiently stressed is that, only if these facilities are granted to us, shall we be able to educate good citizens for the State itself. We shall see in greater detail later why this is so. The State, therefore, has the grave obligation of giving us every facility, not merely for the secular education of our Catholic children, but also for their spiritual and religious education because, although education may consist of several different things, in itself it is *one whole*. The idea of education is to produce and to mould a unified personality, and if one of the elements in education is either neglected or frustrated, then that unity will never be achieved satisfactorily. For these reasons we are fighting, and shall go on fighting, to maintain our Catholic schools and also the full rights of parents to use them how and when they choose.

You may ask what this has got to do with the subject with which we are dealing at the moment, namely education in the home and family. Simply this, that school education should be a continuation of that given in the home by the parents, and is in no way a substitute for it. Teachers, however competent they may be, are only the delegates and the representatives of the parents; and in consequence, the parents have the right to see to it that the teachers to whom they delegate the task of helping in the education of their children should be fitted for that task, not merely from the point of view of secular learning, but also from the religious aspect. Also, this problem of our Catholic schools implies that, while present conditions endure, the duties of Catholic parents are liable to be more onerous than they were before. In those cases where children have to be sent to non-Catholic schools owing to the obstacles put in our way by government policy in this matter, it falls on the parents to see to it that the religious education of their children is adequately provided for, and that means that they will have to be prepared to supply much of that religious training themselves. It is not a mere matter of teaching them the answers to the questions in the Catechism. We have to build citizens for the Kingdom of God, and there is much more to that than merely teaching them the truths of Faith and the obligations of the Catholic moral code. We have to teach them to *be* Catholics and to live and think in a Catholic way.

There is, however, yet another reason why the duties of Catholic parents are more difficult nowadays than they were, shall we say, in the time of our own parents. Without over-exaggerating the modern difficulties, all must admit that the system and methods of modern civilization are not conducive to the living of a good Catholic life in the world as we understand that obligation. It is not so much that man's inclinations towards evil have changed, because they have remained much the same ever since the Fall. The difficulty seems to come from the fact that, in our time, more people have actually followed those evil inclinations and have revolted against the moral law. There has been a slow but effective drifting away from religion. In past ages those who broke the Commandments of God at least admitted that they had done wrong and that they would like to keep that law if they could. Nowadays people refuse to admit that their actions are against the moral law. In a word, the sense of sin has been lost, and with it the idea of the need for God's help and His pardon for wrong-doing. The revolt against God is much more open and unashamed.

In our parents' day life was much more simple. There was very little need to contend with the influence of the cinema, for example, with its doctrines of freedom from all duty towards God and its glorification of sex in all its forms. The newspapers were much more " sedate " in every way and did not cater—at least to the extent they do nowadays—for depraved tastes in sensationalism, not to mention other evils of the modern Press which are no less dangerous even if more subtle. Nor is there any need for us to speak of the modern trends in literature, particularly the novel, which in many instances has become the chief instrument for the propagation of doctrines which are radically opposed to the teachings of Christ and of His Church. As a result of all these influences the whole atmosphere of modern life has become tainted with religious indifference and immorality which goes under the specious name of freedom from inhibitions and controls. The fashion today is to make a show of indifference to religion, and that does far more harm than anything else, particularly among the modern youth. We are living as Catholics in an era of world history which is, in many ways, far more dangerous than the times of active persecution in the past, because now there are new methods being used in the campaign against religion which are more delicate and subtle. The circumstances of our modern civilization have brought about this change, and we are expected to live in the midst of this poisonous atmosphere and to bring up our children in it. On our part it would be stupid, if not definitely criminal, to refuse to recognize these difficulties or to act as if they did not exist. We must face the facts as we find them. On the other hand, it is no use our being over-pessimistic about these difficulties. What we must do, as Catholic parents, is face up to them with a courage born of our Faith, in the sure knowledge that God, who never fails His children in their hour of need, will not leave us to fight against these evils without the aid of His grace, which is not merely sufficient for us but which alone can bring us safely through all our trials.

For these reasons which we have outlined, and for others too, modern Catholic parents need great supernatural courage. Above all there is need of a firm resolution which will be put into effective action that our children will be given the very best education which we can provide for them, both spiritually and materially, so that their characters may be fitted in every way for the struggle which we know to be before them in the world. From the very first day they go to school they are bound to come into contact, in an ever-increasing degree, with the atmosphere of materialism and indifference which pervades modern society. For this reason the education which they receive at home is of supreme importance. It is the family life which will bring them safely through the trials of this life to their eternal happiness in heaven.

As you can see, then, it is of supreme importance that you, as parents, should have a clear idea in your minds from the very beginning of the difficulties you have to face and also of the great dignity which is yours. There is no one, neither the State nor the school—not even the Church—who can perform this task as well as you can. It is your great privilege to be the pivot on which the whole education of your children turns. Those human souls have been placed by God in your hands. That constitutes your obligation and according to the manner in which you fulfil it, so you will be judged by God.

Obviously no book can ever give you all those little individual directions which will suit your children exactly, mainly because there is a large element of truth in what all parents think, at least in their hearts, that there was never another child just like theirs! Apart from that, so many individual factors have to be taken into consideration in each individual case that it would be quite impossible to discuss them all in one book. The main purpose which the present writer has in mind is, not so much the laying down of hard and fast rules for individual cases, but rather to guide you in your task by discussing certain general principles which you yourselves can work out in actual practice. These principles will apply not merely to the question of religious education—although, because of its great importance, that branch of education will receive special attention—but also to education as a whole through the various stages of the child's life. Thus we shall endeavour to deal with such things as the preparation for parenthood, the preliminary education of the child in the home and in the family, the early school days, the whole of school life, at least in so far as it concerns the parents, and also that most difficult period of all, adolescence. Finally we shall have something to say about vocational guidance and the preparation for marriage. Throughout we shall keep in mind the basic principle which has been explained in this chapter, i.e. the parents' obligation to prepare good citizens of the State and of the Kingdom of God on earth, the Church.

Parents sometimes wonder why a book on this subject should be necessary at all. Surely Nature herself gives us all the guidance we need to bring up our children? In answering this question we must avoid two extremes. It would be a great mistake to imagine that book learning alone is the important thing. Very often the instinct which a mother has about her children is much more useful than any book. At the same time we must not think that books on this subject of child education are therefore useless. On the contrary, they can save us from making a great many mistakes. Without such books our education of our children would often be a " hit-or-miss " affair, and we cannot afford to take that risk because children are rather delicate things to handle. This is true not so much of their bodies but of their characters. A false move at the wrong moment can easily influence the whole of the child's future life, and it is that kind of mistake which can be so easily avoided by knowing something about the general principles of education. There are bound to be a certain number of problems arising in every family and most of them have very simple solutions. Frequently a book can put us on the track of those solutions by indicating the general lines which our handling of such problems should take. Above all, it is necessary that Catholics should have books at their disposal which have been written

by Catholics, for the simple reason that our Faith must pervade
and perfect the whole of our life, including this primary obligation of the religious and secular education of our children.

Remember too that, although education has always the same
end in view since the coming of Christ at least, i.e. the training
and formation of souls for heaven, it is still true to say that
different periods of the world's history have demanded slightly
different methods, since each generation has to deal with its
own special problems affecting the growing child. As an
example of this we have already mentioned the materialistic
atmosphere in which our children will have to live. The special
problems of our generation demand care and attention to detail
which was not required a generation or so earlier. Here again
a book is useful, because it can not only make us fully conscious
of these special problems, but also it can provide some kind of
an answer to them which, if not fully satisfactory in every
individual case, will at least serve as a guide to parents in actual
practice.

Also Catholic parents are in special need of some general
literature on this subject of child education because, by the very
nature of the case, they have to deal with certain moral problems
which do not affect other parents quite so much. We are not
speaking of the natural law, which is the same for us all, but of
such elements for sanctification as the Sacraments of the Church,
which have to be fitted into the child's training as an integral
part of his life, not as something which is in a section apart.
The whole idea of a Catholic education is this integration of
the supernatural and the natural which can never be understood
completely by any non-Catholic, however well intentioned and
competent in other ways. It is much better that such help
should come from Catholics who both understand the difficulties
and can give advice either as parents or as priests.

Once you understand both your obligations and the difficulties
which face you as parents, the next thing to stress is the great
importance of prayer. God is always willing to give us His
help and guidance, and this is especially true in the case of
parents who are trying their best to fulfil their obligations in
this matter of the education of their children. In many cases,
however, God has conditioned His help on our prayer, and for

that reason one of your most important tasks is to pray to Him for all the grace you need to carry out your duties to your children in a fitting manner. You should begin this campaign of prayer from the first moments of your married life, asking Our Lady's intercession, as the Mother of Christ, and that of St. Joseph, His foster-Father. Think occasionally of the example given us by the saints, especially the case of St. Monica, mother of St. Augustine, who never ceased praying for the conversion of her son, even when things seemed most dark and hopeless. It was due to her prayers that he finally became a great bishop and saint.

Lastly, we can find a great justification for a book such as this, which deals not merely with the religious aspects of education but also with the secular, in yet another quotation from Pope Pius XI's Encyclical on the Christian Education of Youth:

" For the love of Our Saviour, Jesus Christ, therefore, We implore pastors of souls, by every means in their power, by instructions and catechisms, by word of mouth and by written articles widely distributed, to warn Christian parents of their grave obligations. And this should be done, not in a merely theoretical and general manner, but with practical and specific application to the various responsibilities of parents touching the religious, moral and civil training of their children, and with indications of the methods best adapted to make their training effective, supposing always the influence of their own exemplary lives."

This chapter has been written in accordance with the wishes of the Pope as expressed in those words, in order that you may have, at the very outset, some idea of the scope of your parental obligations in this matter of education. If no mention has been made of such things as the obligation to look after the physical health of the child, his food and clothing, etc., that is merely because those things are taken for granted here. They will be dealt with at length in the chapters which follow. Your main duty is first of all a clear understanding of the fact that the obligation of educating your children belongs primarily to you. You can delegate others to help you in that task from time to time, but the main responsibility still remains on your shoulders.

In producing these children you have co-operated with Almighty God who created their souls and placed them in your care. Therefore that primary obligation and end of all good education, i.e. the salvation of your child's soul, must be kept in view all the time if this task is to be fulfilled in a fitting manner. The duty, as you can see, is a serious one, but at the same time the graces necessary to perform it worthily will never be lacking, provided you ask for them in your prayers.

CHAPTER TWO

PREPARATION FOR PARENTHOOD

I T IS A MATTER FOR REAL CONCERN HOW FEW PEOPLE MAKE any preparations—apart from the strictly material ones— for the great obligations of the married state. If any preparation is made this is usually limited to the collecting together of the necessary money to assure a reasonable start in life, together with a few lessons in cookery, perhaps, and home management. The real truth of the matter is, of course, that the remote preparation for marriage should have been made long before, during the years of our own education, and especially during the final stages of our life in and with the family. Education is one whole, and should fit us in every way to take our part in the world. For that reason we shall have a good deal to say about the parents' task in preparing their children for this obligation when, in the final stages of this book, we come to deal with the last few years of the children's life in the care of their parents. However, one or two of the basic principles which govern this remote preparation will not be out of place here, addressed to those who are thinking of getting married.

One of the most important factors in any happy marriage is, naturally, the character of the husband and wife; and character is largely a matter of good habits. As we shall see later on, one of the main purposes of education is to surround the will with a certain number of good habits which help us to act according to general moral principles. These habits cover a very wide field. Some of them are habits of thought; others govern the will itself, thus making it easier for us to act according to the dictates of our reason. Others, in their turn, govern the basic inclinations of our human nature, in order to make sure that we rule *them* instead of allowing them to rule *us*. Now, one of the most important elements in any remote preparation for the married state is to make sure that you, as an individual, have acquired these good habits. In other words, before we can assume the obligation of teaching and educating others we have to subject our own character to a severe test. In this matter of education we pass on what we have learnt from others, whether they be our parents or our teachers, together with the accumulation of our own experiences. In order to know fully what we have to try to produce in the character of our children we must first of all know, from our own experience, what is of advantage and what is of disadvantage, and this knowledge must cover the general fields of which we shall speak when we come to deal with the question of education in general and the purpose of it.

Consequently, make sure that your own character is well formed before you enter into this state which carries with it the obligation of forming the characters of others. If there is anything in your make-up which you know will not be of use to you, and which may even be the source of positive harm either to your partner in marriage or to your children, then make a firm attempt to overcome it and to acquire the opposite good habit *before* you get married. Even if you do not manage to overcome all your bad habits before marriage, at least you can know what they are, and so save yourself a good deal of unpleasantness. Perhaps a few examples will help you to understand exactly what this preparation implies. If you know that you are inclined to be very selfish, for instance, then you should attempt to cure yourself of that long before marriage, because there is nothing which will cause so much trouble in your married life as wanting your own way all the time and not knowing how to give and take. Marriage is definitely a " two horses in one cart " affair, and it will not work satisfactorily if one horse is pulling one way all the time and the other is digging his heels in! Again, you may have a habit of being untidy. That will have to go if you are looking forward to a married life of reasonable happiness and tranquillity, so see to it before you get married, and don't, whatever you do, leave it until after the wedding, in the vain hope that everything will turn out all right in the end. Have you learnt to control your bad temper, especially in the early morning ? If not, then now is the time to learn, because there is nothing so disruptive of domestic happiness as this. It usually means that while one partner goes off to work in a mood which is by no means conducive to hard work, the other will stay at home with plenty of time to prepare stinging retorts for the evening return of the beloved. It will also mean that your children may be subjected to constant scenes of domestic strife, which is not a good factor in their education. Sometimes conjugal bad temper is worked off on the children almost unconsciously, which is even worse for them. It is not fair, either to your future partner in life or to your children, to leave the correction of these bad habits until after marriage—it takes too long, for one thing, and often, while you are engaged in it the harm is done. This harm may not manifest itself at once, but it is sure to do so later in your life together. You should be able, with the help of a little reasonable self-examination, to think of other examples for yourselves, but if in any doubt consult your friends, or perhaps better still, take notice of the things your enemies say about you, because some of them may be true!

Then there is the very important question of your choice of a partner in life. If you were asked, when in your right mind, to choose a companion for a long journey or for a holiday you would not choose on the facts of mere looks or money, would you ? They would probably be the last qualifications which you would look for. Nor would you choose someone who might leave you in the middle of the holiday to go off with someone else. Yet there are many people who choose a companion for the grave obligations of the married state with far less care than they would choose a partner for a holiday. Remember in this connection that your own personal and primary obligation in life still obliges you, even although you are married, namely, the salvation of your own soul. That is all-important, and in the married state it implies certain things which are often not considered deeply enough. In the first place, you will also be expected to do all that you can to help in the salvation of the soul of your partner in life as well as the souls of your children. Also you will have to work out your own salvation in the family circle, and not apart from it. Therefore your choice of a partner in marriage will have to be governed primarily by this consideration. You need someone with whom you can be reasonably sure of saving your soul. That must never be forgotten, because if you fail in that primary obligation then your whole life, and not merely your marriage, has been a failure. It is with these factors in mind that you should set about the task of choosing your partner in life.

Obviously, you are going to have a better chance of living in harmony with someone who thinks and feels as you do, at least on the more important subjects—and one of those subjects is religion. That brings us naturally to a short discussion of the question of marriage between people of different religious beliefs. Now, when non-Catholics read books on this subject, and when they find out that the Church does not encourage mixed marriages, they frequently take offence ;—just as such persons are almost sure to take offence at what we are about to say here. Yet there is no need for them to do so if they would only think for a moment about this most important subject. Consequently, let us begin with a word to the non-Catholic who chances to read this book. The Catholic Church has nothing against you, as an individual. She is thinking all the time about the Catholic partner to your marriage and also of the children. She does not like mixed marriages because she knows from bitter experience the evils which can follow from them. That does not mean to say that all mixed marriages turn out badly, by any means, or that Catholics are necessarily better living people than non-Catholics. It means that, in the main, non-Catholic marriages (i.e. what we call mixed marriages) carry with them certain difficulties and certain inconveniences which do tend to impede the perfect happiness of marriage and the perfect fulfilment of the ends for which it was instituted by God.

The importance of a good Catholic marriage cannot be over-estimated. Think of it for a moment. Marriage means a complete union of two people with their very different characters and temperaments. This union cannot be confined to one department of life or to another—it must be complete in every respect if that marriage is to be a real success. You can see at once that there will be a very important factor missing in that union if the two parties are of different religious beliefs. For one thing there is the simple disunity of setting forth in different directions on a Sunday morning for church, with the added factor that the children will have to go with the Catholic party! Or perhaps the non-Catholic does not go to church at all, with the consequent bad example for the children, who soon start to ask questions on the subject. Certain common topics of conversation on Catholic subjects have to be ruled out, either because the non-Catholic party does not know anything about those topics or else because they only lead to arguments. That means a constant strain for the Catholic, whose religious life thus has to be set apart, as it were, from the ordinary married life. Again, sometimes the non-Catholic is full of suspicions that an organized attempt is being made to bring about his or her conversion to the Catholic Faith. This leads naturally to a feeling of resentment and often to accusations that Catholics are hypocritical, setting themselves up to be better than others, and so on. Again, this factor may not appear either before marriage or even during the early stages of married life, but it usually raises its head sooner or later. It is for this reason, among others, that Pope Pius XI writes in his Encyclical letter on Christian Marriage: " If the Church occasionally on account of circumstances does not refuse to grant a dispensation from these strict laws (provided that the divine law remains intact and the dangers above mentioned are provided against by strict and suitable safeguards) it is unlikely that the Catholic party will not suffer some detriment from such a marriage."*

Nor must we forget for one moment the possibility of a difference in outlook on several important moral matters. Apart from such things as fasting and abstinence, there is the very difficult question of what is called " birth-control." Now we are not even hinting that non-Catholics are not religious in their own way or anything stupid like that ; it is just that they have not exactly the same moral outlook as Catholics on many points. We do not deny that there are cases of good and happy mixed marriages in which the non-Catholic party does every-thing possible to make it easy for the Catholic to practise his or her religion. That is not the point ; because for every good

---

* Pope Pius XI, *Christian Marriage*, C.T S. trans., p. 40.

mixed marriage there are several which are unhappy and basically un-Catholic. That fact, which the Church knows only too well from the depths of a long and varied experience in such matters, has led her to be very opposed to such marriages from the point of view of the Catholic partner and also from that of the children, who frequently grow up either slack in their religious duties or with no religion at all. Given all possible advantages, marriage is a difficult business at the best of times, but if there is this initial difficulty of religion then it may very easily become a failure, or at least lead to a life-long struggle in which the partner with the stronger character will emerge victorious over the weaker member. Some people attempt to argue that such marriages are alright so long as it is the mother who is the Catholic. That is a very fallacious argument, because the father is just as important as the mother in this matter, and often has more force of character. We need not mention here the difficulties which frequently arise with regard to the education of the children in such mixed marriages, because they are only too obvious.

For these reasons, and for others which need not be mentioned here, choose a Catholic partner if you possibly can, and there is a much greater possibility of your marriage being a real success. If you have already chosen a non-Catholic, then think of the future and do not be led into hasty action by the whims and the feelings of the present moment. Marriage in the Catholic Church is for life, remember ; and you have to think even now of your future children and of their Faith, not to mention the salvation of your own soul together with that of your partner. Perhaps it will be possible to convert the non-Catholic before your marriage, but if that is not possible, then the least you can do is to make up your mind now, and also make it quite clear to the other party, that all the necessary conditions which have to be promised before the Church will give permission for a mixed marriage are going to be carried out to the letter. As you probably know already, the non-Catholic has to promise that all children born of your marriage, without exception, will be brought up in the Catholic Faith, and that there will be no attempt to interfere in any way with the Catholic's religion. Also the non-Catholic will have to have a certain number of instructions in the Catholic attitude towards marriage, as a safeguard to the Catholic party.

Once you have begun to think of a certain definite person as a possible future partner in marriage then, above and beyond the question of religion, think of that individual's character. You have to *live* with him or her, remember, and there is a question here of a co-partner in a life-long enterprise in which the education of your children is a most important factor. Is this person's character one which is fitted for that task ? If not, then you will certainly have to think again. Take your time, and do not be rushed, because once this is done it cannot be undone. Above all, pray that God may aid you in your choice. His grace will always be at hand if you ask Him for it, especially in a matter so very important in every way as this. Exchange views and opinions on all the really important matters, and discover the other person's mind on all those questions which you know are bound to come up sooner or later in the course of your married life. Remember that love at first sight is something which only belongs to the realm of the novel. What we can have in real life is a sexual attraction to someone at first sight, and that may easily not be real love at all. The very foundation of real love is respect ;—indeed, I would go further and use an even stronger word, " reverence," because love, if it is true love, is essentially a very holy thing. With this reverence as a basis, and not mere physical attraction, there is every hope that you will be able to make a success of your marriage and also of your parenthood. Without it as the basis, the possibility (I hesitate to say the probability) of failure is staring you in the face from the very beginning.

Although not a thing which one can insist on, it is certainly very useful in many ways if the two people who are going to be married mutually agree to a medical examination before their marriage takes place. There are several reasons for this. Go to a Catholic doctor and tell him why you are asking for a full examination, i.e., because you are going to be married. In that way he will be on the look-out for certain things, and may be able to give you good advice which will make all the difference during the first few months of your married life. In this way you are also making quite sure that you are capable of having healthy children. It is also a good opportunity for asking certain questions concerning married life about which you may possibly be a little uncertain. Get him to give you a certificate to state that you are fit for the married state and then show that to your partner. In this way you will have saved yourself much worry, perhaps, later on.

If your partner is also a Catholic, then you are entitled to have a Nuptial Mass at your wedding, and this is such a very great thing that you should always insist on having it, together with the great blessing which the Church gives so solemnly to those of her children who are entering into this state of life. Give the priest plenty of time by going to see him well before the date when you wish to be married. So many people are disappointed because, owing to the fact that they leave such things until the very last moment, they find that there are difficulties in the way.

If, on the other hand, your partner is not a Catholic, then do remember that you will have to take him or her along to the priest, not only to sign the promises which are a necessary condition for the dispensation in this case, but also for a certain number of instructions on the Church's viewpoint on marriage as a Sacrament. The Church very wisely insists on this, not only because the non-Catholic may thus become interested in the Faith and want to know more about it, but also so that he or she may at least know fully what is expected of those who marry Catholics, as well as the Catholic moral viewpoint on certain important questions affecting marriage and children. Above all, during this time of preparation for your marriage, don't forget to pray very hard indeed, because you are entering into a state of life which is difficult and which has many and grave obligations attached to it. You will need all the help which God can give if you are to live up to that high vocation to which He has called you.

Once you are married, then start as you mean to continue. Remember that one of the very best preparations for the future education of your children is a good Catholic life, lived in accordance with the law of God and the Church. If this is lacking, then all your other attempts at teaching are liable to consist of so many empty words without good example behind them, and that will not count for very much. Children learn far more easily by following the example given to them by others, especially their parents, than they do by any number of words ; and unless you begin to train yourselves from the very beginning to give that example, then you will most probably find that, when the time does come, you will fail badly. Consequently, make it a rule of your married life that you will both attend Mass together whenever possible ; that you will go to Confession and to Holy Communion at least once every month (it should be possible to do more than this, but we are stating the minimum), and that you will say the Family Rosary every night, together. These attempts to put your Faith into practice will not only sanctify your life together, but will also be the very basis for a living example to your children later on, and something which they will always remember. Aim at making your marriage truly Catholic in every sense of the word, and that, from the very beginning, because your first and primary obligation is to save your own soul and that of your partner, together with those of the children whom God may entrust to your care. In this connection you can have no better example to follow than that of the Holy Family, and you should put yourselves and your family under Its care.

Lastly, the mutual knowledge which will be built up during the first years of your married life should help you to create a really domestic and happy atmosphere for your children who are to enjoy it with you. Learn to expect " squalls " now and again, because they are inevitable, even in the best of families. Learn at the same time how best to bring those unhappy moments to a speedy and a successful conclusion. It is during these early months and years of preparation that you can learn best those essential lessons of mutual " give and take " which are so very necessary for your future happiness. Do not leave it until the children have actually arrived before you learn how to avoid the major quarrels by tact and understanding, but do it from the very beginning. You will notice the benefit of this later on.

If you have used this time of preparation carefully and well, then, once you know that a child is coming to complete your marriage union and to bless it, you will know exactly what to do. Just go along quietly, preparing yourselves mentally, physically

and spiritually for that great event.   Get a Catholic doctor and
also a Catholic nurse if you possibly can, and above all—this to
the future mother—go along to the priest and ask him to give
you the special blessing which the Church has provided for
women who are going to have a baby.   It is a blessing in which
the Church prays to Christ to bless and preserve both you and
your child from all harm, that the birth may be a happy one,
and that you may all reach heaven through His intercession
who was also born of a woman while being at the same time the
Eternal Son of God.   The Saviour who blessed in such a
wonderful way the simple marriage feast at Cana during His
life on this earth will be no less ready to bless your marriage and
to give you all the graces which you will need, as parents, in
order to carry out in a worthy fashion all those obligations which
arise from that state of life to which He has called you.

Once your baby has been born the next important step is its
Baptism.   There should be little or no need to mention here the
importance of this Sacrament from every point of view.   As
you know, it is absolutely necessary for salvation, and so you
should not let any consideration make you run the risk of your
child dying without having received this Sacrament.   If he is
perfectly healthy, then have him baptized as soon as possible,
let us say within a week at the very latest, but even earlier if
you can.   If, however, the child should not be very healthy, or
should be taken ill before that time, then there is only one thing
to be done, and that is to have him baptized as soon as possible
and in your own home, if necessary.   Send for the priest and
tell him why you need him.   In case of really urgent need, and
if the priest cannot be had in time, then anyone may baptize.
That is one of the reasons why it has been suggested that you
should have a Catholic doctor and nurse if that is at all possible.
The method of baptism is very simple ; all that you need to do
is to pour some water on the child's head and say at the same
time these words :—" I baptize thee in the name of the Father,
and of the Son, and of the Holy Ghost," having at the same time
the intention of doing what the Church does in her ceremony of
Baptism.   The general rule, then, is, when in doubt, baptize!
We cannot make too sure in this matter.

Normally, however, you will be able to have your baby

baptized by the priest in church. Usually such baptisms take place on Sundays, in the afternoon, but in any case you should send someone along to the presbytery to see the priest beforehand and to arrange the time with him. Before the actual ceremony takes place you will have one or two things to think about. In the first place, a Catholic child should have a saint's name, the whole idea being that the child is put under the protection of that saint whose name he or she bears. What a very silly thing it is to give a child such names as May or June, when there are so many saints' names with rare and wonderful associations for the Church to be had for the asking ! If you need any help in this matter of choosing a name for your child there are two little books sold by the Catholic Truth Society which will be of help to you. One is called *Saints' Names for Boys* and the other *Saints' Names for Girls*. You will be sure to find all that you need there. In some Catholic countries there is the custom of giving the child the name of the saint whose feast day falls on the child's birthday. If that does not suit, at least you should remember those grand old English saints whose names mean so much in the history of our country.

There is also the obligation of providing Catholic god-parents. It is no use asking non-Catholics to perform this office, because on the one hand the Church does not allow that, and on the other they could never hope to fulfil the obligations which it implies, however ready they may be to do their best. The god-parents are supposed to watch over the Catholic education of the child in case anything should happen to prevent the parents from giving it. Consequently, this is not an obligation which can be lightly undertaken, by any means. If you would like some Catholic who cannot be present at the actual ceremony to be the god-father or god-mother, then you must get someone to stand proxy for them at the ceremony, and also you should get their consent in writing and show it to the priest.

We have neither the time nor the space here to give a full description of the ceremony of baptism, but there are one or two things with regard to it which must be said. In the first place, this should be a family feast in every way. Only too often we do not remember with sufficient gratitude the great gifts of God which we receive so frequently during life. This gift of Baptism is one which Christ won for us by His Passion and Death on the Cross, and we should all learn to appreciate it to the full.   On this day and at this ceremony the grace of God is going to flow into the soul of your child for the first time, making him a Christian, giving him the full right to be called a " child of God " in the most perfect sense possible for any creature. Through this ceremony he acquires the right to heaven—a right which it is your obligation to bring to perfection by his education.   For that reason it is a very good thing if you can all go to Holy Communion on the day of the Baptism, but if the mother cannot manage that, at least the father should go.   If you can, read through the prayers and the ceremony of Baptism before you go to the church, so that at least you have some idea of what God is doing in the soul of your child through the ministration of His priest.

Once the mother is able to get out again she should go to the church and give thanks to God for all the graces which she has received and also to receive the official blessing of the Church. This ceremony is usually called " churching," and because so many people seem to misunderstand it, perhaps it is worth while explaining a little.   In the first place, it is not necessary to be churched before going to Mass or Holy Communion, as so many people seem to think.   Indeed, it is not necessary at all, but it is a very good and holy custom, because it is the official thanksgiving to God for having brought both you and your baby safely through the difficulties of child-birth.   In the course of this ceremony the Church blesses both you and your child, and calls down God's grace on you all, that you, as the parents, may be given all the helps you need, and that your child may profit by your efforts to bring him up as a good Christian.   The Church also prays that both you and your child may come to the reward in heaven which God has promised for those who love Him.

CHAPTER THREE

WHAT IS EDUCATION?

BEFORE SETTING OUT ON A JOURNEY, IT IS ESSENTIAL TO KNOW where we are going and also to have made up our minds as to the road we are going to take. Indeed, before undertaking any task, however small, we must have some idea of what we are aiming at if we are to accomplish it successfully. If this is true of ordinary, every-day affairs, how much more will it be true of the great task which lies before you as parents. Unless you have a reasonably clear idea from the very beginning of what you should aim at through the training which you are going to give to your children, then you will have little chance of producing anything—except possibly chaos. Consequently, in this chapter we shall make some attempt to discuss education in general, at least in so far as it concerns the parents.

It will be clear in the course of this discussion that we are using the word " education " in its widest sense and are not restricting it to any one of the many branches of education. We have already stressed the fact that the parents constitute the main factor in the education of their children, and that they have both the right and the duty of watching over the whole field of that education in order to direct it towards its final end or purpose. Consequently, they have to know what that purpose is.

A leading Catholic educationist has given this brief but clear description of what education should be. " It is," he says, " that culture of mind, will and emotions which, while adapting man for a particular calling, disposes him to achieve an excellent personal and social life within that calling." The whole object of education is personal happiness, not merely from the point of view of the material world and its comforts,

but also from that of the supernatural. Man is a composite
being, made up of soul and body, and he has to earn heaven for
himself by means of a human life, lived in accordance with the
law of God and with the help of those graces which God will
give him so abundantly. It is, therefore, impossible for us to
see this question of education in the right light if we attempt to
separate the merely human in life from the supernatural.
Religion—and notice that by this term we do not mean mere
attendance at church—is something which must influence the
whole of human life, and especially the development of character.
It should fashion our thoughts, our emotions, decisions and
actions in accordance with God's plans for our ultimate happiness.
Once again, first things must be put in the first place! If the
soul, with its ultimate destiny, were to be neglected for the
merely human or material aspect of education then we would
fail completely in our duty as parents. At the same time the
human aspect must not, and indeed cannot, be neglected
altogether, because it is the basis on which grace works and
through which we achieve our eternal salvation. The whole
object of our education, then, should be so to form our children's
characters that they may be perfectly fitted to live their human
lives on this earth in such a way that, through them, they may
gain the eternal life of heaven. Ruskin saw one aspect of this
question when he said that education is not a means of getting
on in the world ; it is a means of staying pleasantly in your
place there.

As you can see, it is not a question of instilling mere knowledge.
On the contrary, knowledge by itself is not much use unless it
takes its rightful place in the complete personality. The secret
of education from the Catholic point of view lies in the formation
of a character which will know what is right, true and good ;
and which will be able to act in accordance with that knowledge
because it is in full possession of all those habits of mind and will
which alone can assure that decisions will be effectively carried
out in actual practice. It is only when all these conditions are
fulfilled that a man can be said to be well educated. If we may
sum this up in a rather trite phrase, the whole idea of education
is to help the child to live, rather than to help him to make a
living!

The result of education from the parents' point of view, then, should be a man or woman who is in every way supernatural in outlook—one who thinks, judges and acts in harmony with the example of Christ and the law of God. To that end we have to develop those natural inclinations and characteristics which are to be found in every human being. We shall have to guide, teach and organize in the child those habits and skills which will aid in the fulfilment of his purpose on earth and which will serve to bring him to the perfect happiness of heaven. In a word, we have to train our children to *live*, and to perform that vital act in such a way that, by their lives, they may achieve a certain degree of happiness in this world through their fulfilment of its social and personal obligations, at the same time directing all those efforts to the final end of man, the vision of God face to face.

Pope Pius XI indicates in general terms how this can be achieved. " Christian education takes in the whole aggregate of human life, physical and spiritual, individual, domestic and social . . . in order to elevate, regulate and perfect it, in accordance with the example and the teaching of Christ."* This Papal teaching contains at one and the same time a perfect summary of the tasks before you and also of the reasons why your training is of such importance for your children's future. Man has to gain heaven by taking his rightful place in this world. Therefore the education of the child naturally implies a preparation to take that place without fear. As the years of adolescence draw to a close and the state of perfect manhood or womanhood draws ever nearer the final shaping of this character should become ever more apparent. The Pope outlines for us briefly the means by which this shaping of character is to be accomplished. The training we give to our children must tend towards the formation of correct relationships between the child and the various orders of reality with which he has to come into contact and in which he must play his part. Let us examine that important statement for a moment.

Man is essentially a composite creature, belonging at one and the same time to many orders of being. First of all, he is a *person*—an individual, having a soul and a body joined together

* *The Christian Education of Youth*, C.T.S. trans., p. 45.

to form a little world of its own. He is also a member of a family—another little world, and a very important one! He is a citizen of a certain State and Country, having corresponding rights and duties towards his fellow citizens. Lastly, and most important of all, he is a member of the Mystical Body of Christ and of His Church on earth. Man's complete and perfect education, then, will be something which will fit him to take his rightful place in each and every one of those different orders.

If we examine them closely we shall notice that his relationship with the last of these orders, i.e., as a member of the Mystical Body and the Church on earth, does in fact pervade all the others, because they are all connected with it. Thus, it is because man is a member of the Mystical Body of Christ that he must know how to govern the little world of his own person in accordance with the demands of his membership with Christ. There will be certain laws to be obeyed, things to be done and things to be avoided which govern his personal relationship with God. His attitude towards other members of the family, especially to his parents, will also be determined to a certain extent by his membership of this Mystical Body, because he will have to render obedience, love and respect to his parents and be ready to help them in their temporal and spiritual needs, not merely from purely natural motives, but mainly because it is part of God's law that he should do so. His attitude towards his fellow citizens of the State and towards the civil authority will also be governed by certain laws which he knows of through his membership of the Mystical Body. Once that general principle has been grasped your task, as parents, becomes a little clearer. It means that you should see to it that your children know how to live in relationship with those different orders of being in such a way that through their lives they may earn heaven for themselves. But how is that to be done?

In general we may reply that it is done by the correct formation of the child's character, but that reply is still far too vague, and consequently we must go on to ask just how that result may be achieved in actual practice. Naturally, many of the details will have to be dealt with in later chapters, but it will be possible for us to outline here the main principles which must govern us in our performance of this important task.

It is no exaggeration to say that the whole secret of education turns on the formation of good habits ; and in this respect our main task, as parents, is to produce in our children those habits of mind, will, emotions and self-government which can regulate effectively all the powers of the soul and body in relationship with those different orders of being and reality which we have just mentioned. Thus, we shall have to help our children to build up those habits, both spiritual and physical, which help them to govern themselves and their own personal relationship with God and with His laws. These we may call personal habits. We need to cultivate in them good family habits, too, together with certain social and religious habits which will enable them to fulfil all their duties with regard to the State and the Church in a fitting manner.

In this connection it is as well for us to notice that, when we speak of habits, we do not merely mean those which regulate our external conduct directly, but also those which refer to our thoughts and our decisions. Thus, intellectual formation does not consist in a mere collection of facts or an ability to manipulate words or figures. Primarily it is the habit of assessing Truth, especially Divine Truth, together with a prompt submission of the mind and the will to that Truth even though all our natural inclinations may rebel against it. It is the ability to judge all things under the aspect of eternity rather than by the standards of this world, and a prompt moral reaction in accordance with that judgment. This will only be achieved after a long period of training, which we, as parents, must be able to direct along the right paths in order to attain that end. Youth is especially a period of formation, and we must never forget that.

Therefore we are out to develop what is good in the child and to remove, or at least control, what is not good by building good habits both of thought and of action. Here it will be useful to say a word or two about some modern tendencies in education. Some people are of the opinion that every child is good by nature, and that, provided he is left more or less to himself, he will develop normally. Nothing could be further from the truth, and it is our obligation, as Catholics, to say so clearly. The basic error in this theory comes from the fact that it ignores completely the element of Original Sin—if, indeed, its defenders have ever heard of such a thing! Such people try very hard to prevent the introduction into education of certain very necessary factors, such as physical correction or the teaching of a positive moral law, on the grounds that such things only tend to build up what are called repressions and inhibitions. To their way of thinking, the child should either be allowed to follow all his natural inclinations without let or hindrance, or else he should have all the reasons for and against explained to him and then be permitted to choose for himself. Such theories are nonsense, and should be treated as such.

To begin with, owing to the fact of original sin, not all the tendencies of our human nature are good by any means. They become good or bad according to the education which the individual receives, especially during the period of childhood. Thus Pope Pius XI, from whose famous Encyclical letter on Christian Education we have already quoted, says : " Every method of education founded, wholly or in part, on the denial or forgetfulness of original sin and grace, and relying on the sole powers of human nature, is unsound . . . Such are those modern systems which appeal to a pretended self-government and unrestrained freedom on the part of the child." Much as we would like to affirm the contrary, we are bound to confess that human nature, after the Fall, is a nature which has been wounded by sin and despoiled of grace. It carries within it the marks of sin in the form of ignorance of the moral law, uncontrolled tendencies which lead it to evil more easily than to good, and the seeds of rebellion against God. All those things have to be corrected by means of education. It is interesting to notice that the very people who hold this absurd theory are also those who insist on the great part played in the development of character by inherited traits, and, as we know through the teaching of science, not all inherited traits are good ones by any means.

As a consequence of original sin we are all inclined to seek for those things which please us and to ignore or refuse to do those which do not fall in with our own wishes and inclinations. Self is the most important element in our original make-up, and indeed it has to be in order to help in the preservation of the individual. But, since we have to live in constant relationship with God and with other members of the human race, it follows that this element of self-will has to be very strictly trained and controlled, otherwise we would become quite impossible both from the point of view of our lives as members of a family and also as citizens. The good order and discipline of both the State and the family demand that very often self should be renounced for the benefit of society as a whole. Neither has grace absolute dominion over self, at the beginning of our lives at least—to which fact all sin is abundant testimony. We have to acquire that dominion by a period of strict training under the guidance of others who have already learnt how important that dominion of self really is and also the best methods of acquiring it. This can only be achieved by a slow process of acquiring all the habits which are necessary to safeguard our relationship with those four orders of reality with which we are constantly in contact. The following graphic representation of the end in view in all education may help us to grasp this fact a little clearer.

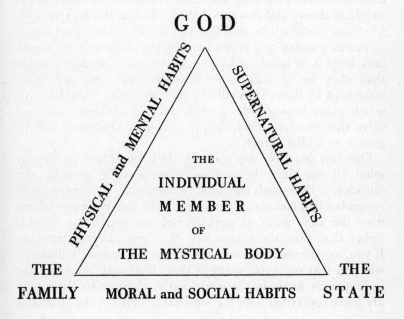

GOD

PHYSICAL and MENTAL HABITS

SUPERNATURAL HABITS

THE
INDIVIDUAL
MEMBER
OF
THE MYSTICAL BODY

THE
FAMILY   MORAL and SOCIAL HABITS   THE
STATE

In that diagram, as you can see, the relationship between the individual and the Mystical Body of Christ pervades and directs the relationship of that individual to himself, to the family and also to the State and civil society.   To that end he is surrounded by habits of thought and judgment, moral principles and action which alone will enable him to fulfil all his duties in a fitting manner.   That is the finished product of your education of your children, and it is as well to keep it in mind from the very beginning.

Thus, it will be clear that we are not free to bring up our children just as we like.   Rather, it is our obligation to set to work on a plan which has already been laid down for us, at least in its general lines, and that plan is divine in its origin.   It will also be clear why we have laid so much emphasis on the preparation for parenthood which is necessary if this work is to be carried through to a successful conclusion, as well as the need for a good Catholic life lived together as members of one family. It is because, as we shall see later, mere knowledge of the Faith and of the moral law is not enough.   With all of us it is true to say that one ounce of example will teach us much more than a great weight of theory and precepts.   With children this is even more true than it is of adults, and that fact can be of very great use to us in our training and education of those children if we would only keep it in mind.   Children see far more of their parents than they do of their other teachers, and they are more influenced by them, especially by their example.   Also the love which exists between the parents and the children serves to drive that example much deeper into their characters and to give it an added influence.

One last word on this subject!   It is important to keep in mind all the time the end we have in view, namely, the salvation of these souls entrusted to our care.   If we manage to remember that fact always then we shall be able to see everything from the view point of eternity and the everlasting Truths, rather than from the narrow one of merely material interests. If you, as parents, keep that end always before your minds you will find that you avoid many of those fatal mistakes which are so frequently made in the education of children by those who are more concerned with the material interests of the child and the family than they are with the supernatural destiny which is all-important. Very often you will find that it is a great help to think of those solemn words of Our Lord, " What doth it profit a man if he gain the whole world and suffer the loss of his soul ? "

For that reason also we have stressed the importance of the duty you have of praying for your children and for the graces which you need to educate them properly. When you are in doubt as to the line of action you should take, even perhaps after having given it deep thought, then there is only one thing left for you to do—pray about it and ask God to guide you. If you trust in Him He will see to it that both light and grace follow upon your prayer, for the simple reason that He too has exactly the same interests at heart as you have, namely, the salvation of your children's souls.

CHAPTER FOUR

THE EARLY YEARS

THE EDUCATION OF THE CHILD DURING WHAT WE HAVE CALLED
in the title to this chapter the " early years " will, of course,
cover several chapters of this book. Here we shall confine
ourselves to those general principles which will have to govern
your conduct towards the child during the baby stage, i.e., up
to the time when he begins to take a visibly conscious interest in
the things around him. That time is not long in coming, as
you will soon find out in actual practice, and sometimes it is
only a matter of months after birth.

The fact has already been mentioned that education is one
whole, and that principle has an important application here.
Education is a unity in the sense that it should be continuous.
That means to say that your child's education starts from the
very first moment of his birth and will continue until his death.
To think that your duties as parents come to an end when your
children reach a certain age is just as bad a mistake in its way
as the opposite one, i.e., imagining that your obligation does not
begin until your child can take a conscious interest in things
around him. During this baby stage there are certain things
which have to be done, some of which apply to the child
directly and others to you.

In the first place, you can inculcate good habits in accordance
with the age of the child, while at the same time training yourself to avoid those things which can cause trouble later on.
Secondly, you should prepare your mental attitude towards
certain branches of education, determining at least roughly how
you are going to put those general principles into effective
action. Lastly, there are certain very definite preparations
which should be made for the next stage and which should

not be put off with the excuse that there is plenty of time.

We have mentioned as our first point the formation of those good habits which are in proportion to the age of the child, as well as the avoiding of certain things which are almost certain to cause you trouble later on. Observation has proved that some general remarks on this subject are by no means useless.

Some parents seem to think that because a baby in arms cannot talk he has very little consciousness of what goes on around him and no particular feelings with regard to the circumstances of his life during this early stage. Nothing could be further from the truth. A very young child, a few weeks old, manifests certain signs which show quite plainly that there are feelings at work within him which are at the very root of the formation of the human character, such as, for instance, those of love and hate, pleasure and pain. It is true that the sensations which arouse those feelings at this age are few, but they are vivid and nearly all connected with you. Therefore your conduct towards him at this stage matters a great deal for the future formation which you hope to give to his character. Thus, your own habits of cleanliness and punctuality, especially the routine for washing, feeding and playing with your baby, are important and should be kept to as far as is practical, in accordance with the child's needs at the time. If you are not regular with regard to the time for feeding your baby and for giving him his bath, then you are obviously going to put him in a bad humour and are also well on the way to getting him into irregular habits. You are upsetting his routine, which is much more important than your own, and you are liable to find in consequence that you are having trouble with him at night and will begin to wonder why. Also you will find that you tend to be in a hurry, especially over his bath, and thus deprive him of his pleasure without any necessity. Remember that it is during those times that he gets a chance to exercise his muscles, and also his pleasure serves to fix his love and attention on you more than on other things. That is important, because it is the breeding ground for his confidence in you. It is natural for mothers to want to nurse their babies, and it is certainly very natural in babies to want to be nursed ; but here again a certain routine must be observed. Over-nursing is just as bad for a healthy child as is the lack of the proper and natural demonstrations of love and affection.

That last remark brings us naturally to a discussion of some of the things which you have to learn to avoid if you wish to prevent much worry and trouble later on. Since one of these things is intimately connected with this question of nursing and affection we can begin with that.

In general small babies learn much more quickly than most people would ever imagine. They soon get to know what is pleasant and what is unpleasant and also learn to seek for the pleasure in their own way, usually by crying for it. Now that natural manifestation of desire for their own way has to be brought under control from the very first because it contains the root of much selfishness later in life. If you get into the bad habit of picking up your baby and nursing him every time he cries then you are asking for trouble, because that child is soon going to discover that he can get anything he likes out of you provided he goes the right way about it and he will soon discover the right way by trial and error. You will become a tool in his hands instead of his educator and his guide. This is not a doll given to you for a plaything, but a human soul and body which has to be trained in the right way. Learn therefore to train your children from the beginning to appreciate the fact that you are not going to pay any attention to unreasonable requests for nursing and they will soon give up the unequal struggle. You may think that this has very little to do with education, but even a little observation of babies and their ways will soon prove the opposite. You are sowing the seeds of future obedience in the mind of the child almost unconsciously, and that is a great step forward.

This does not mean that you should fall into the opposite error and never play with or nurse your child. That would deprive him of those demonstrations of your love and affection which are his right and which form an important part of his life during these early stages. Also, if he is ill and needs your attention, then, of course, you must give it freely; but a little experience will soon enable you to distinguish between the reasonable and the unreasonable demands for attention. You will soon learn to distinguish the cry which indicates pain and the one which is a sign of bad temper or a wish to be petted and made a fuss of for distraction purposes. Have your definite times for nursing and for playing with your baby and keep to them. If you can only do that, then you are doing both yourself and him a very great service.

Try to imagine the child's world during this early stage of his life and put yourself in his place for a moment. Every day he is becoming more interested in the things around him. The sense of sight, aided by that of touch, is growing more acute. His hearing and memory are both developing rapidly, becoming accustomed to sounds and leading him to attempt to repeat them. How wonderful everything must seem to the child and how new! Try to understand exactly why this should be and also see those factors which are helping at the moment to bring about a full and perfect education of your child. These varied experiences are all necessary that he may learn slowly to take his place in those different orders of reality which we mentioned in the last chapter. Since these experiences are, in the main, pleasant ones, they induce him to do this almost automatically, because they capture his attention and his interest. At the same time, however, there are other factors and experiences which tend to hold him back, and thus develop in him those habits of control which are so very necessary for character formation. It is easy to see what these factors are, at least in general terms. First of all, he is so very dependent on others for everything, and he soon comes to realize this fact. His own scrappy knowledge of the outside world is so unreliable that he can easily mistake one thing for another. We have all seen a child trying to catch hold of a stream of water flowing from a tap as though it were a piece of string. Naturally, these inhibiting factors are not quite so obvious in the baby in arms as they are in the two-years-old child, but they are there nevertheless.

That is why it is important that you should begin as you mean to continue, making it quite plain to the child that he is loved and wanted by you, that your protection will always be there when it is needed, while at the same time making it equally plain that not everything he wants will be forthcoming exactly when he wants it. We have all seen older children having fits of screaming and rolling on the floor in temper in order to get

4

their own way, but it is not always easy for us to realize that the root of that temper lies in early childhood—in the baby stage, in fact. We say, and we are right, that such a child is " spoilt," but more often than not we fail to think of the undoubted fact that such spoiling started at a very early age, otherwise it would never have developed to such an extent.

That is why, as our second point, we have mentioned that, during this early stage, you should prepare your own mental attitude to this question of the future education of your children at least along general lines. For example, there is the matter of obedience to authority. What attitude are you going to adopt in the near future with regard to that ? Are you going to rule the children, or are you going to let them rule you ? Is your rule going to be one of love or one of fear, and how are you to carry this into actual practice ? All these things need thinking out long before the first occasion presents itself when you tell the child to do something and he refuses to obey you. If you have not given this matter due thought it is quite easy for you to be caught out when that happens, and then you may be either too easy with him or too severe. Again, what is going to form your attitude towards such things as your children's play periods ; is it going to be your own will and pleasure or theirs ? Children soon feel the injustice of not being allowed to make any noise while they are playing, or not being allowed to play as they wish much more than you might think. Even a small baby soon shows definite signs of this desire, when he picks up a spoon or some other hard object and throws it on the floor, for instance. That is not necessarily " being naughty " at all, but is usually prompted by an instinctive desire to use his hands and the throwing muscles of the arms, together with the great pleasure he gets from hearing the spoon fall on the floor. This whole question of the importance of play-time for children will receive a good deal of attention in the course of this book, but at the moment it will be sufficient for you to determine your own general attitude towards such things, because it will not be very long before certain situations present themselves when you will have to decide what you are going to allow and what you are going to forbid—and on what grounds. Think of it from the child's point of view, not from your own.

Now we come to what is perhaps the most important preparation of all, namely that which will be necessary for your first steps in the religious education of your child. This preparation should not be left too long, because now is the time when it can be done in peace and quiet. Later on it will be more difficult.

First of all, let us say a word or two as to the end and purpose of your religious training of the child.

We have already insisted that all education aims at the perfection of the individual character by means of good habits which surround the intellect, the will and also the emotions of man in such a way that they will lead those different faculties easily towards a knowledge of what is right and what is wrong, and also to actions in accordance with that knowledge. Therefore it will be no surprise to you to hear that religious education too is largely a matter of building up good habits. During the early years of the child's life not all the senses play an equally important part in development, and in a way this remains true all during life, although in later years this preponderance of one sense over the others is usually compensated for to some extent so that it is not so easily noticed. In the early period of a child's life, however, it is definitely the sense of sight which plays the most important part, followed as a close second by that of touch. This information will be of great use to us in all our attempts at education during that period, particularly in religious training. It means that our main appeal should be made through those two senses, although we do not exclude the sense of hearing altogether.

In this matter of religious education we must never allow ourselves to forget the end in view. The object of religious training is not mere knowledge—how many parents and teachers have made that mistake in the past! The end in view is the love of God. If we can be reasonably sure that we have so arranged our religious and secular training that we have led our children to a deep personal love for Christ and for God then we may rest assured that we have fulfilled our obligation as parents. If we have concentrated our attention on mere knowledge then we are very liable to find that we have failed in our object. Knowledge is necessary—but only because it is a prelude to love. For that reason parents should do all they can, even before the birth of their child, to develop in themselves this deep personal love for God, because once they possess it then there is every chance that they will be able to pass it on to their children. If this love is missing in the parents, then their example will counterbalance all their teaching, so far as the children are concerned, and it is here that we see the beginnings of so many failures and the reason why children tend to leave their Faith when they leave school.

Keep this object of all religious instruction always before your minds, because on that will depend the success or failure of your training, and not on the mere knowledge of the Catechism answers or prayers, etc., no matter how necessary those things may be in other ways.

Now let us see what preparations you should make while your child is still in the baby stage.

Putting into actual practice the general rule that the appeal to the young child should be made through the senses of sight and touch, you can buy and set up in conspicuous places pictures and statues which you know will have an appeal for children. They should be placed where they can be easily seen by the child, and that is especially true of the bedroom where he sleeps. You can also make a simple little altar or bracket of wood and set it up in the corner of the bedroom with a statue on it, preferably a statue of Our Lord as a small child with His Mother. Remember that it is not religious art that you are trying to teach, and so there is no need to spend a great deal of money on these things. Get statues and pictures which are in fairly vivid colours, because those appeal more to the sense of sight in the young child. This does not mean that you have to fill the room with religious pictures, to the exclusion of others, such as those of animals, etc., which also appeal to the eyes of the child. All these things are useful, because they can be related to God later as His creatures.

There is, however, one very important thing which you should prepare now while you have plenty of time, and that is a religious scrap-book. This idea will not be a new one to those of you who have read the previous books in this series, but for the benefit of others it will be as well to explain it here in some detail.

The basic idea behind the religious scrap-book is simply this, that the child finds it much easier to assimilate things through the senses of sight and touch at first, and also where religion is concerned, through the Sacred Humanity of Our Lord. They find in that Humanity a constant example which they can follow, and surely that was one of the reasons for the Incarnation! Like your own child, Christ was once a little baby, and then grew through childhood and adolescence to perfect manhood under the care of Mary, His Mother. The idea of the scrap-book is to express this Model in a graphic form and to group round Him all the other religious instruction which needs to be taught in the early years. It is quite simple to make, although it does need a little time and care, together with a certain amount of imagination if it is to be done really well.

You will need, first of all, a large book with blank sheets of paper in it—a drawing book is the best for this purpose. Then make a collection of religious pictures and also others which will fit into the religious teaching as a whole and stick them in the book. This should be done in a definite order, so that they may form groups round which you can give your verbal instructions later on. Naturally, the whole thing has to be done with imagination, so as to produce something which will interest the child and capture his attention. Stick the pictures in firmly, not too many to each page, and then decorate the blank spaces round them in any way you choose so as to make each page a surprise for the child. Remember what you are out to accomplish, and then make your plan of the book so as to achieve that object. To help you, here is a suggested list of subjects in the order in which they should appear, but, of course, there is no reason why you should not change this order a little if you think fit.

The first group should always be pictures about the childhood of Jesus. This means pictures of the Nativity, the Holy Child, the Holy Family, Jesus surrounded by the animals, the Three Wise Men, etc. It is a very good idea to include here, on a page by itself, one of those little paper Cribs which pull out and show the whole scene as if it were in relief—this never fails to interest the child. Leave a few pages blank after this section (and, indeed, after every section), because you are bound to come across more pictures later on and then you can add them to your book in the correct group. Also these blank pages will help you in another way later on, when you start giving oral instruction to the child. Then one of the best ways of fixing in his mind the story of the Incarnation is to " build " the scene on paper while you tell the story by sticking the pictures in one by one, with the child's help.

You can follow up this group with a smaller one on the boyhood of Jesus and then continue with His manhood and especially His Public Life. In this section try to find at least one picture of Jesus with the children. If you cannot find exactly what you want, then you must invent it. Stick a small holy picture of Christ in the centre of a page and then around that centre stick some pictures or photographs of children—your own rather than others. Leave the scenes of the Passion and the Death of Christ until later, and pass on to your next group, which should illustrate the Creation. This should not be at all difficult, because you can have some pictures of Jesus with the animals and also stick round those either natural flowers which you have collected and pressed in a book to dry, or else drawings and pictures of flowers and animals. The natural flowers are the best for this purpose, because they attract the child's attention more easily. Indeed, this section of your scrap-book can easily be the most colourful of all, especially if you use your imagination on it.

Next will come a section on the angels and saints, followed by one on Our Lady. This should offer no difficulty, but do remember to include, if you can, a picture of the child's own Patron Saint and also those of the family. After this can come a general section on prayer, the Rosary, etc., and the pictures for this can be obtained quite easily, because you can get the pictures for the Rosary section in an attractive folder which pulls out to show the whole series. Cut off the section on the Sorrowful Mysteries, and use that for your next group, which is about the Passion and Death of Christ. Here, too, pictures abound, and once again you should be able to obtain from a Catholic bookshop a folder of the Stations of the Cross which will do very well for your purpose either whole or cut into individual pictures. End this section with some pictures of the Resurrection and the Ascension.

Remember that it does not matter what pictures you use for this scrap-book provided they are full of colour and attract the child's attention. Old Christmas cards, pictures cut from books and the usual holy pictures sold in Catholic shops will do.

Later in the course of this book we shall have a good deal to say about the actual method of using this scrap-book, but this will be enough information for the moment to enable you to make one for yourselves. It need not cost a great deal of money ; in fact one of the most attractive things about it is that it is well within the reach of all. More important than the money spent on it is the time you are willing to give in order to make it really attractive and interesting for your child.

If you have any older children in the family and have not made one of these scrap-books before, then it is a good thing to get them to make one for the baby for when he gets a little older. In this way you will help those older children to develop their religious sense and also give them an idea of their responsibility towards their younger brother or sister. You are also training them for something which will be very useful when they themselves become parents. Keep them on the general lines which have been laid down here, especially to the order of subjects, but allow them to use their imaginations on the decorative parts of the book.

If the older children are not yet old enough to undertake such a task, at least you can let them into the secret and allow them to help you find pictures for the book and also to stick them in the different groups. This will give you good practice in the use of the scrap-book, because while you are actually making it you can use the sections to teach them more about God and about Christ. Don't think that this is a dull and uninteresting task, because you will soon find that your imagination gets to work on it and that it can be a fascinating thing.

If you follow out these simple instructions and begin on the scrap-book while the child is still very young you should have a most useful and efficient instrument to hand when the time comes to begin your religious training. Such a book, once made, will last for years, and there should be no need to make more than one for your whole family, as you will see when we discuss the method of using it. Take your time over it, and do make it as attractive as possible. Of all methods of teaching religion to very young children, this is by far the most effective in actual practice.

CHAPTER FIVE

THE FIRST STEPS

BEFORE WE CAN DISCUSS THE GENERAL PROCESS OF EDUCATION during these early years, that is to say from babyhood up to the age of three, it will first of all be necessary to develop still more a few of the points which have already been dealt with, especially one aspect of the final end in view in all education. This subject will be dealt with in many places in this book and from very different angles, because of its great importance.

We have already defined our object in education, i.e. the formation of good spiritual, mental and moral habits which, in their turn, will construct a really strong character, able to stand up to all attacks made on it and to meet any situation with confidence. The art of forming these good habits in your children is not one which comes by instinct, nor can we afford to rely on any " hit-or-miss " methods. Therefore, certain general principles are given for your guidance.

In the first place, you know that habits are formed by the repetition of acts ; and it would be foolish to suppose that one act is going to be sufficient to form a good habit or remove an evil one already formed. For that reason these early years are very important in the education of your children, to such an extent that it is true to say that the roots of your future success or failure may very easily lie in the use you make of them.

By far the most important of all these good habits which we are out to form, both from the spiritual and the secular points of view, are those which govern the will. In that connection it is very necessary that we should know where the strength or the weakness of the will really lies. We are so very accustomed to speak of a " strong " or a " weak " will without understanding what those terms mean that some explanation of them is necessary. It would be ever so much better if we used other terms to describe this power of the will, such as a " good " or " bad " will, because that is really what we mean. The act of the will is of exactly the same strength in all its actions and choices, and in that sense there is no point in describing it as strong or weak. What really makes for a strong or weak will is the strength or the weakness of the motives we have, either for action, or for the necessary perseverance to carry through the decisions once they are made. That explains how it happens that we find certain individuals who are reputed to have very strong wills in one direction, let us say in their business affairs, and yet are as weak as water in other things, for example, in the education of their children. They give in to the children in everything and allow themselves to be swayed by every whim and fancy the children express. Why is that ? It is because the motives are at fault, and not the will-act as such. To train the will efficiently this fact has to be clearly recognized.

It means, in actual practice, that our task as parents calls upon us to provide motives at all the various stages of their lives which will lead them to act correctly and so form good habits as time goes on. We shall also have to provide other motives for avoiding things we know to be wrong and thus avoid also the formation of bad habits. It will also be obvious that it is of little use to attempt at this early stage the development of rational motives ; instead we shall have to rely on others which are more in accordance with the age and the development of the child. These motives, which form such an important part of the child's education during these early years, are mainly reduced to two, i.e., the love of the parents for the child and also parental authority.

Of these two motives the stronger should always be parental love. Let us see some of the ways in which this parental love can and should be manifested during this early period of the child's life. First of all, in order to understand the importance of this love, it will be necessary for us to say something about the mental development of the young child during this period of its life.

In the very young child it is possible to notice two very

definite pathways along which mental development proceeds. There is first of all the question of habit formation which depends on certain physical factors, such as feeding, crawling, imitation of sounds, attention to voices, and—a very important element— the evacuation of bowel and bladder. But there is also a very clearly defined emotional development, because there are at least three of the basic human emotions which soon show them- selves in the young child, i.e., rage, fear and love. At first all the child's attention tends to be concentrated on himself and it is only later that he begins to find an interest in the world around him. Thus, when he needs something and does not get it at once he is quite likely to scream and cry, manifesting all the signs of rage. A sudden noise, or the removal of his mother's supporting arm rather quickly will bring to the surface easily recognized signs of fear. In the presence of his father and mother, when he hears their voices or feels their caresses he soon shows obvious signs of pleasure and of love for them. Later on we shall deal at length with the physical factors mentioned above, and so it will be sufficient here to concentrate for a while on the emotional influences, of which parental love is the most important.

It is of great importance during this early stage that you should do your very best to see to it that the things which are liable to cause such emotions as fear, rage, jealousy, and especially feelings of not being wanted or loved, should be excluded as far as possible. The infant's main task during this period is to grow and develop, and for that he needs an atmos- phere of peace and contentment. For that reason the mother should feed the child herself wherever that is at all possible, and nothing except physical disability should be allowed to prevent her doing so. During those times of feeding there is a mutual flow of love and affection between mother and child which is very real to him and easily assimilated. He feels that his mother is the source of one of his most important satisfactions and pleasures ; thus, very early in life he associates his mother with his comfort and with his love. He feels that he is wanted and loved, and that is all-important to him and gives him confidence. If the child is fed artificially, then, since anyone who is at hand can do this, there is the danger that this great motive for love and confidence will be checked at its source.

For the same reason you should set aside definite periods for playing with your child, and this is true not merely of the mother but also of the father, whose affection is every bit as important to the child. During those periods you should show him, by your actions, words and especially by the tone of your voice that he is loved and wanted. This may not seem so very important to you at this stage, when he does not seem to understand a word of what you are saying, but experience has proved that it is very necessary for the future development of character and especially for the correct orientation of those emotional factors which govern that development.

Nor should your love confine itself to such direct methods as the ones we have just mentioned, because it should also incline you to avoid, by mutual consent, anything which might serve to create an atmosphere which will give rise to emotional disturbances in the life of the child. Children, even at this early age, are even more sensitive to atmospheres than grown-ups ; and thus family quarrels are very dangerous, especially if little or no attempt is made to keep them from the sight or hearing of the child. He soon learns to detect the difference between certain tones of the voice, and so parents should learn from the very beginning to be unselfish in this matter and to think more of their children than they do of themselves. Their attitude towards each other in the home is very important, and many of these family disturbances can be avoided by the use of a little tact and mutual understanding, especially if the parents have discussed beforehand their attitude towards such things. Remember that the young child is especially sensitive to the emotional reaction which he feels in his mother who caresses him when she herself is emotionally upset.

In a word, then, if the child is to develop as you would like him to do you will have to see to it that he is surrounded from the beginning with an atmosphere in which these basic emotions are brought under effective control. Example is the best teacher in this, as in other things, and the child needs to be guided by people who are themselves emotionally mature.

The same thing is true of those other emotional factors we have already mentioned, i.e., fear and rage. In such matters you can do much to safeguard your child by avoiding all things which might produce these unfavourable reactions. For instance, it is a fairly simple matter to prevent the majority of those loud noises in the house which are liable to frighten him, such as the banging of doors and so on. We can try to associate those things which normally produce a fear reaction with joy and laughter and even with play. We can allow him to see strangers under favourable conditions, for example, instead of thrusting them upon him when it suits us, without any thought for his reaction. We should avoid showing fear ourselves in his presence, especially as he grows a little older, and we should not use fear as a motive for securing obedience during infancy —there is no need for such methods at this age.

Rage and anger may also be avoided by removing many of their causes. If the child is suffering from physical pain or from bodily discomfort then he should be attended to at once and not be forced to await your convenience. Avoid unnecessary hampering of his freedom of movement—one of the commonest causes of anger in the young child. In the same way, try to avoid all unnecessary interference with his infant activities. If these are not to your liking, or you think that they are in some way harmful to the child, then it is ever so much better to divert his attention to something else which will interest and distract him.

Even though the motive of love is the most important of all in the child's education, there will still be a place for parental authority, and we shall discuss this matter in various places in this book under its different aspects in accordance with the age and the development of the child. Here, at the very outset, the important thing is for you, as parents, to acquire a right attitude towards your own authority, and indeed, the right ideas about authority in general.

First, it must be kept in mind that all authority exists, not for the benefit of the person who exercises it, but for that of the subjects over whom it is exercised. If this fundamental idea is overlooked by those who wield authority, then it will not be used correctly and many evils will inevitably follow. Our authority comes from the fact that we hold a certain position in life rather than from any personal merit of ours. Should this authority be regarded as absolute, then it only becomes dictatorship and tyranny of the worst type, arbitrary in its decisions and failing utterly to fulfil its essential rôle in education. It is not for nothing that St. Thomas Aquinas teaches us that children are completely under the control of their parents until they attain the full use of their own reasoning powers. We cannot deal with our subjects as we think fit. They, too, have their natural rights which have to be respected, and if we do not respect them, then we can expect and indeed deserve to meet rebellion, and that against the whole idea of authority, which is just what we should be out to avoid. Applying this doctrine to parents, we may say with absolute truth that the parents exist for the children, and not the children for the benefit of the parents. Does this sound very trite and obvious? If it does, then remember that there are many parents who act as though the contrary were the truth and as if their children existed for their benefit alone. The Sacred Scriptures tell us—and parents are very fond of quoting this text—that children should obey their parents, but we are also told on the same divine authority that parents should not anger their children to the point of making them rebel against authority. This is undoubtedly what St. Paul means when he says : " Fathers, provoke not your children that they be not discouraged."

You will not go far wrong in this matter if you realize that the sense of obedience to authority is something which has to be built into the whole structure of your children's characters, and not something which can be imposed on them by force. Also remember that the motive of mere authority is not at all the best of all motives, and that it should be replaced as soon as possible by the rule of reasoned motives. Later on you will have to rule your children by getting them to rule themselves, but that period of their lives will be dealt with when we get to it. At the moment the point for you to realize fully is that your children are not slaves, given to you by God to obey your every whim and wish. They are human beings with rights of their own, and those rights have to be respected. You must act always in the light of this truth.

We are now in a position to sum up the obligations of parents at this stage of their children's lives in one sentence : " Be positive, be patient and be persevering." Let us develop those qualities a little.

1. Be positive

Our efforts, in this matter of education, should be directed towards getting our children into good habits which will enable them to act in the right way in certain given circumstances. Now, although this will mean that we shall have to prevent the child from doing certain things which we know, from our experience, to be wrong or to be bad for him, that does not imply that we should fill the child's life with a series of " don'ts " all the time. There is perhaps nothing which is quite so annoying to the child. It is really " nagging " of the worst type, and what is even more important, it is bad education. Almost all our guidance *can* be positive if we care to make it so, and that is particularly true of these early years. Above all, never become one of those parents who always say " no " on principle. Do not show impatience, however much you may be tried, because if you do, then you are giving the child a very powerful weapon which he will not hesitate to use later on. In fact, you will be teaching him all the time just how he can best annoy you, and he does not forget those things easily. Anyone who has seen a child use this weapon knows just how powerful it can be. It is such a very natural reaction and defence that it is best not to give him the opportunity of using it at all. Put your commands in a positive manner, rather than a negative, wherever possible. If you really must stop the child from doing something, then distract him with something else rather than merely give him the negative command. You will soon get into the way of doing this with a little practice, and now is the time to start.

2. Be patient

We cannot expect to educate children in six weeks or even six years, and nature has planned that this task should take a long time purposely. This is true of all the senses and faculties, but it is even more true of the will, because as the child develops so there will be given him more opportunities of using his own will and using it correctly. Go slowly, therefore, and with great patience. Try always to put yourselves in the place of the child and see things from his point of view rather than from your own. Never get annoyed, at least not outwardly, during these early years. As we shall see, there will be a place later on for just anger in this process of education, but it is not yet. Observe the child closely, because each individual of the human race is unique, and so the general lines of education will have to be modified for each individual. It is no use thinking that everyone can be dealt with in exactly the same way, and it is here that your prudent judgment should be exercised. Therefore get to know your children intimately ; observe them as you would other people's children, if that is possible. A child of this age has no real personal problems, and it is an important part of your task as parents to see to it that none develop through your handling of him.

Do all you can never to lose your temper with a child during this period of his life. This you will find fairly easy during the first year or so, but it will become more difficult as the child gets older. You should also make a great effort never to lose your temper with each other, especially in front of the child. Again, this may not seem very important while the child is so young, but it is. For one thing, you are getting yourselves into bad habits, and for another we must never forget the receptivity of these young children, who are extremely sensitive to atmospheres. Such domestic quarrels upset the young child very much more than parents imagine ; they frighten him, and may easily sow the seeds of many future difficulties. Thus, a child may very easily connect a certain room in the house with these quarrels, and if that happens to be the room where he eats his meals then it is simple to see how this can be connected with many feeding difficulties later on in life. Such a child, especially if unduly sensitive, may easily eat slowly and without appetite, or may even refuse to eat at all on occasions, and thus cause you much needless worry. Also such quarrels can easily set the child against one or other of the parents, or at least give him an unnatural fear of one of them, a thing which must always be avoided at any cost.

At the same time it is natural that a clash of wills between parents and child should come sooner or later. In such cases you should keep in mind, as a general principle, that it is fatal to allow the child to dominate you even once and so win the battle. We have all seen cases of parents who were in fact dominated by their children and what a pitiable spectacle it is.

Be firm, therefore, and make the child obey you provided that you are sure you are in the right. This means once again that you must see the situation from the child's point of view as well as from your own. Find out whether the particular thing you command is really something which matters in the education of your child or whether it is merely a whim or fancy of your own. Also, judge it in the right perspective, to see if it is something which is worth making a fuss about, because quite often parents are inclined to insist on something which is not really worth all the energy they expend on getting it done. Once you have made up your mind on those things, then act with firmness and decision, according to the age and the development of the child. Never give an order unless you are fully prepared to see to it that the order is obeyed. For this reason unnecessary commands or useless comments are a mere waste of time and only serve to undermine your authority in the eyes of the children. We shall have much more to say on this question of authority and the manner of enforcing it later, but, in passing, it is worth while mentioning that now you should reap some at least of the benefit of not giving in to all your baby's whims and fancies, especially in the matter of being picked up and nursed.

3. *Persevere*

Your main object is to produce good habits in your child, and that is, of necessity, a task which demands time. Constant repetition of acts is necessary in order to root a habit deeply. Therefore routine is essential. It is not enough to show a child how to do a thing once or twice; it should be repeated until the lesson is learnt. Your task now is to learn the value of constant and persevering repetition, without anger or even annoyance at failures. In education, as in so many other things in life, it is the slow plodding without giving way to despair which wins through in the end.

In the present chapter we have contented ourselves with a brief exposition of those general principles which should govern your actions during these early years. In the next chapter we shall endeavour to give practical advice on the things which should be taught during this period and also on the lines your education should take, especially in the matter of religious training, which is the most important from every point of view.

5

CHAPTER SIX

EDUCATION BEGINS

IN THIS CHAPTER WE SHALL DEAL WITH SOME AT LEAST OF THE practical applications of the general principles which have already been discussed in so far as they affect the secular and the religious education of the child from birth up to the end of the third year of his life.

Such things as physical illness and general elementary hygiene are altogether outside the scope of this work, but in general it might be as well to point out that parents should be neither too anxious about their children's health nor too neglectful. Experience teaches us that such a warning is necessary, because far too many parents treat their children as though they were semi-invalids, thus sowing the seeds of trouble in later life. Remember that a normal baby is one of the healthiest things in Nature, but at the same time be on the look-out for signs of physical illness and get a doctor's advice at once if you are in any doubt, especially in the case of the first child. After you have had a little experience to guide you it will be much easier for you to tell almost at once whether these physical signs demand immediate medical attention or whether you can deal with the first stages of the illness yourselves.

One of the best indications that your baby is healthy is his weight. A normal child usually gains between six to eight ounces per week during the first few months of his life, so that the birth weight is usually doubled within the first five or six months. During the second half of the first year the child should gain between two to four ounces weekly, and thus the birth weight is usually trebled during the first year. However, there may be variations either above or below the average height and weight, and these need not worry you unduly because the child may still remain well within the limit of the normal. It is safe to say that a child who shows a scale of weight and height which is between seven to ten per cent. below the average for his age is below the normal standard required for good health and should be examined by a doctor. Get a good book on this subject and follow it ; then you should have little difficulty.

Here we intend to confine ourselves to the field of education, and thus we shall only touch on the physical when it has some bearing on that subject.

It is taken for granted that you have followed the advice already given and have not given in to all your baby's whims and fancies, especially in the matter of being picked up and nursed every time he cries for attention. You will also have laid down a definite routine for such things as the bath, feeding, sleeping, play, etc. Thus, by the time the child reaches the age of one year he will have become accustomed to this idea of routine. Apart from these important factors, the general education during these early years will concentrate on the formation of other good habits both of cleanliness and punctuality. Let us deal with the question of cleanliness first.

If you wish to avoid such distressing things as bed-wetting or constipation in later life then now is the time to begin the development of good mental and physical habits towards that end. It is really surprising how few parents make any real attempts to teach such good habits from infancy. They seem to take it for granted that nothing much can be done until later in life. This is a mistake, but at the same time we must not demand adult standards from the young child.

In actual practice we should give the child every opportunity of acquiring such good habits early in life by putting him on the pot after each feed. At first there may be no response, but quite soon he will come to realize that we are pleased if he gives up the stool at the right time and in the right place, especially if we show our pleasure by the tones of our voice and do not insist too much if nothing happens. Sometimes the child who responded readily to our suggestions during infancy may show a tendency to relapse into the old habits of irregularity once he begins to walk or at times of emotional upset. There is nothing very surprising in this, and we should not scold him for it. Patience and much gentleness is required in this matter if we are to gain final success.

By the time the child reaches the age of three you should have achieved your object, and once you are reasonably sure of him then it is a good thing to leave him alone during his morning visits to the lavatory, thus allowing him to manage for himself as soon as possible. The important element in this training is to get the child to correspond with you through love and not from fear of scoldings.

As the child grows older this regularity of the habit becomes even more important, and for that reason we shall deal here with its main outlines once and for all. By the time he reaches the age of five or six all tendency to bed-wetting should have disappeared except on very rare occasions when there may be some other reason for it. We shall mention later in this book the methods which may be used to counteract this habit should it persist beyond this age. By this time, too, the child should be well accustomed to attend to the wants of Nature at certain definite times. This is of much greater importance than parents generally realize, and care should be taken to see to it that the child acquires the habit of doing this after breakfast *every morning*. Once school age has been reached, make sure that the child gets up in time to have his breakfast in comfort and then attend to this matter without undue haste. Older children and adolescents in particular are very careless in this matter, and have to be carefully watched and given good advice.

Do not allow your children to get into the habit of taking laxatives without real necessity. In the vast majority of cases this can be avoided altogether by the cultivation of good habits of regularity, good diet and the juice of an orange taken first thing in the morning before breakfast. More people should develop this habit in their children. In summer the orange juice may be replaced by other fresh fruit juices if necessary. Should a mild laxative be required, the best one for older children is liquid paraffin in small doses, because it is non-habit forming and also is not assimilated into the system. The use of other drug-laxatives should be reduced to the very minimum.

If all difficulty in this matter were dealt with in childhood and adolescence then there would be much less trouble in adult life than there usually is. It cannot be over-stressed that the cultivation of good habits in childhood is the real solution to the problem of constipation and such like ills. We should not consider the bowel movement as being merely a physical thing, because it has a large mental element in it and that can be efficiently educated. Don't allow your children to be lazy in this respect. Also make quite sure that they get sufficient fluids to drink, especially during the summer months.

This idea of the cultivation of regular habits also applies to such things as rising in the mornings, washing and sleep, not to mention such things as the regular hours for meals and good habits in eating. These good habits are formed very early in life, some of them during infancy, and although the times for these duties may undergo a certain change as the child grows older, the idea and the habit of regularity should be maintained and developed. We have mentioned the time for going to bed at night, and the whole question of the hours for sleep is so important that a special word or two about it will not be out of place.

First of all, remember that small children need sleep, and plenty of it. A baby will normally sleep most of the time, but even when the baby stage is over the young child should get into the habit of sleeping for an hour or so before dinner every morning. You will find this morning habit much more useful than the more usual afternoon sleep for the simple reason that it does not interfere with the child's rest at night. The morning habit leaves them free for play and for walks in the afternoon and so makes quite sure that they are healthily tired when bed-time comes.

Once the child passes out of the baby stage then you must not allow him to acquire irregular habits in the time for going to bed. Make a fixed time and keep to it. Naturally, this hour for bed will have to be revised as the child grows older, but the important thing is to get the habit of regularity. Most children soon acquire a great facility for employing what may be called " delaying tactics " when the time comes for going to bed, but once they have found that such tactics do not have any effect on you they will soon drop them and will obey you promptly. This is especially true if they have been played with for half an hour or so before bed-time, and this play is not a bad thing provided you see to it that the games are not over-exciting. In that way you will avoid much trouble. In cases of over-excitement a little glucose in water given just before going to bed is a useful and entirely harmless sedative. The custom of giving children a sweet to suck on going to bed is not, however, good, because they may fall asleep with the sweet still in their mouths and also such a practice tends to make them feel thirsty and so they are constantly waking up and demanding drinks.

Children should be accustomed from infancy to going to bed in the dark, and if they get into this habit you will find that they usually lose all fear of the dark, since that fear is one which is not born in us ; we acquire it from others. Therefore don't be afraid of the dark yourselves, or at least do not show this fear in front of the child, and you will find that the children will not develop it at all. We shall deal with some exceptions to this rule about sleeping in the dark later.

If you wish to avoid trouble over feeding later on in childhood, there are a few simple rules which should be observed once the infant has been weaned. Make both meals and meal-times as attractive as possible. This can always be done with a little imagination and ingenuity on your part. The room itself should be clean, light and airy. The child's plates, cups and so on should also be clean and interesting. One system which gives good results is to use plates of the Pyrex type and to paint flowers, birds or animals underneath so that they show through the glass. Transfers are sold for this purpose. Good habits in eating should be taught as soon as possible, but always without making meal-times periods of continual correction. This rule should be observed throughout the whole of childhood. Show the children what to do and do not grumble at them all the time if they fail to carry out your instructions perfectly. Above all, do try to make the meals attractive not merely by varying the food as much as possible but also by variety in the methods of presentation—half the battle with children.

Once the child begins to feed himself—and most of them soon insist on this—then make sure that he has every chance of learning quickly and easily. Put his food on a dish in a large enamel tray or on a piece of oil-cloth so that any mess can be ignored and easily cleaned up. Make sure that his chair is of the right height to allow his arms free play and that it is close enough to the table. It is not much use putting his food on a plate which is either too flat or very shallow, because he will spend most of his time chasing it round the plate with a spoon if you do that. Give him either a flat plate with a square rim (these are usually made especially for babies), or else a deep dish. The spoon should be small, otherwise he will attempt to put too much food into his mouth at once ; but it should have a deep bowl to make things a little easier for him. A piece of crust held in his left hand will give him something much better to push the food with than his fingers. The cup for drinking purposes should be small, but with a large handle. Remember that he will be able to deal with it much better if you do not put too much liquid in it at a time and that it is better for him to drink after the meal than during it. He will usually get very angry if you attempt to hold his hand and guide it, so that it is really much better to let him experiment for himself.

Punctuality is important for meals, as also is patience and good temper, not merely with the children but also with each other. Never allow meal-times to develop into family debates, especially heated ones, because that is not good for anyone's digestion and there is a very special reason for avoiding this when the children are at table, as we shall see.

So far we have dealt with certain questions with regard to the general education of the child during these early years. Now we must consider religious education, as far as it is possible to give it during this period of the child's life.

We presume that you have already made the preparations described in previous chapters of this book, so that everything is now ready. It is time to put those preparations into actual practice. In the other books in this same series you will find this question of religious education developed for you throughout the whole of childhood. Consequently, here we shall endeavour to stress a little more some of those points which are of the greatest importance.

There may be very little you can do so far as the child is

concerned during the baby stage, but you can make sure that you acquire good habits yourselves, and they will have their full effect later on. You can hang religious pictures on the wall of the child's room where he can see them, also make and erect that little altar we mentioned before, with its statue of Christ and His Mother. We do not know exactly when a small baby develops the faculty of distinguishing objects clearly, but it is certainly much earlier than people think. Get into the habit of making the Sign of the Cross over your baby when you put him to bed at night, and go down on your knees at the side of the cot and ask Almighty God to bless and protect him during the night. Any form of words will do for this prayer, but in case you should need a definite formula here is one which is very suitable. "Dear God, keep my baby under the care of your Divine Providence while he is asleep. Send your holy angels to watch over him, especially his guardian angel. Give me all the graces I need to bring him up to love and to serve You. Holy Mary, Mother of the Child Jesus, I put my baby under your protection. In the Name of the Father, and of the Son and of the Holy Ghost. Amen."

This idea of the parents blessing their children before going to bed is an old Catholic custom which might well be revived. Try to observe it all your lives, because it serves not merely to call down God's blessing on the children but also it impresses on them the idea that their parents stand as God's representatives—an idea which must be learned before they can love you as they ought.

As soon as the child can distinguish a picture of his Mother or Father then he can also recognize one of the Child Jesus and Our Lady. Get into the habit of showing him such pictures and repeating for him the Holy Name. He will soon pick it up and then begin to say it for himself. Once he begins to talk, you can soon get him to say " Goodnight, Jesus " and " Goodnight, Mary " on going to bed. You might give him the pictures to kiss as he says these words.

At this stage you can also take the child's hand and make the Sign of the Cross on him with it—there is no need to say the words just yet. The movements will soon become automatic, and then you can get the child to do it himself.

As soon as he shows a definite interest in picture-books then you can begin to use your religious scrap-book. The first steps in the use of this book are very simple ones, because there is no need for many words ; all you need to do with the child is look at the brightly-coloured pictures and repeat to him the names of Jesus and Mary. Here are some simple suggestions which will help you in your use of the scrap-book at this stage.

You must choose your moments to bring out the scrap-book, that is to say, when the child is ready and willing to sit quietly on your knees as you turn over the pages to look at the pictures. There is no point in trying to interest him in it when his attention is directed elsewhere. Remember that the whole idea of this book is bound up with the fact that its use should be considered a special treat and should be understood as such by the child. This is important because such special treats impress themselves on the mind of the child. So choose your moments when both you and he are ready and willing to give some time to this pleasure.

This also implies that the book should not be given over to the child to do with as he pleases, but should be kept in a safe place for the parents and the child to use together. Such moments of real intimacy are very precious to the child and this will help your religious instruction very much if you make the most of it. If you give the book into the child's hands, then not only does he miss the great pleasure of using it with you but also you will soon have to make another scrap-book!

If you have an older child, you may permit him to show the book to the younger one at times but do not neglect this duty altogether yourselves. Once religion becomes connected in the child's mind with the idea of parental love and intimacy you have achieved something very great indeed, and have provided a motive for the love of God which is of the greatest importance.

For grace before and after meals it is sufficient, to begin with, if you make the Sign of the Cross on the child with his hand and later get him to do it himself, adding the words when he knows them. All present should make this sign with him, and you should try to remember this at every meal, because it is on these small things that your future success will depend.

Once the child reaches the age when stories of all kinds appeal to him, you can extend the use of the scrap-book by telling him simple stories about the pictures. Remember that they must be simple stories and that it is a good thing to introduce variety at times by giving him some pictures of the Holy Family or the life of Christ together with some coloured crayons. The idea behind this has many applications which you can discover for yourselves. The child learns, not merely by seeing and touching, but in most cases by doing things. Such simple actions as the colouring of these pictures will fix them and the stories connected with them very firmly in his mind.

In most cases this story-telling stage can be reached by the time the child is three years old, often much earlier than that. However, there is no need for you to hurry at this point, and you should keep pace with the actual development of the child, never taking a step forward until you know from certain definite signs that it is time to do so. Patience is the great virtue now as later. Remember, too, that you must never do anything which will tend to make the child dislike religion or the periods of religious teaching.

This religious training should expand gradually until the child reaches school age, but since we shall deal with the question of education between the ages of three and six in another chapter we can postpone detailed discussions of this development until then. There is one point which still remains to be dealt with here, and that is the question of the importance of play for the young child's development.

A child—very rightly—spends much of his time in play. He finds an ever-increasing interest in his small toys, in his companions, himself and the world around him, as well as his own experiences in contact with that world. This play is not only important from the point of view of physical development but also from that of mental expansion and character formation. During these periods of play he gets opportunities to exercise and develop his muscles and also learns to control them better. He develops his senses and perfects his mind. Through this play he learns to control his balance, to appreciate distances, colours, shapes, and so on. We should, therefore, never underestimate the value of play for the character formation of the young child.

During the first six months of his life the child is mainly concerned with the joys which he has in the use of the sense of sight and touch, and so we should give him some old toys, not merely to interest him and keep him quiet, but also to educate him. Rattles are useful for this purpose, and so are old cotton reels joined together on a piece of string and, if possible, brightly coloured. Bright colours, especially the shades of red and yellow, seem to captivate his attention most of all. Once he enters upon his second year of life then we should provide him with a collection of wooden blocks or bricks. Indeed, during this period almost anything can become a toy for him, since he now takes a very great interest in the world around him. During the second and third years of his life we should also try, even at some cost to our sense of good order and tidiness, to provide him with some sand to dig in and also some water to play with. This can nearly always be done during the summer months at least in a space in the garden set aside for that purpose. Why those two simple elements should exercise such a great effect on the character development of the child is something which remains a mystery to us, but the fact is that they are of great importance, and so you should do what you can to provide opportunities for their use. They certainly develop co-ordination of muscles and control.

During the third year he continues, to a great extent at least, his former activities, but it would be as well to add to his pleasure some old sheets of paper together with a collection of coloured chalks or crayons. These provide a source of never-ending entertainment and also train his sense of distance and perspective as nothing else can. It is also possible to retain his interest by telling him simple stories from illustrated books, provided they are not beyond his understanding, and also by allowing him to " help " you around the house. Give him a small duster or an old piece of cloth which can do duty for one and he will be quite happy.

It should be kept in mind that, during these years, the child's play is not by any means simply a " game." He plays for quite another reason, i.e., because it is Nature's way of developing the long muscles of the body and of training him in co-ordination and muscle control. It also develops his senses. Those restless movements which are sometimes so very trying to grown-ups form part of Nature's plan for his education, and we must learn to appreciate them as such.

Just as we do, the growing child needs fresh air, and as much as possible should be given him. Provided the baby is well wrapped up there is no reason why he should not be placed in his cot near an open window provided he is safe from draughts. Sunlight is good for him, too—as indeed it is for all young growing creatures, provided we take care to see to it that he gets it without being burnt by the direct rays in the summer months. A child does not like the direct sunlight on his eyes any more than we do, but if it is allowed to get at his whole body it will do wonderful work on the bone structure and the skin, aiding the body to resist such things as colds and infections in general much more than any amount of medicine will ever do. Later in life one of the very best ways of getting fresh air, sunlight and also exercise for the body and the senses is the daily walk, and wherever possible this should be a part of your routine, even if it has to be a short walk.

A child's clumsiness at this stage of his development is the natural accompaniment to his efforts to learn muscle control, and so we should not scold him when he falls over or drops those things which he is trying to carry safely into the kitchen. However annoying such events may be for us, they are very necessary for him. Give him big objects to play with, to hold and to carry and you will probably find that he does quite well, because it is the coarse muscles which develop first, while the finer ones will take a little longer to learn co-ordination. That is why he holds a pencil in his entire fist, and finds it so difficult to use his fingers at first. Encourage him all the time and you will soon see positive results of your training.

CHAPTER SEVEN

PROBLEMS OF EARLY CHILDHOOD

THE TITLE OF THIS CHAPTER NEEDS SOME EXPLANATION. IN the first place, it is intended to be a transitional chapter, which will discuss some of the more common problems which are liable to arise during childhood, i.e. from birth until the age when the child can go to school. Thus it takes us a little further than the previous chapters of this book, which have dealt with general principles of education and mainly from the point of view of the young child up to the age of three. Some of the problems which are mentioned here may never occur at all in the case of your child, while others may be found earlier or later, according to his development. There is very little use in trying to give a definite time limit for such things, because individuals differ too much either through heredity, environment or some other circumstance. It is neither fair nor correct to attempt to " type " individuals too readily.

Very young children have no problems. That statement will probably be hotly contested by some of our more " advanced " psychologists, but it is nevertheless true. Up to the age of three the problems exist, not in the mind of the child, but in those of the parents, and it is during those early years that many of the seeds of future personal conflict are sown. Nor can we be expected to deal here with all the possible problems which can arise in individual cases, but only with those which are almost certain to present themselves unless they are guarded against by careful action on the part of the parents. Other problems which arise from either physical or mental abnormality, and which thus need expert medical treatment, are also beyond our scope.

Having thus limited the field to which this chapter refers it will be as well to begin our study of these problems by repeating something which has already been mentioned before, but in greater detail. There are seeds of future character abnormalities and of conflicts in every child by his or her nature. These have to be watched and guarded against very carefully during the early years of childhood. They are especially important because they have some effect on practically every department of education during those years and also later on. Such factors are the child's smallness in comparison with the world around him, his physical weakness which does not allow him to overcome obstacles as easily as he sees other people overcome them ; the unreliable nature of his judgments and knowledge, which naturally leads him to make many mistakes, as also the fact that he cannot see very clearly the connection between events as we see it. Perhaps a few simple examples of these factors will help to show us how they can affect the child in his relations with others and also in his relations with the world about him. His smallness and weakness naturally imply that all physical effort to overcome difficulties and obstacles is much greater in the child than it is in adults, and requires a mental attention which he is often not able to give. The very simplest actions, such as putting on his clothes and doing up buttons, for instance, which we find so simple, are great tasks to the child, because he has not yet acquired the habits which make such operations easy. The very acquiring of these habits takes time and energy, together with repeated effort, and since every child, by his very nature, is selfish in the truest sense of that word, i.e., tends to look for self gratification and pleasure instead of hard work and effort, he tries to rely on others rather than go to the trouble and effort of acquiring such habits.

It is also due in the main to his smallness and weakness that he begins to know the meaning of fear, and all fear is a very important factor in the life and the character formation of the child. On the one hand, he is always on the lookout for new experiences, because that is the only way to develop knowledge, and all children want to " know " things. On the other hand, experience teaches him that some things are not what they seem to be at first sight. Often, if he trusts to his eyes, they look nice and the source of pleasure, but on closer acquaintance they are nasty and cause pain. Thus, fire may be very nice to look at, but when you touch it it burns. Again, he can crawl upstairs, but the getting down again seems to need a new and a complex mechanism which he does not seem to possess. All these experiences, especially if they have the added circumstance that his parents show fear at times, tend to produce a fear in him which may easily become exaggerated and so the cause of much future trouble.

The very knowledge which he longs for with increasing desire as the years unfold, seems uncertain and shifting. Thus, he learns that one particular thing which he sees quite often is called a chicken, and then, a few days later perhaps, when he applies this newly-acquired knowledge to a duck he finds that he is wrong. It is all so very difficult. This limitation of his knowledge makes him still more uncertain of himself, and so serves sometimes to increase his fears. Then again, it is so very difficult for the small child to see the connection between events, because he lives very much in the present moment. Today may be Monday, but to the small child there seems to be no intrinsic impossibility in the fact that tomorrow may be Saturday. All these factors, which are so very real to the child, even if unconsciously as yet, must be taken into consideration during these early years, because, as we shall see, they have very important applications in the whole field of education.

Consequently, one of the most important rules which parents have to learn and to keep in mind is that they *must* try to see things from the view point of the child and not from that of adults. That is what we meant when we said that, in early childhood, the main problems are in the minds of the parents rather than in that of the child. Let me give you some practical examples of this principle as applied to your efforts to educate your child correctly.

It is perfectly natural for the child to do those things which he knows or thinks are pleasing to him, and he has still to learn that other people have to be taken into consideration and that his parents have to be obeyed. This takes time, patience and above all love, if it is to be done without breaking the child's will into pieces. We must not expect the children to do things which we want them to do all the time, because there are sure to be countless occasions when their inclinations pull them one way while our knowledge of what is right and wrong pulls in the opposite direction. In such instances we have to educate the child by making him do the right thing gently, firmly, but all the time with love and understanding of his difficulties. It is not easy for him, remember, but we can make it a little easier by the methods we use. Unreasonable anger on our part or scoldings will only serve to produce rebellion on his, and that is not good for our authority. Let us see just one example of this before we pass on. Most babies soon learn to find comfort and pleasure in sucking their thumb, but then, most babies also get out of it quite soon and very easily. Parents, on the other hand, often get very worried about this habit and wonder what they should do about it. Some go to the extreme lengths of tying their child's arms so that he cannot suck his thumb, others put gloves on him, in which case he merely sucks the glove, and so frustrates that attempt to prevent his pleasure quite simply. What should we do? That depends on the circumstances and also on the individual. If he is a very small baby then there is every chance that he will soon grow out of it, so that he can be left alone for the time being unless he is doing it most of the day and very vigorously, in which case he might deform his mouth or dwarf his thumb. Then steps will have to be taken. If he is older, then we shall find that he usually only sucks his thumb for a short time when going to sleep and very seldom during the day, and in that case there is no need to worry about it because he will get out of it naturally. Sometimes a woolly doll or animal taken to bed with him and cuddled in his arms will prevent it altogether and at once. Don't attempt to tie his arms down or anything like that because you will only succeed in making him very angry and so cause more trouble. Make sure that his hunger is fully satisfied, because that may easily be the cause of the thumb sucking. If the child is no longer in the baby stage, but has passed the age of three, then you may have to deal with this situation gently, either by withdrawing his thumb or, better, by giving him interests outside himself which will distract him. You may even go to the lengths of giving him a boiled sweet after he gets into bed, and that will probably do the trick. We have already said that this practice of giving children sweets to suck in bed is not a good one for several reasons, but in this case it is better to depart from the general rule, because you have a legitimate reason for so doing. If, in spite of all this, the habit persists into later childhood, say after the age of six, then you have a problem on your hands, because there will be a reason for the thumb sucking which probably lies deep in the child's character. We shall have something to say about this later, when dealing with the problems of older children.

By the time the child reaches the age of three his life may have been complicated by the addition of yet another child to the family. Now, this event is of the greatest importance and very much will depend on how it is handled. Consider it from the child's point of view for a moment. He has held the centre of the stage up to now, and all the attention of the parents has been for him alone. He knows, in a vague way at least, how much he depends on them for everything, and thus he is perfectly capable of resenting the new member of the family and of considering him as an intruder who is coming between him and his parents. The key to the answer to this problem lies not so much in the child as in the parents' attitude towards their children. If they make unfair distinctions between the two children, favouring one to the exclusion of the other, then they are asking for trouble and may expect it. If they get into the habit of contrasting the conduct of the baby with that of the older child to his obvious disadvantage, the same is true. Remember that the very position of any individual child in the family circle by reason of his age may have a great influence on his development. There are special problems connected with the eldest child, with the youngest and with the intermediate ones, not to mention the only child, who by reason of his special position is a problem on his own. We shall have something to say about those cases later on. At the moment we are concerned rather with the parents' attitude in regard to the new baby and the former one. In general it should be kept in mind that this situation is of the greatest importance, and that you can do much to ease it if you are careful to do all in your power to make up to the older child for the decreasing amount of attention which is naturally paid to him at certain times. This problem, like so many others, carries with it its own danger signals. Thus, if you find that the older child is especially difficult at such times as feed time for the baby or bath time, then you can be fairly certain that you have at least the beginnings of this problem on your hands. Fits of temper, biting, scratching, lack of interest in the baby, waking up at night and screaming for attention—these are all signs of the same thing, and show that you must take steps to correct your attitude to the older child. The method of dealing with it is, fortunately, simple and effective, as a rule. It consists in giving to the older child slightly more attention at other times than he has been accustomed to receive. Thus, if he is difficult while the baby is being fed, then you can promise him a special treat once baby has been attended to, and, of course, you must keep your promise. This treat should be something which concentrates your attention on him and which implies intimacy and affection. Thus, once baby has been fed you might settle down in a chair with the older child and tell him a story or play with him for a while.

Generally this difficulty tends to show itself in the first child more than in the others ; however, if you are wise enough and careful enough to avoid any over-demonstrations of affection for the younger one then you can meet this difficulty and overcome it almost before it appears. Remember that it is perfectly natural for you to have preferences, but it is a very unwise thing to show them in any way at all. Equal attention, where possible, is the only safe rule in this matter, especially when your children get a little older. It might be as well to mention here that it is normally a bad thing to delegate your parental responsibilities to the older child by giving him charge of the younger one. This very seldom solves the problem, and may even increase the older child's feelings of resentment. Give him added sense of responsibility in other ways if you like, but not over the younger child. All children feel this jealousy for the newcomer, although not all show it equally, and thus it is a problem which should be ever-present in your mind when the new baby arrives. You can do much to prevent it ever becoming a real difficulty to the older child if you are careful to show him that he is still wanted as much as ever before and still loved.

In the long run, of course, the problem solves itself, because there is nothing so good for the education of the child as a large family in which one child will find splendid allies in the others. They alone can understand and enter fully into his world of childhood, and he soon learns to appreciate this fact very much. Also this problem is usually less acute when one baby follows soon after the former.

We have mentioned the fact that fear plays a very great part in the development of the character of the young child. It would be no exaggeration to say that fear is also at the very root of the vast majority of the problems which you may have to meet with in the up-bringing of your children. Perhaps its presence may not always be detected, and sometimes it is not always easy to recognise as fear, because of its many disguises, but it is there all the same. There are two very obvious manifestations of fear, however, which cannot be overlooked here. One of these is the fear of the dark. This is something which is not inherited, but which is acquired either from you, or from circumstances or perhaps from some unpleasant experience. The very small child, especially if he has been used to sleeping in the dark from birth, is not, by nature, afraid. If, of course, you are afraid of the dark then you can expect that your child will also learn to acquire that fear, too, and you must do all that you can to prevent it, and never show that fear in his presence. Among the unpleasant experiences which commonly produce this fear in the child we need only mention two. One is the very stupid habit some people have of hiding in dark corners and then popping out at the child with a loud " boo! " This is a common trick of older children in their dealings with the younger ones, and it should be prevented or stopped as soon as it shows its head. In the same class are all " horror " stories and " bogey men ", and we would do well to remove all such things from our list of stories.

One of the best preventions which can be of great use in this matter is your religious education of the child. We have already mentioned the little wooden altar in the child's room, with its statue or picture of Jesus and His Mother. If you have already got the child to say " Goodnight, Jesus," on going to bed then it should be quite easy to bring home to him the idea that Jesus and Mary are going to be with him all the night through, and will look after him. In this way the sense of loneliness which is one of the causes of this fear tends to disappear. It may even be necessary to place a little lamp in front of the statue for a few weeks, but do not start this until all other means of over-coming this fear have failed. By the way, if you must keep a cat in the house when there is a young baby (not at all a good thing), do see to it that the cat cannot jump up on the child's cot or bed during the night, because there is nothing quite so frightening. Dogs are not usually offenders in this, especially if they have been well trained.

One of the consequences of this fear may be bad dreams at night. These can, of course, be caused by other things, such as the cutting of teeth or over-excitement before going to bed. The first thing you must do with regard to these dreams is to observe how frequently they wake the child during the night and, if possible, connect them with the true cause. If you cannot find any other cause, then you may be quite sure that they are the results of fear. Usually the child wakes up crying or shouting for his mother and there is no apparent reason for the alarm. He will give as his explanation that he was dreaming. If this happens after you have retired for the night yourselves there is a great temptation perhaps to take the child into your bed with you and comfort him, thus avoiding getting cold yourselves. This is not a good way of dealing with this evil, because you are not teaching the child to rely on himself. The best method is to pick the child up for a while and comfort him and then, when the worst appears to be over, put him back to bed again, staying with him for a few moments longer until he settles down. Most children respond very quickly to this and soon fall asleep soundly. This method may demand more or less heroic self-sacrifice on your part, especially during the winter, but it is easily the best method of curing this evil without forming any other bad habits at the same time.

Once the child reaches the age of three years, and perhaps even before that time, the very controverted question of punish-ment is sure to arise. A general word or two on this subject may help to clear the air of prejudices.

Naturally, all excessive punishment or strictness is wrong. That may be concluded from what we have already said about authority in general and parental authority in particular. Any authority which acts as if the subjects of it possessed no rights whatsoever, but merely exist for the benefit and the convenience of the person wielding that authority, is starting off on the wrong foot so far as education is concerned and is bound to come to grief sooner or later. The child is a person with rights, some of them belonging to him even before he is born into the world and while he is still in his mother's womb. Those rights must be recognized and respected if correct relationships are to be built up between himself and his parents. His special difficulties must also be understood and allowances made for them. Any use of authority which implies an ignoring of these fundamental principles is evil, and will merely lead to an increase in the sense of weakness, fear and insecurity which are already in the child owing to his special circumstances in the family and in the world. Consequently, our first duty as parents is to assess correctly our position and our authority with regard to the child. We have to understand quite clearly that he, like us, has rights which we must respect. Unless we do acquire this right attitude towards the child we shall only do more harm than good by our correction, because we shall only increase the child's sense of insecurity, instead of leading him gradually to build up his own character and so stand on his own feet.

The other attitude to punishment which is much more common nowadays than it ever was before is equally wrong, because it tends either to suppress correction altogether or at least to adopt methods which, by their very nature, are bound to be ineffective. Such an attitude does not take into consideration the fact of original sin! In its extreme form this attitude means that we should leave the child alone entirely, allowing him to find out by personal experience what is right and what is wrong. That opinion and attitude cannot be supported by any Catholic, but there are some who maintain that at least all physical correction is wrong and harmful. We should never forget that, even in the law of God, punishment is an integral part of contrition and of pardon. As usual, the middle way contains the truth, and here are some general principles which will help parents to acquire a right mental attitude towards this question of correction and punishment.

In the first place, all punishment should be just, proportionate to the offence and also intelligible to the child.

When we say that punishment should be just we mean that it should come from a justice which is tempered with mercy— a thing which we all expect when we deal with God but which we sometimes forget in our dealings with others. It is not just, for example, to keep a small child waiting in suspense for a long time while we deliberate what is to be done with regard to a certain offence. If any punishment is needed then it should follow at once on the offence. Again, justice must be observed in the kind of punishment which we administer. All humiliating punishments must be ruled out completely, as should all "psychological" punishments, for example that of not speaking to a child because he has done wrong. "Nagging" must be avoided too, because in any case the child soon gets used to it and turns a deaf ear, so that it has no effect. If you ask a child who is old enough to talk reasonably about such things, what he does during this "nagging", you need not be at all surprised to hear him reply, "I think of something else." How very much better it is to administer one quick sharp physical punishment and then forget all about it. The children, too, prefer that method.

Punishment should also be in proportion to the age of the child. One would imagine that there should be no need to stress this point, but in actual fact experience shows that there is. It must also be in proportion to the offence itself as seen from the child's point of view rather than from our own. Thus, a child can see no difference between breaking a cheap plate, for which he receives little or no rebuke, and one which is, shall we say, valuable. If punishment is withheld in the first case and sharply administered in the second then the child feels that an injustice has been done, and he is right. If a certain mode of conduct which is normally allowed when no visitors are present is corrected sharply when they are present then the child only becomes confused. He cannot see the connection between the presence of a visitor and a certain mode of conduct. He is perfectly right, because there should be no difference.

We should also remember not to demand too much from the very young child, out of all proportion to his capabilities. The real test to be applied in all cases is whether the child knows perfectly well that he is doing something wrong, and especially if he does it with malice, because he knows that it annoys us. This sense of moral responsibility is soon born in the young child, but naturally, it has to grow with him and so will become much more acute as he grows older. To punish without taking this factor into consideration is very wrong, and should always be avoided.

This is partly what we mean when we say that all punishment should be intelligible to the child. It should be administered with justice and mercy, preferably the latter prevailing, and in proportion to the offence and age of the child. Lastly, it should be intelligible to the child, in the sense that he knows he has done wrong and that he fully deserves the punishment which is administered. Provided this fact is clear to the mind of the child then punishment does him no harm at all, but, on the contrary, a great deal of good. He knows that it is administered with kindness and affection, and that his parents do not really like to punish him at all. That makes a very big difference.

There are some mothers who think that it is the father's duty to administer such punishment as may be required by the day's misdeeds, and thus, instead of dealing with such situations as they arise, these mothers insist on telling the child "Just wait until your father comes home!" Now, nothing could be more harmful than this. In the first place, such a mode of conduct only serves to make the father an object of hatred or at least fear to the child, who connects his home-coming with a recital of his faults and the administration of punishment. This is all wrong. Also this method of acting means that either the offence has long since been forgotten by the child or else it has been on his mind most of the day, instead of being corrected at the time and then forgotten. Parents who act in this way are sometimes surprised when, later in life, their adolescent sons or daughters refuse to confide their problems to them, while doing so freely to other adults.

Never administer punishment when in a fit of temper. If you know perfectly well that you are far too angry to punish calmly then do not punish at all. It is far better in the long run.

Neither should you indulge in that type of punishment which consists in manifestations, often too prolonged, of disapproval. Worse than this even is the refusal to admit that the child can do anything very well, and which manifests itself in a refusal to praise the good which he does. The contrary should be our method. Praise the good done by the child and reward it, so that he soon comes to see that being good pays dividends in many ways. Later on in his life you will be able to supply far more perfect motives, no doubt, but these preliminary ones are by no means to be despised.

Punishment can often be made to fit the crime in a most surprising fashion, and if administered quickly and cheerfully, will be found very effective. Some examples of this method may be useful, but it should be remembered that it is only really useful in older children, i.e., from the age of six upwards. If a child has been told not to make a certain noise, for a real and not for a purely imagined reason, and still persists in ignoring this command then it is often very effective to take him out into the garden or into another room and force him to continue making the noise which has been the cause of all the trouble for five minutes on end without stopping. Often it is only the fact that the particular action has been forbidden which makes it so attractive, and the child will soon learn that it is no use being attracted towards such forbidden things once they themselves are made a particularly odious punishment. A child who persists in whimpering for nothing after being told to stop can often be cured for good and all by being made to stand up and produce the same noise for five minutes without stopping. One or two applications of this method are often sufficient to remove some evil which has resisted all other methods.

There are certain punishments which should be avoided altogether, and we have already mentioned some of them. Perhaps we might add to that list such things as sending the child to bed without any supper, shutting him up in a room by himself (often no punishment at all to certain types of children), putting the child in a dark cupboard, all long-term punishments, all attempts to make the child look or feel ridiculous, especially by holding up one of the other children as an example of good conduct (how irritating and ineffectual this is, and how harmful to both children). The same may be said with regard to punishment as the result of tale-bearing by another child, all deprivation of love and affection and in general anything which will humiliate or degrade the child. Contrariwise, there is nothing whatever wrong with a slap administered at the right time, either on the hand in the case of younger children, or on other more effective portions of the person in the case of older children. " Boxing of ears " however should be out from the start, because often fathers in particular do not know their own strength, and also a good deal of harm can be caused without intention, even to the extent of deafness. Use your hand, and never an instrument, to administer such physical punishment, because in that way you will be able to control your strength better and will know the force you are putting into the blows.

In general, with younger children there should be no need to administer physical punishment at all, because a word of reproof is usually sufficient to let them see that you do not approve of their action. Also it should be possible to avoid most of the situations which call for punishment with a little tact on your part during these early years.

Make up for punishments afterwards by proving to the child that you have now forgotten all about the offence which brought on the punishment, and that it has been paid for in full. He appreciates that, and also sees the justice of the punishment better. Remember that very often indeed you are the real cause of the act which calls, so you think, for punishment, because you have not been careful to distinguish between those things which a child can be told to do or not to do with profit and those which are really impossible. You should learn from the beginning to classify things into at least three groups. First come those which are the objects of real and prompt obedience, such as the time for bed, getting up in the morning, putting away toys which are getting in everybody's way, not answering back, not biting other children or hitting them, clean hands at meal times, not running across the road, and so on—a list which you must complete for yourselves. In the second group we should place those things in which the child is to be given complete freedom. This will cover such things as the way he arranges his toys in his cupboard, the games which he chooses to play at the time set apart for play, the choice, at least on some occasions, of where he goes for his afternoon walk, how he spends his pocket money, however little it may be. Such things, and others which you can add to the list, should be made the objects of the child's own free choice, and see to it that it is free in every way, even though you do not happen to agree with that choice on every occasion. Lastly, there is a large group of things which cannot and should not be made the object of obedience, because the child has not complete control over them or perhaps because to make them the object of commands would be to make him worse instead of better. Into this group fall such things as biting nails, stammering, shyness with guests or other children, refusal to play with certain children, and so on. To make those things the objects of formal obedience is generally to lose our child's respect and confidence. Far better to attack them indirectly by encouragement and by kindness.

One last word—don't command unless you are sure that the thing you are telling the child to do really matters, and also that you are willing to follow your command up should it not be obeyed. Don't impose things just because you feel like it, or forbid something just because you do not happen to like it. Don't be arbitrary. Always give a child due warning if you are breaking in on something which he is interested in, such as playing, reading or drawing. You don't like being interrupted yourselves when you are in the middle of an important task, and nor does he. If you take the trouble to tell him that in five minutes time he will have to put away his toys and get ready for supper or bed then he will be much more likely to obey you when that time comes, and thus both of you will be much more contented. Also learn to be a little tactful, and do turn a blind eye occasionally, when you know that it can be done without any harm to the child's future character.

If you follow these few simple rules then you should be able to avoid many problems which sometimes arise because parents have not acquired a right attitude to this whole question of punishment. You may have noticed that nothing has been said here with regard to punishment in connection with refusal to say prayers, and so on. That is because we shall have something to say about that later on. In general it is not a good thing to make such refusals the occasions of punishment at all. There are other ways of dealing with those situations, as we shall point out when we come to them.

CHAPTER EIGHT

FURTHER PROBLEMS OF EARLY
CHILDHOOD

POPE PIUS XI HAS WARNED US ALL, IN HIS ENCYCLICAL ON THE
Christian Education of Youth, that we must not be mere
theoreticians in this matter of education, but that we must
be prepared to give practical guidance whenever that is possible.
For that reason we shall insist all through this book on the
practical problems which confront parents and others who are
interested in the education of children.

Closely connected with the question of punishment, which we
have discussed in the last chapter, is that of spoiling. We have
all seen spoilt children at some time or another and have probably
condemned out of hand the parents who were responsible for
allowing such a thing to happen. Now, above all things, it is
very necessary in this matter of education to take all the different
factors into consideration. In the first place, spoiling implies
much less danger than does the opposite extreme—too much
harshness. Also, it is much more easily eradicated later in life.
This does not mean to say that we are vindicating completely
those parents who insist on spoiling their children, but it does
mean that there is at least one good aspect of this matter which
is all too frequently forgotten.

However, since spoiling implies bad education it should be
avoided as far as possible. This can usually be done provided
that the following dangers are guarded against. In the first
place, never allow the child's wishes to dominate you, and make
that a rule from the cradle. If the child is given in to all the time
when he is still in the baby stage then obviously he is going to
expect (and most probably receive) the same treatment throughout the rest of his childhood. Then will come the inevitable
clash once he goes to school and finds that he can no longer have

his own way. This is proved to be only too true during the trying period of adolescence and even later in life. Consequently, he may quite easily develop problems which might have been avoided altogether had his education been conducted on a more sound basis. Normally, however, the spoilt child soon learns that his attitude does not pay, and so he is forced, at the expense of wasting a good deal of time which could have been used to greater advantage elsewhere, to change his whole outlook on life. This is a pity, and principally because it does involve such a waste of time. The child's character should have a unified development, beginning in the cradle and ending with complete manhood or womanhood. Instead of this, there has been an unfortunate break in this continuity. Another danger is that, when and if such a child becomes a parent himself, he may go to the other extreme in the education of his own children, and thus fall into the error of over-discipline, which is far worse than spoiling because it tends to destroy all sense of confidence between parent and child.

A second point which we have to consider if we wish to avoid spoiling our children is that they are so very much more attractive when they are not spoilt. There are few things more degrading for parents, did they but know it, as a spoilt child, and there are also few things so unattractive in themselves. Consequently, it is very much to the child's own social advantage that he should not be spoilt. It is, after all, so very easy to avoid, if we will only make the initial effort.

Discipline must always be observed in the family circle, and if that discipline is maintained then there will be no spoiling, you may be quite sure of that. So, let parents make up their minds, not so much not to spoil their children, but rather to see to it that there is real discipline in their families, and a discipline which has love and kindness as its foundations. This implies a correct attitude on the part of the parents to the whole question of punishment which we have already dealt with, at least in its general principles. Also, parents must realize fully the harm they are doing to their children by spoiling them. A child whose slightest wish is his parents' law, and who knows no correction save gentle words of protest which he ignores completely after a time, is in for a very big shock when he comes up against the world of stern reality and competition. Nearly all such spoilt children develop many faults which others generally manage to avoid. They are nearly always very proud characters (the basis of many, if not all, sins), they are also inordinately ambitious and ruthless in their dealings with others who stand in their way. They are usually mean in their dealings with other children, and are the first to despise their parents for their weak attitude towards them. The children who really grow up to love and to respect their parents are those who have been brought up under a firm but kind discipline and who come to understand later on in life all that they owe to that attitude on the part of their parents. Also the spoilt child soon develops a grasping personality, selfish in the extreme, and completely unaccustomed to self-control. For all these reasons, and also for others which it is not necessary to stress here, we should be extremely careful never to run the risk of spoiling our children.

Another problem which may easily present itself during these early years, up to the time the child goes to school, is that of lying. Now, before we can deal with this problem correctly it will be necessary for us to know certain facts about the life of the young child which are well known and yet at the same time frequently forgotten.

It has been said that the child lives mainly in a dream world of his own construction, and while this is sometimes the case, it is not absolutely true. A young child does very often manufacture a dream world in which he spends a good deal of his time, and this is especially true of the pre-school years of growth and development. That does not mean to say that he is living in this dream world to the complete exclusion of the world of reality—not by any means. The contrary is, in fact, the truth. He is very interested in the world of reality, and only too keen to learn more about it. Thus, although many of the child's lies are really only applied fantasies, this is not the only, nor even perhaps the root, cause of lying in children. When a child tells us, for example, that he has seen a dragon at the bottom of the garden, very often he himself believes that he is speaking the truth, especially since dragons are, after all, very rare beasts, and he has not yet come across one in real life. That is a typical example of the applied fantasy. However, there is a vast difference between such exaggerations—they cannot strictly be called lies—and the real, bold lie of self-excuse or defence, when, for instance, the child deliberately says that he " has not done it " when we know perfectly well that he has, and can prove it with the evidence, perhaps, of our own eyes. What is the exact difference ? Let us examine these two cases for a moment in greater detail.

Knowing how very vivid the imagination of the young child can be, especially when it is working on the manufacture of that world of dreams of which we have spoken, it is very easy for us to see that he can confuse the images which he finds in that world with those which come to him from the world of reality. At first he only realizes very vaguely that such a transfer is taking place, and so he can be excused from the charge of telling a deliberate lie. A lie always implies that we are saying something which we know to be false, and in this case the child is saying something which he believes to be true. It is not a lie, to him at least, and so should never be punished as such by us. Our task as educators is to lead him gradually to meet and to recognize the outside world as it really is, not as he creates it for himself. Such transferred fantasies are best ignored completely or perhaps met with a smile, as though the whole thing were a game.

The other case is very different, but even here we should do our very best to get to the root of the trouble and not allow our judgment to remain on the surface. What is it that makes the young child tell lies of excuse ? The root cause is usually fear of some kind.

We have already made it quite clear that the young child is justified, to a certain extent at least, in feeling afraid. His very smallness, his feeling of relative weakness and helplessness, all these factors go to make him feel fear. To laugh at such fears and to ignore them altogether would be a grave mistake, because they are very real worries to him, and we must deal with them in that light. Such fear in one form or another is at the very root of most of the problems which crop up during childhood, and sometimes in later life as well. If it is dealt with sympathetically now he may be cured altogether. Generally it is true to say that the first real lie is born of the fear of punishment which he hopes to escape by telling the lie. It is untrue to say that there is, in every child, the innate tendency to lie. It is, however, quite true to say that there is, in every child, the root fear which can, unless it be corrected and adjusted, serve to make lying almost second nature. Usually the fact that a child is continually telling lies indicates some grave fault in his education, and that can generally be traced back to the parents. What exactly has gone wrong?

The child fears punishment for wrong-doing; that is very natural. He fears it so much that he is willing to escape from it, if he can, by telling a lie about the facts—and that, too, is natural, at least the first few times it happens. What is not natural is that such a course of action should persist, because it indicates a clear flaw in our methods of education. Consequently, we must ask ourselves how we are going to deal with this matter of lying in childhood.

First of all, we must remember that the fantasy of the child's mind, narrated as a fact, is not a lie, and must not be dealt with as such. Nor need we pay much attention to other types of fantasy-stories which will crop up sooner or later, and which do not imply any attempt to escape from punishment or from personal responsibility. The lie which has to be dealt with, then, is that statement which the child knows to be false and which has been made in order to escape from punishment or from responsibility.

The remote cure should have been applied long before such lies appear at all. The child should have been taught, from a very early age, to have such great confidence in his parents that he need never fear them, or their anger. This will serve to do much to off-set the fear which is the cause of the lie. He should have been brought up in such a way that he is by this time fully accustomed to discipline administered with firmness and kindness. But even all this will not generally stop him from trying on the idea of a lie at least once or twice in order to escape from punishment.

The very first time this happens it should be brought to his notice that, instead of making his punishment easier, the lie only serves to increase it. That is certainly the very best method of dealing with this matter in its early stages. Even the smallest child is open to a certain amount of reason. Your child should know that it is wrong to tell lies, at least if your training has been complete and good. This should be impressed upon him again, together with the idea that the lie adds to the gravity of the original offence. Then the punishment should be applied at once, and perhaps even added to because of the lie. Once or twice should be quite enough to get it firmly fixed in the child's mind that lying does not pay. But that is by no means enough, because we are out to educate our children for their whole lives, not merely for the relatively few years of their childhood. Consequently, the child should be given a little talking to once the offence and the punishment for it are both safely over. This should be done with kindness, as between very good friends. He should be told that to lie is evil because it is also an offence against God who has given us our tongue and speech so that we may tell the truth. God loves him, and so is sad when He hears those lies, however small. The other disadvantages of lying should be clearly pointed out, if possible in the form of stories, e.g., that people will never believe him at all if he lies (the story of the boy who cried "Wolf!"), even when he is really speaking the truth. When he comes to go to school he will find that lies are punished much more heavily there than this one has been at home. Also he can be told that, if he owns up honestly when he does something wrong, then he *may* possibly escape the punishment, or at least it will not be so heavy. If you are careful to make opportunities for putting this last observation into actual practice with the child for a while, it should serve to remove that basic fear which is at the root of the lie.

If dealt with in this way, lying should soon disappear, and then, later on in life, you can tell the child that the lie told in the confessional is much more serious than one told in ordinary life. In this way, as you can see, by our general education we prepare our children to be good citizens of the State and also of God. The main thing is to be sure that your child will tell the truth, especially to the priest in the confessional. That is of prime importance for his future life, and perhaps even for his eternal salvation. Your task is to prepare for that even now.

While we are talking about fear we might return to something which we have already mentioned, i.e., the fear of the dark.

7

Apart from what has already been said, you will have to remember that, once this fear does rear its head, then it is once more a very real thing to the child. Be patient and kind with him, therefore, because it is no use scolding him for it, since he cannot help it and certainly does not want to be afraid. Put the small lamp in front of the statue on his little altar for a few nights at least, to help him, and whatever you do, once he has been put to bed, let him hear that you are moving around the house. In other words, prove to him that you are somewhere near at hand, even if you are not actually in the room with him. Leave his door open a little and let him hear you while he is going to sleep. The most important thing in the cure of this evil is to restore the child's sense of self-confidence, which is lost through this fear.

Another manifestation of fear which sometimes causes a good deal of trouble is bed-wetting. Let us be fair to the child once more. If the parents have taught him good habits from the cradle then, in nearly every case, this problem will not arise, at least not as a problem. It occurs in most children up to the age of six or so, and is then commonly due either to fear of getting out of bed unaided or in the dark, or sometimes to mere laziness. A gentle remonstrance on these occasions should meet the case, provided that you have not to accuse your own conscience of not forming good habits in your child from the beginning. If, however, this habit of bed-wetting becomes frequent, and especially if it persists after the ages mentioned, then you have a real problem on your hands, and one which has to be dealt with.

Once again, in the vast majority of cases, the root reason for this habit, even though that reason may be very much disguised at times and hard to detect, is fear. Let us attempt to strip this fear of its disguises for a moment and look it straight in the face. Sometimes it is due to the fact of a new arrival in the family, and the older child is being neglected a little, or at least has that impression. In such cases this habit is the child's way of calling attention to himself, and he is quite willing to take all the very unpleasant consequences, because by it he is gaining the attention which he feels is not otherwise being supplied. In this way the fear-reaction of the child is being converted into a means of exercising power over his parents—and a very effective means at that ! This feeling of not being wanted, no matter what the cause, is frequently at the root of this habit, as can be proved very simply by its prevalence in the cases of illegitimate or unwanted children.

The habit may be due to the fact that you have not provided an easily accessible pot and lights for the child, especially for one who is afraid of the dark. In this case you are to blame, and it is no use putting all the blame on to the child, who is thus being forced to overcome a very real fear of the dark in order to get out of bed. Correct these mistakes and all may be well.

Environment may have something to do with this trouble, as we saw very clearly during the last war, because it was a frequent bother in the case of children who were evacuated from their homes and put with strangers. Once their confidence returned the trouble ceased. This environment may easily be in the home itself, and there have been many cases where this problem arose because of rows and disagreements between the parents, again through the fact that such squabbles increase the child's feeling of fear and insecurity.

Thus, having discussed at least some of the more common causes and disguises of this fear which give rise to the problem, we must attempt to find some solution to it. Naturally, only general rules can be given here, and much will depend on the parents' ability to discover the real manifestation of this basic fear for themselves by a rigorous examination of their consciences.

First of all, if this habit is very frequent after the age of six or seven, a doctor should be consulted to eliminate possible physical causes of it. If there is no physical cause, then other methods will have to be used. Naturally, success will depend on our being able to discover the real cause for the habit, and for that we have to rely on the honesty of the parents. Since fear is, in nearly every case, the real reason at the back of it, that fear will have to be detected first of all, and then removed, sometimes by a process of trial and error. Thus, you can try putting a small light in the child's bedroom, especially if he is afraid of the dark. Above all, do all that you can to increase his self-confidence and also to prove to him that your affection is not lessened or changed by this unpleasant habit, and that you do understand his difficulties, while at the same time being ready and willing to help him all you can. On some occasions a simple sentence, spoken with love, will serve to cure this habit. For example, you might tell the child that you know it is difficult, but you also know that he is going to do all that he can to help you to make him a clean boy again.

If there should be anything wrong with the general atmosphere in the family, then, of course, you have the obligation of putting that right before going any further. This may be due to several causes, of which the principal ones are rows which take place either before the child or at least when he can hear them; perhaps the child is being ignored a little due to the arrival of a new baby, not to mention the much greater evil of his not being wanted at all. Once you do hit on the cause and correct it you will be very surprised to find that the evil disappears almost at once. Remember that punishment for this habit is worse than useless, and that, until the real reason for it is known, cheerful encouragement is the only thing you can do in all justice. In cases where the habit persists in spite of all that you can do there is only one thing left, and that is to get the child admitted into hospital for observation. You will soon find out then if there is a physical cause for the habit, because if there is not, then it will cease almost as soon as the child is admitted into the hospital, and will start again when he comes home.

Another common problem of childhood is nail-biting, and this, like thumb-sucking, is only to be dealt with directly when it persists into later childhood and adolescence. The general treatment is the by-now-familiar one of training the child's sense of security and confidence. This will soon end the habit if you are patient. Give him interesting things to do to take his mind off the nails and the thumb, and you will succeed very quickly.

When, however, these habits of nail-biting and thumb-sucking persist longer than normal then we must take some steps to cure them, as far as we can. Above and beyond increasing in every way the child's sense of confidence in us and in himself, there is one method which has been discovered by recent research which really does cure a good number of these habits, especially the ones which have become unconscious through long practice. This method consists in making the habit a conscious one rather than unconscious.   Naturally, this cure cannot be used in the cases of habits which affect the moral order, such as masturbation in adolescence, but in the case of these purely physical habits it is well worth trying.   The basic element of the method is simple.   We make the child do the action which forms the main element of the habit consciously rather than unconsciously. This tends to bring it under voluntary control much more easily and often succeeds where other methods have failed.   It often has a very good effect in cases of very slight speech defects.   For instance, when a person stammers slightly it is often useful to make them repeat the actual sound they have made while stammering over a particular word.   This brings the vocal cords and the whole of the speech mechanism under voluntary control and thus tends quite naturally to cure the habit.   It is also particularly successful in such things as typing errors which are often being repeated and also in cases of spelling mistakes which are involuntary.   To make such mistakes voluntary and conscious seems to put the correct method naturally into the brain.   It may seem rather a peculiar method of correcting physical habits, but it definitely works.   Remember that it may never be used or advocated in the case of bad moral habits, because we may never do good that evil may come of it, and also because those habits are normally conscious actions in themselves.

Another difficulty which sometimes arises in the case of slightly older children is that connected with their meals.   This problem does not always manifest itself in quite the same way in all children.   Sometimes it is confined to slowness in eating, while at others it takes the form of refusing to eat at all, or eating with obvious reluctance and under pressure.   Perhaps it may be a question merely of particular dishes.

If the refusal to eat is only very occasional then there is no need to do much about it unless it is an obvious manifestation of temper or disobedience, in which case the suitable punishment should be administered.   Nature knows that, at certain times, it is not a good thing to put food into the stomach.   If you leave the child alone then Nature will provide the cure for that in her own time. If you must do something then just give the child a glass of milk or failing that orange juice and leave Nature to do the rest. The child will soon get hungry and then will return to normal again provided that there is no other cause for the refusal to eat, and that will soon manifest itself.

If, however, this refusal happens many times and there is no physical reason for it then it does fall within the scope of this book. Once again, nearly every time our old enemy, the child's fear, is at the root of the trouble. The main difficulty is to discover what exactly is causing the fear. It may quite easily be due to undue severity on the part of the parents at meal times. We have already pointed out that meals should be made attractive to the child from every point of view. Naturally, bad manners have to be corrected here as at other times in the daily life, but that is no reason for making the life of the child a misery at table. So many people who are really over-anxious to educate their children well fall into this error. Better by far to make a mental note of the mistakes and then to correct them gently after the meal is over than to make the whole of the meal-time unpleasant to the child by constant nagging. Again, the child frequently connects the particular room in which he has his meals with unpleasant facts or happenings, especially with family rows. Parents must control themselves during meal-times and should make a very firm resolution never to indulge in arguments or bickerings during those times. These domestic rows are a constant source of worry and of fear to the child, and that much more than most people realize. It may need a good deal of self-control on the part of the parents to avoid them altogether, but that control is their duty, because of its necessity for the well-being of their children. There is, in point of fact, no excuse for ignoring this warning.

If the reluctance to eat is connected with a particular kind of food then it is not a bit of use insisting that the child must eat it, and not serving him with anything else until he has done so. There are other methods of dealing with this which are more effective and also much less harmful. If the child will not eat fat, for example, then there is really no need to worry, because that can easily be supplied to his body in other and more attractive forms. If it is a question of cabbage (many a child's bugbear), then, again, there is no need whatever to lay too much stress on that particular vegetable, good though it may be for health, because there are others which have the same health-giving properties. Orange juice will supply the deficiencies, and all will be well. Also, there *are* other vegetables than cabbage, and you must learn to consider the child's tastes a little. It may even happen that the method of preparing or presenting the food leaves much to be desired and so has something to do with this reluctance to eat it. Try new methods and see what happens. Serve it up more attractively and in smaller portions, and remember that it is no use making the child's life a misery simply because he does not want to eat certain foods. That is all wrong, and serves no useful purpose.

Slowness in eating is a little more difficult to cure, perhaps, but it usually has a less dangerous origin, being due to the fact that the child becomes distracted during meals and thus takes much longer over them. Cure the distraction and you will have removed the cause of the slow eating. Try smaller portions, attractively prepared and as varied as possible. See to it that the child does not eat between meals (always a good rule in any case), and also that he has a certain amount of healthy exercise in the open air which will tend to make him hungry. Attractive preparation and presentation of meals is half the battle here.

A young child who normally says grace quite cheerfully will, however, occasionally rebel and refuse to oblige us. This may be due to obstinacy. Here one of the very best cures is to give to each child in turn the privilege of saying grace for the whole family for a week at a time. In this way the saying of the family grace at meals will come to be looked on as an honour, and not as a cross to be bravely borne, or alternatively, as a means of annoying parents. In the case of any reluctance to say grace just take away the privilege for the time being from the offender and give it to the next child. This will cure the evil without making religion odious to the child—a thing which must be avoided at all cost.

We have mentioned several possible causes for these various difficulties, but there is one more which must not be entirely overlooked. It is always possible that the child may be making these things a means to annoy his parents or perhaps to impose his will on them. This is very true of difficulties with meals and also the refusal to say grace when asked. Judge the case very carefully first, and then, once you have made up your mind that there is no other cause but this one, you must deal with it according to the general rules which we have laid down with regard to punishment in general. But do remember one thing. If the difficulty should manifest itself in the matter of grace before and after meals then be very careful. Here you are in a difficult position, because there are two contrary things pulling you in different directions. On the one hand, we must not do anything to make the child hate religion or blame it for all his punishments or even for some of them. On the other hand, parental authority must be upheld. As a general rule, it is much better to run the risk of losing a certain amount of parental authority rather than to punish for offences which hold an element of religion. It is a golden rule which cannot be too often insisted upon that you should never punish for a purely religious offence, nor indeed, when it can be avoided, for those which even approach to this standard. We shall see in the course of future discussions that there are certain religious means which tend to overcome this difficulty for you, and you should use those rather than the physical means of punishment for such offences.

We do not claim that all the possible problems which can arise in the course of childhood have been dealt with here, nor indeed that these particular problems have been solved in every case, because individual children differ too much to make such a thing even possible. However, the general rules and lines for your conduct have been laid down, and they apply to every case without exception. If you follow them carefully you will at least have no difficulty in deciding for yourselves when you have a problem on your hands, and that is, in itself, a great step forward. Only too many parents do not recognize the elements of a problem in their children when they see them, and consequently a number of children run the risk of being seriously handicapped in later life when a simple use of these general rules would have brought about a complete cure much earlier in childhood. Don't imagine problems, but at the same time realize that they may possibly arise in the case of your child, even though you may have taken all possible steps to avoid their causes. If this chapter does no more than help you see these causes in actual practice, then it has done its work, because in that way you will have a much better idea of some at least of the things which you should avoid as parents.

CHAPTER NINE

THE PRE-SCHOOL YEARS

As OUR KNOWLEDGE OF THE FACTORS WHICH INFLUENCE THE development of the child increases so it becomes more evident that these pre-school years, which take in that middle period between the ages of three and six, are of vital importance for the future mental and physical well-being of the child. This period is necessarily a formative one, and on it will depend to a very great extent the mental health of the child later on. This means that the parent-child relationship should be perfected during these short years. But, before going on to deal with those matters, let us say just a word or two about the physical health of the child.

Just as this period has a great influence on the mental development so, too, during it, the foundations are laid of the whole bodily structure, and for that reason your efforts should be directed towards nutrition and exercise, together with the utmost care in preventing infection as far as that is possible. Any physical defects which manifest themselves during these years should be dealt with at once. It is really surprising how much can be done in this way if things are taken in time. Such things as sight defects, stammering, bad hearing, etc., should receive immediate care and attention, and from experts. Only too frequently such things are left until the child goes to school, and then are discovered for the first time, whereas they should have been noticed and dealt with much earlier in life.

So far as the general education of the child is concerned, there are three main things which we have to aim at. We have to complete the basic formation of his character so far as the family atmosphere is concerned, and develop those good habits which we have already discussed in previous chapters.

Secondly, we have to do all that we can to bring out the social side of that character, and lastly, there is much to be done with regard to his religious education. Let us deal briefly with those three things in order.

The good habits which are formed during this period are seldom if ever lost completely. Be on your guard, therefore, and develop as far as you can good habits of punctuality, kindness, and moderation in dealing with others. Increase the child's knowledge of what is right and what is wrong, and see to it that he acts in accordance with the knowledge which he possesses. These good habits will include in a very special way the habits of truthfulness, open dealings with his parents and confidence in them. Respect for others should be insisted upon, and so should that obedience which is based on at least a vague knowledge that parents and others in authority stand in relation to the child in the place of God and with His authority. You should be able to get this idea across in the course of your religious instruction, and especially through your stories about the Holy Family.

The child must also learn by experience (and be corrected where he goes wrong) that he must give in to others sometimes, and not always expect to have his own way in everything. This affects, not merely his parents and those in authority over him, but also his companions and friends, as well as the other children in the family. He must be made to see, in other words, at least as far as he is capable of seeing it, that others, too, have rights and that those rights have to be respected. This habit is much more easily learnt than one would expect, especially if it is taught properly—the play period is one of the best times for this. Again, the normal habits of cleanliness and tidiness have to be deepened and developed during these years. The child should be given gradually more and more freedom in such matters, under supervision, of course, until they become second nature to him. He might be given a special cupboard for his toys, and be allowed and expected to put them away neatly after use. That cupboard should be respected by the family, and thus he will learn to leave other people's things alone unless given permission to touch them. Slowly, as these years unfold, the child should be taught to depend ever less and less on his parents for things. Naturally, this will have to be done slowly, and you cannot expect it to happen all at once.

At the same time, this separation must not interfere with the growth of a real family atmosphere, which is of the greatest importance. The child should acquire an ever deepening sense of love and of confidence which will last all his life. This will depend to a very large extent on the good will and self-sacrifice of the parents, who must learn to show themselves always ready to listen in patience to the child, to play with him and show him a deep personal affection without any loss of parental authority.

We have already had something to say about the importance of play in the development of character. Indeed, play is always important for a child, because it is during those periods that the child brings about many contacts with the outside world. It may seem that he lives and plays in a dream world of his own, but, if you observe him closely, you will see that such play nearly always has some connection with the external world of reality of which he is becoming ever more and more conscious. You will understand what is meant by this if you watch a little girl playing at " mothers and fathers ". There you will notice a very perfect imitation of her parents, for example—a thing which makes itself very plain in the repetition of phrases which we can recognize as our own. Even the very gestures are those of grown-ups, which are being imitated in a childlike fashion.

It will perhaps be useful if we indicate here, before going any deeper into this matter of play, those things which interest a child between the ages of three and six. Physical exercise is a necessity during these years in order to develop the long muscles of the body—which is one reason why it is almost impossible for the child to keep still for very long. Such things as running, jumping, throwing things, lifting, rolling on the floor are very useful, and we should provide the kind of clothes which cannot be harmed very much by such activities. Competition games are popular, too, together with pattern toys, simple puzzles, large coloured cubes or blocks, animals and dolls in general, clay for simple models, and perhaps the favourite of all, the blackboard and chalk, which supply a very real childish need. Lastly, do try to give your child some opportunities of playing with sand

and with water. We do not know exactly why it is so, but these two elements have a very great influence on the child and somehow help him to express himself in a way which is not possible by any other means. One of the easiest ways is to provide a sand tray, with small models, if possible, which can be constructed into a home or a farm on the tray. This is a fascinating thing to a child and gives him hours of real pleasure. So far as the water is concerned, it should be a fairly simple matter to allow him to help in the watering of the garden or else to give him a small bath of water in a place where he cannot make much of a mess. This, together with a small boat or two, will be all that he needs for happiness.

All children of this age love dressing up, and you should help them to cultivate this taste for the dramatic by all the means in your power. You will find it very useful in many ways.

In general, a skilful mother or father can use the time of play to teach many things, including truthfulness, the simple courtesies of life such as " please ", " thank you " and so on ; even prayers ! It is so very easy to direct children's games that it seems strange that so many parents leave their children to play by themselves without making any attempt to use this very valuable opportunity. This does not mean, of course, that we should be always interfering, but that we should not ignore this most useful of all mediums for teaching. Some examples may not be out of place. A dolls' tea party, for instance, can be used to teach good manners at table or even methods of addressing people when introduced to them, and all this without detracting one bit from the pleasure the child gets out of the game. This also helps to overcome the child's natural shyness at meeting strangers, and children thus trained soon become very simple and natural in their manner when meeting others, especially grown-ups. The same dolls can be used to teach truthfulness. If you make one of the dolls knock something over and then get her or him to say that she or he did not do it you can follow this up by presenting the whole problem to the child for his solution. You will then see how much of your own training has gone home to the child or not as the case may be. Before putting the dolls to bed they must be made to say their prayers, and this is a good opportunity for getting the child to repeat small prayers to them and thus help his own memory of them, all without leaving the field of play. We shall have more suggestions to make later on with regard to the possibilities of the play period in the teaching of religion, but these examples will suffice for the time being to show you how very important this play is in the education of the young child. Learn to use it as such.

Here are a few general principles which can guide you in the matter of the development of the emotional side of the child's life. In the first place, understand him fully, and his own particular difficulties. Then apply your guidance to help him— a thing which must be done kindly but firmly. Don't give in to all his whims and fancies, but at the same time don't impose your own will on him simply because you feel like it. Have a real reason for all you command in this matter. Avoid all emotional disturbances yourselves, and you will go a long way towards helping your child to avoid them, too. If you are constantly giving way to bad temper, moods of depression and the like then you can expect your child to imitate you in that. In this matter it is important that the mother should never attempt to talk to the elder child as if they were both of the same age, discussing all the events of the day, and perhaps most of all the shortcomings of the father! This is a very bad thing, and usually accounts for the " old-fashioned " type of child, who speaks and acts as if he or she were an adult.

If you follow out these general principles carefully then you should find that your child is taking an ever-increasing interest in the outside world of reality, and that his relations with that world develop quite normally. You, on your side, have to see to it that this development is not hindered in any way. His companions, that is the other children in the family or those from outside, are very important factors in this development, because it is mainly from them that he learns unselfishness and the general rules of give and take which are going to be so important later on. Thus, it is a very good thing to encourage him to meet other children, gradually at first, and then more and more as time goes on. Watch them at play together, and see what you have to improve, remove or introduce in your child's character. Judge the whole thing in an impartial manner, because you cannot afford to make mistakes by being too lenient or prejudiced in your judgments, or by always thinking that your child is better than other people's—however natural that feeling may be. This companionship will give you an excellent opportunity for curing such evils as tale-bearing, than which there is nothing so destructive of social character, because it means that the child is not standing on his own feet as he should and also that he tends to consider himself better than other children. Gentle correction here with good advice as the child grows older will soon effect a cure. In general, this element of companionship teaches the wise parents much more quickly than anything else exactly what they have to do to bring about the necessary development in their children's characters.

Gradually the child must also get used to meeting other adults apart from his parents. This is a very good way of testing how far his attitude to the outside world has developed and how far it still needs to be improved. The child who gets behind a chair or into a cupboard when a stranger comes into the room is not going to be any match for the world until that habit of mind is broken down. Don't think that you are going to succeed in this all at once, because here great patience is needed.

This ability to meet and to stand up to the world of reality is not, however, confined to meeting people. There are also personal situations to be faced and the child can be prepared for those by a gradual emancipation from parental control in such elementary matters as washing, dressing, feeding himself and so on.

If you find that such things as temper-tantrums are beginning to develop in the character of the child during this period then you can usually effect a prompt cure by following out this simple method. At first such things are best ignored, because they may be just demonstrations to call your attention to the child, and once he sees that they fail in their object then he will soon stop them. If, however, experience and trial prove that they are really demonstrations of anger then the best thing to do is to isolate him in a room by himself, without any show of anger yourself. This, together with a little attempt to reason with him when he is normal again should meet the situation, especially if it is combined with the religious education, as we shall see later.

By far the most important of all our efforts during this formative period of the child's life are those we make to complete as far as possible at this stage the religious education of his whole character. It may be stated with truth that there are unlimited possibilities for the religious training of the child during these years, especially so far as his whole attitude towards religion is concerned. There is so much to be done and so little time to do it in that we must have a plan and must stick to it. Nothing can ever quite make up for the lack of this training, and it does form one of our most pressing obligations. Let us see first of all what we have to aim at and then how we can achieve that aim in actual practice.

The aim is a very simple one to put into words, which does not mean that it is equally simple to effect. We are out to give to our children a very deep personal love for God and for his religion. Nothing must be allowed to frustrate that purpose, and everything else must be subordinated to it if we are going to succeed in giving a really worthwhile education to our children.

In order to accomplish this aim it is necessary to develop both the child's religious knowledge and also his life of prayer, so far as he is capable of being developed at this age. The scrap-book comes more and more into the picture during these years between the ages of three and six. We have already made a beginning with it by showing the child the pictures and by naming the people we can see in them. Now we shall have to extend its use to cover actual teaching.

Begin with the life story of Christ and tell the story while following through the pictures, starting with the angel's visit to Our Lady to tell her that she was going to be the Mother of God. Go slowly and gently, not expecting too much at first, and you will be surprised to find out how quickly the child remembers the story by this method and is able to repeat it. Tell some of the other simple stories from the Gospels, especially the one of Christ and the children, which always attracts attention. Those parents who would like to have some specimen talks of this kind can find them in one of the other books in this series.* Remember that your aim is not, and never should be,

* *Christopher's Talks to the Little Ones* (Burns Oates).

mere knowledge, because that, of itself, never saved one single soul. What you must produce is a deep personal love for Christ, for His Mother, the angels and the saints, and thus for God and for His religion. This can only be done successfully if you are careful to choose the right times for your work with the scrap-book and also if you are willing to devote yourselves wholeheartedly to this task. Naturally, your own love of God will have to be very great, otherwise you cannot hope to achieve much in the case of your children. This means, in actual practice, that your own religious life will have to grow and deepen together with that of your children.

All those means must be used for this great purpose which will serve to make religion attractive to the child, and none must be attempted which would serve to make it disagreeable or disliked. Among these many means at our disposal we find things like the play times. Here it is quite useful to use the dolls to play the Nativity, or as children who have to be taught their prayers, and in many other ways. Nor are the dolls the only means at our disposal. Get the child to reproduce the drawings which you will find in the other books in this series ; they are not only very easy for a child to draw but also very attractive to the children. They serve to fix the religious ideas which they represent very simply and easily. Have them colour pictures of the crib, the whole series of the life of Christ, and so on. Let them build a crib for themselves at Christmas time, and put the presents they are going to receive round the crib instead of using the old traditional " stocking " method.

As they grow older, take them on visits to the church and show them the statues and the altars. Tell them that this is Jesus' home and that He loves to see them there and to listen to what they have to say to Him. Don't be afraid to take them to Benediction and even to Mass. You will soon be able to keep them reasonably quiet, and if necessary you can always take a soft toy or a small picture book with you to engage their attention should they begin to wriggle about too much. They will learn slowly, never fear.

Prayers have to be learnt, too, at this stage, slowly at first, and then more quickly as time goes on. By the time the child goes to school he should be able to say the Our Father, the Hail

Mary, the Glory be to the Father, together with the short acts of faith, hope, charity and contrition. Morning and evening prayers have to be taught as well, in simple forms suitable to the mental capacity of the child at first, and then added to as time goes on. These prayers should never be left altogether unsaid, but naturally, if the children are tired after a long day in the country or something like that, then it is of very little use to take them through all their night prayers. The best thing to do in such circumstances is to get them to make the Sign of the Cross and then tell Jesus they love Him, and so to bed.

At first you will have to begin by saying the child's prayers with him, but as soon as possible you should confine your part in these prayers to " hearing " them, so as to make quite sure that they are said properly. In your form of night prayers there should always appear some kind of an act of contrition, however short. This has many uses ; for example, by means of it many small faults can be corrected. Thus, when the child refuses to say grace you can make that a reason for saying a special act of contrition that night, together with a promise that he will not offend in that way again. Such things as not telling the truth, selfishness, bad temper and so on yield very readily to this simple method. We have made no attempt here to give a definite formula for these night and morning prayers, mainly because most parents already have the form which they were taught as children. However, once again those who wish for one will find suggestions in the other books in this series.

Although it may be possible to delegate your religious instruction of the younger child to the older ones, that is not a thing which should always be done. Remember that those moments which you yourselves dedicate to his religious instruction are moments which soon become very precious to the child, which means that the instructions are connected in his mind with your love for him. This in its turn implies that the instruction will go much deeper than the mere words you use, and tends to become a happy memory which will remain with the child all his life and which will also prompt him in his dealings with his own children later on. If you set about your task in this way you will find that, by the time your child goes to school, his religious formation will have been set on a firm foundation which it would be impossible to improve on, and which will be of the greatest value for the future.

Before leaving this subject, it is necessary to issue a warning. We have, up to now, dealt with the positive side of religious education. But there are also certain things which have to be avoided if your training is to have its full effect. In particular you should never do anything which is liable to make religion odious to the child. Fortunately, the old English Puritan Sunday, during which no child was allowed to play games, etc., has almost entirely disappeared—please God, never to appear again! But it does serve as an example of how *not* to treat religion. For much the same reason it does not appear to be a good thing to punish the child for purely religious offences— at least, not at this stage of his development. Thus, refusal to say grace can be dealt with by other and gentler methods themselves connected with religious teaching, and so more effective than any amount of scolding or punishment. Visits to the church and especially Sunday Mass should be made as attractive as possible later on when the time comes. Now, this does need a good deal of self-sacrifice, patience and self-control on the part of the parents. It is so easy to be snappy in the early morning, especially after a longish walk to church, and perhaps fasting in order to go to Holy Communion. But, if you want your children to love their Faith and to grow up to observe its commands then you *must* make that effort. Yet how many times we see cases where it is definitely not made.

Sundays and all the great Feast Days of the Church should also be made days of special treats for the children, and if you use your imagination you will soon be able to think of ways of making them so, instead of days of penance. It does not really matter how small the treat is, but if it is definitely connected in the children's minds with their religion and if it leads them to love God more, then it will be well worth the effort and the time spent on it.

In these troubled times in which we live the Church is insisting more and more on the practice of the Family Rosary. Now, there are still many people who could quite easily say the Rosary in their family circle and yet they do not make any effort to do so. The only reason one can see for this is either laziness or slackness—there can be no other, since the Rosary is a very easy prayer to say and does not take very long. Also the effect on the unity of the family is so very great that one would imagine that all parents would make a real effort to say this prayer in union with their children. There need be no difficulties, especially if the very young children are not forced to attend (let them learn to look on this as a real treat which is reserved for them later on, when they are a little older) and if the hour for the recitation of this family Rosary is fixed for a time when all the family can be present, no matter what their occupations, in the evening. With a little care and attention from all this can usually be done, for where there's a will there's a way! What a great difference this family prayer would make to the individuals and to the whole Church! This prayer brings untold blessings in its train through the powerful intercession of Mary, the Mother of God. This alone has saved many thousands of souls from eternal damnation, and parents, who have for their primary obligation the safeguarding of their children's salvation, should be the first to make effective use of it for that purpose. I hope that all those parents who read this book will make a great effort to put this one counsel into effective practice. There is no doubt about its efficacy.

When the time draws near for the child's school life to begin then it will be up to you as his parents to test his reactions to the whole idea of going to school. It can be stated as being generally true that every child who finds very great difficulty in accepting the whole idea of school has not been educated properly during his earlier years. If you have not been selfish, and have seen to it that the child had opportunities of meeting other children and playing with them, then you should find that he takes to the idea of going to school very easily. Never hold the threat of school over his head as if it were a punishment, but rather as a great day in his life. Usually they like the idea at first, although after the first term you may find that the child is not so very keen, but that is natural and does no harm. It is the first reaction which should be noted and which you should do everything you can to prepare.

Here we are going to take it for granted that you are going to send your child to a Catholic school, if that is at all possible

The reasons for this and its importance have been stressed before, so that there is no need to do more here than to give a brief summary of what is, after all, the main one, namely, the child's religious education. This does *not* mean the amount of Catechism that he will learn. It means ever so much more than that, as you will have realized by this time. The teacher is your representative, and must carry on the work of the home in this matter of religious education. Naturally, then, you will want to send your children to a school where you know that your efforts to bring them up in the knowledge, love and service of God will be completed and perfected along those same lines. This is the main reason why the Church insists on the fact that Catholic children must go to Catholic schools where that is at all possible. There are very few arguments which can be brought forward to justify sending a Catholic child to a non-Catholic school. Education is one whole, and cannot be divided into parts. The religious idea must flow through the whole of the school work, and cannot be confined to the hours of religious instruction. Catholic teachers know that, and so they watch over the children entrusted to their care and do all that they can to protect them from all harm where their religion is concerned. The whole atmosphere of the school is Catholic, and that factor has a great influence on the future development of character. You will not be judged by God on how much arithmetic or geography your children have learnt, but rather on whether you have done all that lies in your power as parents to prepare them well for the supreme task of saving their souls. One of the principal means to that end is the Catholic school.

When the time draws near, then, consult your parish priest on what you should do, and if there is a choice of schools open to you, ask his advice about them, and he will give you all the help he can to choose wisely. Remember that no sacrifice which you may be called upon to make in order to give your children a good Catholic education is too great. This is your great duty, and it should also be your joy—to educate good Catholics who will know, love and serve God all the days of their lives, and who will one day be reunited with you, their parents, before the throne of God in heaven.

CHAPTER TEN

THE EARLY SCHOOL YEARS

IN THE LIFE OF EVERY CHILD THERE ARE CERTAIN DANGER points at which the development of his character can be either stunted or at least seriously hampered unless parents are on the watch for these dangerous periods when the time comes. In general, we may say that everything in a child's life which implies a radical change or an entering upon a new type of existence is dangerous in this way. This becomes more true the older the child gets. Thus, the first step on going to school means for him a real break with the life of ease and attention at home, and also a stepping into a new kind of life where he is very much a member of a small community rather than an individual. It is a very definite milestone in the life of the child, as is adolescence. Changing schools, even because the family has to move into another district, or the change of houses may also bring into being one of these danger periods. The advent of a new member of the family may have the same effect, the death of one of the parents or a serious illness which the child himself has to suffer. All these are danger points which have to be closely watched in order to make quite sure that the child is adjusting his character to meet them correctly. Here, in this chapter, we shall deal with the early school age, i.e., from six to twelve years, and we shall try to discover how the parents' attitude towards the child should develop during that important period. In the chapters which follow we shall also have something to say about the religious education in the home during these years, and also something about the very difficult problem of sex education under some of its more important aspects.

Going to school for the first time is a very big step in the life of the child. Up to now he has lived very much isolated and protected from the world of reality about him. Now he has to take this very definite step forward which will bring him into constant contact with others who are not members of his own family and many of whom he will not like very much. He has to learn many new lessons, applications of those principles which he has learnt at home with regard to self-control, unselfishness, consideration for others, discipline, etc., and such things come a little hard for us all. If you, as parents, have been careful to carry out the instructions given in the previous chapter, and have not isolated the child too much during the last two years of the pre-school age while he was still under your absolute care, then you will probably find that he will begin to settle down to school life fairly soon, once the first few weeks of home-sickness and strangeness have worn off. Don't take too much notice of these few weeks, because it is very natural that the child should have to take a little time to readjust himself after a home life where most things were done for him and where he did not need to take many decisions for himself. If, however, it should persist for a long time, then perhaps you may have to do something about it. Children should be quite happy at the idea of school, and with the school life itself once this first period of strangeness has worn off. If your child shows definite signs of not being happy after some months have gone by it is a sure sign that there has been something radically wrong with your methods of education in the home during the pre-school years. Don't tend to blame this on to the school itself too easily, although in the odd case there may be something wrong there too.

This lack of ability to adjust oneself readily to new situations is found much more frequently in the case of the only child, and the reason is not difficult to understand. Such children can be very easily spoilt by their parents. They receive all the attention in the family circle because they have not had to share that attention with other children. They have also escaped from that magnificent element in all family education, the knocking off of odd corners by brothers and sisters, and as a direct consequence of this, they are by no means so ready to give themselves fully to a life in community as are their more fortunate fellows who have already been forced to adjust themselves to a certain amount of give and take in the family circle. More often than not the only child is at least slightly spoilt by the parents, even the well-meaning ones, and this makes it very hard for him to surrender such a life for that of competition such as he will find in school. Such children are usually self-seeking in their dealings with others, shy at meeting people, inclined to have an exaggerated idea of their own importance in the general scheme of things, and thus, as a natural consequence, reluctant to accept the burdens and responsibilities of school life. The only way to tackle this situation, if it has not been dealt with before the child goes to school, is to encourage him to take his place with the others and also to refuse to give in to feelings of false sympathy for him in his difficulties. Remember that the child is usually prepared to accept what *has* to be without much trouble once it has been proved to him that there is no other way out of the difficulty. We can, then, sum up the difficulties which all children have to face during this early period of their school lives by saying that they have to learn to accept other authority apart from that of the parents; they have to enter into a life of community, in which others have to be considered much more than before and where there is a good deal of competition. Lastly, they must learn to find satisfaction in doing things for themselves which were formerly done for them by their parents. All this takes time.

The mention above of the word " sympathy " brings us to the most important duty of parents during these early school years, namely, the developing and maturing of the sympathy and understanding between them and their children. There should, in fact, be complete and perfect understanding between them before the arrival of that most difficult period of all which we call adolescence. There should also be a certain amount of contact between parents and teachers during this period, together with a frank discussion of the child and his character. Here we must stress the word " frank "—the child's character and possibilities should be discussed both from the point of view of the parents' own observations and also from that of the teachers', which, since it is independent of and different from that of the parents, may often lead to some very interesting and useful discoveries which can have a direct influence on methods of education both at home and in school hours. The vast majority of Catholic teachers would welcome much more co-operation from parents than they in fact receive, and more contact with them.

Unfortunately, quite a number of parents seem to be of the opinion that, once they have sent the child to school, then their own obligation of contributing to the child's general and religious education has ceased. This is by no means the case. There are still many fields in which the parents should work just as diligently as they did before in the days of early childhood. The teachers have authority over the children because they are the delegates of the parents, and not for any other reason. They should continue and preserve the traditions of the family and the home.

So far as the parents are concerned, there is still plenty of room for the religious scrap-book during these early years of school life and up to the time for the First Confession and Holy Communion. They can do a very great deal to help prepare their children really well for the reception of those two important Sacraments. They can not only lay the foundation for the actual doctrine of the Holy Eucharist by their Gospel stories, especially those which deal with the miracles of Christ, but— even more important still—they can teach their children that deep and personal love for Christ in this Sacrament which is going to stand them in such good stead later on. This love is of all things the most important, because it alone can provide the real effective motive for avoiding sin in later life, and thus it can easily prove one of the most influential factors in their eternal salvation. It should extend to the whole of the Sacramental Life of Christ, beginning with the idea of the Real Presence—not at all difficult for a child to grasp—and then later on be applied to the idea of Holy Communion. In all your teaching on this great Sacrament try to be as positive as possible. Stress the idea that Jesus loves to come into the hearts of the children because He can find there innocence and purity. Make sure that they are not content with reciting mechanical prayers after Holy Communion, but get them into the habit quite soon of talking to Jesus in their own words.

This is very useful later on in life when different problems arise, and it is a great pity that it is not more stressed in the children's instructions before Holy Communion. The whole question of the child's prayers and their development is of such prime importance that the following chapter is going to be devoted to that problem. Remember that you cannot expect the child to effect a rapid changeover from childhood without Holy Communion to a childhood with all the advantages of that great Sacrament unless you yourselves are prepared to put in a great deal of spade-work.

Sympathy for the child in his difficulties should, as we have already indicated, develop during this period, and that counsel applies also to such things as his work in school. If your child appears a little backward at first or even a little lazy in his work, don't begin to nag at him or scold him. Leave those unpleasant jobs to the teachers, who will soon get to know the real reason for the backwardness and will be able to correct it in their own ways. It may even be due to some slight physical defect, and in any case, nagging or scolding from you is not going to improve the situation at this point in any way at all. Apart from anything else, it is not conducive to peace and happiness in the child's life: encourage always, and be very patient. You may find that hard at times, but you will thank God later that you did adopt this attitude rather than any other.

This short period from the age of six until the age of twelve should be the happiest of the child's whole life. Whatever you do, keep it that way. Try to make the home life and atmosphere as pleasant as possible. If this was of great importance during the early years of childhood it is even more important now. The reason is simple. The child is growing up, and so he remembers things much more easily and they make a far deeper impression on him. Later on, indeed quite soon now, he will have friends and will naturally want to bring them home—but only if the home atmosphere is one which lends itself to that. It is so easy to make a child feel ashamed of his home, not because it is poor, but rather because of the general atmosphere and because his parents are always engaged in pulling him to pieces before his friends. If you are careful now, during these years, then you will always keep the love and the affection of your children, and they will want to confide in you and to bring their friends home to see you. Later on this is going to make your task very much easier, but you must lay the foundations now. The child is at school, and he is going to meet other children. Quite soon, even without meaning to do so, he is going to compare their home life with his own. That comparison is going to be your first real test so far as he is concerned. You must not fail in that test, otherwise a good deal of your influence will be lost, and you will begin to wonder what has happened to your child because his attitude towards you has changed.

During this period, between the ages of six and twelve, you should make a really determined effort to build up your child's ideals. We all know that the motives which inspire action are the things which carry it through to a successful conclusion, and these motives are not inborn in man, they have to be learnt, and are thus an essential part in general education. Up to now you have imposed these motives for right action as against wrong mainly through the medium of parental authority. Now you are going to have to begin the slow process of substitution. That motive was good enough for the young child, and he could not take in any other, perhaps ; but it is soon going to be questioned, because man is a rational animal and wants reasons for what he has to do. Unless there is another motive which will take its place when the time comes, namely, that of reasoned service, then you will have lost a good deal of hard-won ground. Ask yourselves for a moment what motive means. It is the " why " of an action, that is all. You will then understand what is meant by this substitution. Up to now the child has acted in a certain way because he was told to do so. Soon he is going to act in the same way because he *wants* to and ought to, and there is all the difference in the world between the two sets of motives. If your teaching has been on the right lines then you will find that, slowly, the child's will is coming more and more to the front in all his activities. He will begin to tell the truth, for example, not so much from fear of punishment, but because he wants to tell the truth rather than a lie. The same should be true of all his conduct. You, on your part, must make sure that you supply him with these motives gradually. As he grows older his freedom must be increased. He cannot always be tied to the apron strings of authority. He needs reasons for acting in this way rather than in that. While he is still young these reasons need not go very deep, but as he grows older so you will have to rely more and more on reasons and less on your authority. This early school period is very good training for you both, in preparation for the difficult times which lie ahead.

You must stress little by little the value of moral action for its own sake. You will have to supply simple reasons why it is right to act in such and such a way, and also point out why the contrary is wrong. The child of eight years old is fully capable of understanding simple reasons for things, and these motives should be increased and deepened as time goes on. You can also provide motives which will increase the child's confidence in himself and in his capabilities, and which will thus serve to encourage him. This will also build up that love and affection between the parents and the children which should increase all the time. Thus, little gifts and presents should be given when the child least expects them in reward for work well done or for a difficult moral task well accomplished. This reward motive is not, as some people seem to think, one which is not good enough to be put before the child. Christ Himself encourages us in our own fight by the promise of an eternal reward.

Once school is well on the way to being a success then you will undoubtedly find that sport is playing an ever-increasing part in the life of the child. We have already had an opportunity of dealing with the importance of play in the life of the young child while still under the care of his parents, and exactly the same general principles hold good now. Those games are necessary, not merely for the correct physical development of the child, but also for that of his character. During them he learns something of the team spirit, self-control, muscle control and also courage in practical ways which can hardly be improved. He also accustoms himself to making quick decisions and to using his own initiative. Consequently, although you must make sure that the growing child does not over-tax his strength, this idea of taking part in strenuous games with other children should be encouraged. Make sure that his demands in this regard are satisfied once you are sure that they are genuine. A child who does not take part in such sports and games is very liable to develop badly so far as his character is concerned, and also you may find that you will have trouble later on in other ways as well.

This interest in sport tends to increase as time goes on, and that, too, is not a bad thing, provided that it does not distract his attention altogether from his work. This is a very useful interest to have later on during the troubled years of adolescence, when it will serve to distract his mind from other problems which will then tend to worry him a good deal.

These games will also be a big help to you in your attempts to form good moral habits in your children, because they will soon get into the habit of telling you all about their daily life at school, and that will give you an excellent opportunity of getting home many lessons in truthfulness, unselfishness, charity towards others who are not perhaps so well off as your children are, not to mention several other things with regard to religion in general. These sports and games will also provide you with a fund of general examples in your moral advice to the young child, and they have the advantage of being examples which it is very simple for him to grasp, because he sees them put into actual practice almost every day.

During this period, too, you are going to come up against another factor which is of great importance for the character development of your child, namely, the question of his friends and companions, and a very great deal of your success in dealing with him later on in the adolescent stage is going to depend on the attitude you adopt now. In general, you should do all that you can to encourage good, healthy friendships between your children and others of the same age, while at the same time stopping very tactfully other friendships which you know are not going to be good for the child. During these early school years this is fairly easy, because your authority is a useful weapon and can be used here without it doing any harm. You can almost pick your children's friends, if you go about it in the right way. What is of much more importance for the future is your whole attitude towards this question of friends and companions.

In this connection we have already mentioned the home

atmosphere. Provided you see to it that this atmosphere is always cheerful and happy then your child will want to bring his friends home for you to see them and for them to see you. This is often going to be rather inconvenient, but you must do your best to be patient with them, because this very confidence in you is going to save you a great deal of worry and trouble later on. Therefore, do all that you can to encourage it. Of course, if on some occasions it is too inconvenient, then you must explain to the child and he will understand. Great tact is required at times in getting rid of those you do not want as friends for your children, and in this connection it is very important for you to make sure that you are not acting on mere prejudice or social distinctions. The child cannot appreciate those motives now, much as he may do so later on, so be careful. Sometimes the very fact of your allowing them into the house will make him see that they are not the kind of people he should be friends with, and at others you will just have to endure the situation until such time as you can talk to the child about it. Much of this can be avoided altogether by a tactful picking of suitable friends for your child at the beginning of his school life. He will thus form good habits of friendship which will last him a life-time.

As he gets older and nearer the period of adolescence, then you will have to allow him much more freedom than before. Remember that if you do not allow it he is almost sure to take it anyway, so it might just as well come from you. By this freedom we do not mean for one moment that all parental authority should go by the board—quite the contrary—but rather that the methods of exercising it should change. There will still be plenty of room for authority for some time to come, for instance, in the matter of the time for being in the house at night, for going to bed, and so on. What we understand here by more freedom is rather more opportunity for mixing with the outside world and also less *visible* and obvious supervision by the parents. It also implies more responsibility given to the child. This should be a development which should cover the rest of his life with you in the family circle. The amount of actual freedom to be allowed at any given moment will, of course, depend to a large extent on the circumstances, and that is why no more definite rules can be given. Thus, the age and the character of the child have to be taken into consideration, together with his environment and family circumstances. Here, again, it is your whole attitude which is the most important thing. If your child understands that you trust him and realize his needs then he will usually respond with gratitude, because he will soon see that you are not at all like some other parents who try to keep their children tied much too long to their apron strings and thus limit their freedom and self-expression. He will also be much more willing to listen to your advice, because he will know that it springs from one thing only, your concern for his own welfare. You will have to allow your child to meet and deal with situations on his own much more frequently as he grows older. This is the only sensible course of action for you to adopt, because if your main efforts are always directed towards trying to save him the trouble of dealing with such situations, then he will naturally come to rely on you to such an extent that he almost ceases to be a person in his own right. This is very bad training for the future, when he will have to do without you and rely on his own judgment. We shall have much more to say about this question of the freedom to be given to the child when we deal with adolescence.

Now is the time to say a word or two to the father of the family. Everything which is said in this book is really directed to both parents, unless it is definitely stated that certain sections refer to one or other of them. But, since there is a tendency which is much to be deplored to ignore or make light of the father's rôle in the education of the children it seems necessary to say a word or two about it. Much has been written about the importance of the mother in the family, but little or nothing has been said about the place of the father. This has bad results which are little short of disastrous. In the first place, then, we must insist that *both* parents are necessary for the correct balance of the child's education. The mother has a special place in that education, and one which is of great importance ; but the father also has his, and it is no exaggeration to say that very often his task is, of the two, the more difficult.

During this period of which we are speaking you should endeavour to build up a healthy spirit of real love and confidence between yourself and the children. This can only be done if you are prepared to show them that you are always interested in them, willing to listen to their rather aimless and rambling descriptions of school life as it appears to their eyes. This will serve to build up an attitude in the mind of the child which is always important, but especially later on during adolescence. Very many of the more difficult problems of adolescence would never arise at all if there existed more confidence between the child and the father. Only too often children are afraid of their fathers and have no real confidence in their love for them because of their methods of dealing with them during these earlier years of childhood.

When we come down to the practical level and ask ourselves just how this attitude of mind should be built up in the children, we find that there are certain things which a father who wishes to establish really sympathetic contact between himself and his children must do, and others which he must avoid.

First, he must encourage his children, especially in their school work, which they find very difficult at times, helping them in a real spirit of understanding and union. This spirit becomes more necessary as they grow older. He must be patient with them in their troubles, small as these may seem to him at the time, because later on there will be other troubles which are no longer little ones, and if this sympathy between the father and the children has not been established on a firm basis, then it will be too late to start in adolescence. The attitude must have been there from childhood and given a chance to mature. Self-control will be needed on your part very often to secure this patience, but the effort must be made.

The father must also be willing to take the children for walks at times, and also to talk to them in a spirit of friendly sympathy about their daily lives, their friends, their interests, and so on— in fact, about anything which interests them. You must learn to see things from the child's point of view rather than from your own, and this is something which every father can do, given the necessary good will and love for his children, and it is certainly not too much to ask. After all, it is the father's duty, although it should be clearly understood that it can also be a great pleasure. During such talks and rambles he will come to know his children better ; and that is important, because he can bring to bear on the children his influence and above all his example.   Provided their father has been a real friend to be admired and imitated then the children come to rely on that example more and more as time goes on.   They remember his way of dealing with family situations, both pleasant and unpleasant, his kindness to their mother and to them, his understanding of their problems and his willingness to listen, his way of attending at Mass and at Benediction—all these things leave a very deep impression.   Do you want to know why?   Because they are liable to detect just the opposite in other family circles, for instance, among their friends.   Also because in religious matters they will be guided by that example when they hear from those who are indifferent to religious appeal that religion is a thing for silly women and not meant for men.   Then they will remember their own father, and that example will serve to make such a statement a real insult to one they love and respect.

Just as important as these positive things are the others which fathers should avoid at all costs.   In the first place, remember that much of the happy family atmosphere in the home depends on the father and on his way of acting.   Don't do anything which might tend to make the children look on you as an ogre !   If they begin to think that you are the real cause of most of the family rows then they will soon lose all their love and respect for you, even though they may continue to fear you.   Fear should never be allowed to enter into the picture at all, even when it is a question of punishment which has to be administered.   Avoid all undue harshness in your dealings with the children, together with all manifestations of impatience or lack of sympathy with them in their childish problems.   Don't show yourself unwilling to listen to anything, no matter how trivial it may seem.   Whenever the child is willing or eager to talk to you, do not put him off until later, listen *now*.   Make that a strict rule for yourself and stick to it ; you will have cause later on to thank God that you made it !

Never, whatever you do, allow yourself to become a mere punishment machine.   So often the mother leaves the matter of fitting punishment for offences altogether to the father, so that, on returning home from work, he finds that his main task seems to be to administer correction or reproofs for the day's misdeeds.   This may be necessary now and again, but you should make sure that it does not happen often.   If the children come to connect you with all the administration of punishment then they will grow up to fear you, and that is a very bad thing.   You should be able to arrange things in such a way that the very thought of causing you displeasure will be sufficient to make them avoid wrong-doing.   That is the ideal towards which you should strive, and it is a worthwhile ambition for any father. It will be necessary for you and for your wife to have the same ideas on this subject, so talk it over carefully.

Do not be too exacting with the children where their school work is concerned.   There seems to be a natural tendency to do this in most fathers, and you will probably have to fight down this feeling quite a few times before you achieve self-control.   It is very annoying to see the child producing slipshod homework when you know perfectly well that he can and should do better, but do remember that your scolding will not improve matters half so quickly as a little positive encouragement.   By scolding you may produce better homework, but if that is done at the cost of the confidence and affection which should exist between you and the children then it is by no means worth the price which has to be paid for it.   If you are not pleased with the child's work then tell him so in a quiet and sympathetic manner when the right opportunity presents itself.   He will certainly confess to you that his teachers are not satisfied with it either, or you may find that out from their reports.   Then you will be able to give him both the advice and the help which he needs, without disturbing his confidence in you.

Never punish in anger, and always let the child see that you do not like having to punish him at all, and that as soon as possible you are going to forget the whole sorry business in the hope that it will not be necessary again.

Do not acquire the bad habit of discussing the children in their presence, even though what you have to say about them may be in their favour.   If you wish to praise them (and you should do this at times for their own sakes and for yours), then do it to them directly.

Never be afraid to let them see that your love for them comes before anything else, and that you are willing to give up anything for their sakes.   They will come to appreciate this later on in life, especially if you seem to take it for granted and are not always talking about your self-sacrifices on their behalf.

Before very long you are going to be the only one who can really advise them on certain personal problems, and this is especially true of the boys in the family. Your main interest now should be to build up the foundations of love and confidence on which that advice must rest if it is to produce its full effect. For this reason, if for no others, your own personal, social, religious and moral standards must be as high as you can possibly make them, and you must always give your children good example in these fields.

Excessive drinking on your part can have a very bad effect on your children, and nearly always leads to great fear of their father. See to it that you never make this mistake.

If you can only resolve to put these few simple rules into practice then you will be a real friend to your children as well as a good father, and that is a very useful and a very wonderful thing.

Returning to our general theme, and leaving the fathers of the families on one side for the moment, you will have noticed that special emphasis has been laid on the need for good sound moral values and standards of conduct during this period of the child's training. This is so important that one modern expert in this matter has not hesitated to affirm that *all* the fundamental moral principles which a child will ever acquire have been implanted in his character by the time he reaches the age of twelve. Experience tends to confirm this rather startling statement, so see to it that your task as parents is not performed in any negligent fashion during these years, but to the very best of your ability. This is indeed the golden age, and its possibilities where education is concerned are legion.

CHAPTER ELEVEN

THE CHILD'S PRAYERS

WE HAVE ALREADY DEALT WITH THE QUESTION OF THE religious instruction which should be given by the parents during these early school years between the ages of six and twelve. Now this question must receive more attention, because doctrine or knowledge is closely connected with the love of God which, in its turn, is fostered in the soul by prayer. At the risk of being accused of constant repetition of the same theme, let us make it quite clear that education is one whole—it cannot be divided up into sections or water-tight compartments. Our task as parents is to teach our children how they are to save their souls by living their human life as well as possible, in accordance with the laws of God. We all save our souls by and through our lives in this world, not by trying to separate ourselves from that life and living as if it did not exist at all. True peace and happiness can be found here below, but only in so far as we are living here in order to get to heaven, our true home. Our thoughts, aims and aspirations must be constantly directed towards that goal if we are ever to succeed in reaching it safely. No amount of knowledge will do that for us unless it penetrates the whole of life and makes us live it *in* and *for* God. That is always the aim we have in view for our children. This constant living in and for God necessarily demands an ever-growing sense of the presence of God and also communication with Him through prayer. Prayer is the direct expression of our love for and of our wish to serve Him. In this connection your aim must be to bring your child's life of prayer to such a pitch of perfection that he will be able to stand on his own two feet where God is concerned, and not be blown here and there by every contrary wind. This, in its turn, means that you must make every effort to develop that life of prayer in the child's soul. We have all heard of and known children who seemed to be quite religious in the best sense of that word while they were at school, but as soon as their school life is finished their religious life too seems to come to an abrupt end. The reason is not hard to find. It is because there has been no real attempt on the part of the parents to foster the life of prayer in the child. It has been regarded as one more of those subjects which we learn at school and try to forget as soon as we leave school!

The foundation of this life of prayer should have already been laid, because you will have taught the child a few simple prayers before he goes to school, such as the Our Father, the Hail Mary, the Glory be to the Father, and also a simple form of night and morning prayers. You must now build on that, never being content to leave all the work to the teachers at the school. If the child goes to a Catholic school, of course the teachers will do something to help your efforts, but your part is still of the very greatest importance.

During the first years of school life you should go through those familiar prayers once again, this time with a more detailed explanation. The Our Father does need a little explaining if it is to be said with devotion and reverence. The same is true of all the other prayers you have taught. Once those prayers are well known, with their explanations, so that the child has some idea of what he is saying, then on that foundation you can begin to build up the whole life of prayer, and with great success.

The centre of all prayer in the future is going to be the Holy Mass, together with the Sacramental life of the Church, especially Confession and Holy Communion. Indeed, from the age of five to seven you, as well as the teachers, will be concerned with the preparation for the reception of those two great Sacraments for the first time—a thing which marks a new stage in the child's life as a Catholic. That preparation must be well done.

Part of this preparation will be an explanation of the Mass, at least as far as the child's age and capabilities will allow. Begin with an explanation of the vestments. Tell the child what they are and what they represent. Do the same with the altar, the linen, the candles, chalice, wine and water, and so on. These material things all help very much to capture the child's

attention and also to direct his mind to the doctrines behind them.
If you like to do this with the aid of your scrap-book so much the
better. It will mean that you must cut out and paste into the
book pictures of all the things used during Mass. Give the child
one of those simple little picture prayer books if you like, and then
take him quietly through those pictures during Mass. Remember
that you will have to be somewhere where he can see the altar
and what is going on.

So far as the actual doctrine is concerned, you will not find
much difficulty if you remember to stress these points in a simple
fashion :—

(a). The Mass is a repetition in some way of the Sacrifice of
Calvary. A picture of Calvary explains that quite easily. Point
out that Jesus cannot suffer any more, but what He can do is to
come down on to our altars so that we may love Him very much
for all that He has done for us. That is what the Mass means
for the small child, and he can pick up the rest from your more
detailed explanations later.

(b). Once Jesus is on the altar under the form of bread and
wine, then we can offer Him up to God the Father in heaven as
our prayer. We ask Him to obtain for us all those graces and
blessings which we need so much. Never be afraid to teach the
prayer of petition, because it is the basis of all prayers.

You will have already prepared the way for this teaching
during your earlier instructions with the scrap-book by telling
the child the stories of the two miracles which Jesus did just
before He promised us the Holy Eucharist, namely the walking
on the waters of the sea and also the multiplication of the loaves
and fishes. This will have shown the child that Jesus can do
exactly as He likes with these things which He has made, and
from that idea to the other one of the Real Presence is not such
a very great step for a child. What you must do is to stress
the reality of this Presence by your examples. Point out to him
that Jesus is in the tabernacle just as truly as He was in the stable,
with His Mother and St. Joseph. That He is just as present to
the child during one of those little visits to the church as you
are when you have him on your knee : that the church is Jesus'
home, where He lives and where He loves to see and to talk to
His friends, and so on. These examples count for a great deal,

because they all serve to drive home to the child the main idea, which is the *reality* of this Presence. The fact that we should love to talk to Jesus in church is a simple step once this has been done.

As you can see, the years between five and seven are not so very long for the preparation we have in mind, especially when you remember that you will also have to do your share in helping to get the child ready for his first confession. This task is just as important in its way as the former, because of the great value of confession during adolescence. That value will depend to a great extent on the way you prepare the child now, and especially on your handling of him during the intervening years. Once again, you cannot leave it all to the teachers. A very great deal can be done at home to make sure that the child understands as well as his age will permit what confession means and how to receive this Sacrament well.

Once again, the remote preparation will have been partly accomplished if you have been faithful to the idea of telling him stories from the Gospels. The stories of Mary Magdalene and the prodigal son, for example, are almost perfect material on which to weave the doctrine. So, too, are the many stories of the cures wrought by Jesus on the sick, because sin can best be described as a spiritual sickness, which can sometimes kill the soul if we allow it to do so. Above all, do not forget the stories which indicate the great love Jesus had for little children. They will help your child to have great confidence in Christ and also to see that getting rid of sin is really an act of great love on the part of God.

From this you can pass on to a very brief and matter-of-fact explanation of the doctrine of this Sacrament. The child will accept it quite simply at this age.

After this comes what is by far the most difficult part of your task, namely, teaching the actual practice of confession. Here you must go slowly. Start with some simple prayers which the child can say in preparation for confession. These need not be very long, but one of them at least should be a prayer for God's help to make a good confession. It should sum up all that confession means, and thus by learning it the child is really learning how to go to confession. Some such formula as the following will be quite sufficient :

" My dear Jesus, help me to know what sins I have done ; help me to be very sorry for them and to tell them to the priest who is taking Your place, so that he can forgive me in Your Name. I promise that I will try hard not to do them again, with Your help. Amen."

Follow this up with one Our Father, Hail Mary and Glory be to the Father, said slowly and with devotion, and that will be quite sufficient for the actual preparation. Later on these prayers can be added to at will.

As you know, the preparation for confession includes an examination of conscience, the act of contrition and also the firm purpose of amendment. Let us deal with those elements one by one.

The examination of conscience.

This will not be an easy task at first. We have no fixed method, and indeed it is true to say that there is no single method at present in use which answers all the difficulties from the child's point of view. Perhaps the best way to tackle this problem is to use the commandments as a basis, going through them with the child and telling him what they are all about in such a way that he can understand them. At the same time, you can give examples of the kind of sins which children of his age tend to commit. Whatever you do, never suggest to the child sins which he knows nothing whatever about. This applies especially to the two commandments which govern the virtue of purity. Small children do not understand what those things mean, and it would be very wrong, at this stage, to attempt to teach them very much about such sins. Nor is it any use trying to cover up with some such formula as " I have been rude ", because to the child that expression covers a multitude of things, including answering back to its parents, swearing, spitting at each other and so on. Later we shall discuss this whole matter from another angle, i.e., that of sex instruction. Then perhaps we shall be able to suggest some solution to this difficulty of the sixth and the ninth commandments. At the moment it is better to slide over them quickly and without comment. The moment will come when you have to deal with them in greater detail, but that time is not yet. The examination of conscience in the child's prayer book may help you to see how this should be done.

Contrition.

Sorrow for sin is all-important because of the great lessons it holds for the future, and so this is the point which you must stress most of all. Teach the child from the very beginning that he must spend more time on the act of contrition than on any other part of the preparation for confession. Give him, in a brief form, all the necessary motives for real sorrow, namely, the fear of hell, the love for Christ who has first loved us and died for us on the Cross, and lastly the fact that, just as an act of disobedience to our parents means that we have offended them, so too an act of sin means that we have offended the great goodness of God. Stories about the Passion and the death of Jesus on the Cross are very useful to help the child to get a real true sorrow for sin, even for those small sins which he is liable to commit at this age. Use the Passion with the idea of fostering a great love for Christ rather than with the idea of teaching the child that we have crucified Christ by our sins. That is not a good idea to put into a child's head at this stage. Later it will come in useful, but not yet.

The purpose of amendment.

This is very easily explained by the simple idea which the child can grasp that it is not much use saying we are sorry if we do the same thing all over again immediately afterwards. A few simple examples will easily drive this home to him.

Some children are allowed to make their first confession without ever having seen the inside of a confessional box, or even without having been told what it is like. The very best thing to do in this connection is to take the child to church one day at a time when you know that there will not be many people there and then show him the confessional box so that he will know what he has to do when he does go inside. Let him go in and kneel down, and then close the door on him for a few moments. In that way he will lose all fear of the actual surroundings of his first confession. In general, make sure that you instil a very deep love for this Sacrament in the heart of the child. He must come to look on it as something very great indeed, and not something to fear.

You can and should also provide for the future by telling him that, if ever he does not quite know how to tell in confession something he has done, or is not certain if a certain action is a sin or not, then all that he has to do in confession is to tell the priest so quite simply. You might even suggest a form of words for this which the child can use. Thus, he could say, " Please, Father, there is something I have done and I am not sure if it is a sin or not ". Then the priest will be able, by a few simple questions, to find out all about it and so to put the child's mind at rest. Or again, it may be that something is worrying him and he does not know quite how to confess it. Then he can say, " Please, Father, there is something which I do not quite know how to confess ". Again, a few simple questions will soon remove this difficulty. If you teach this now, then you will feel much more secure when the testing time of adolescence arrives.

Returning for a moment to your preparation of the child for the Sacrament of the Holy Eucharist, it must be stressed once more that you should not leave this preparation altogether to the school authorities. The reason is simple. The main thing which we have to aim at is a great personal love of the child for our Divine Lord in this Sacrament. You are the persons most capable of bringing about this personal union, and you will have failed in your duty if you do not do all that you can in this matter. The doctrine will not be difficult to the child, because small children are capable of assimilating an astonishing amount of doctrine and of understanding it, too. If you have led up to this by a careful use of the scrap-book pictures then you will not have any real difficulty. The teaching which the child is receiving at school will also help you a great deal in this preparation, so the task is a little easier than it may appear at first sight.

Teach some little prayers of preparation—the simple acts of Faith, Hope, Charity and Contrition will do very well as a beginning, together with some simple little prayers to ask Jesus to come into the soul of the child, and to tell Him that there is love waiting there to receive Him. If you can find such prayers in verse so much the better. Perhaps the child's prayer book will be of use to you again here, but *do* make sure that he understands what he is saying and that he does not merely read those prayers mechanically.

The thanksgiving is very important. Stress in your instructions that Jesus is really present within us after we have received Holy Communion, so that we may talk to Him about anything which interests us. He is very interested in such things, too, because He loves us so much. There should be a few moments of quiet recollection after Holy Communion, during which we just think of Jesus within us and repeat over and over again, " Jesus, I love You so much ". This should be followed by a few simple prayers, said with great attention and devotion, including always the act of Charity. Do not let it stop there, however. Make sure that your child speaks to Christ in his own words for a moment or two at least. He will soon get into the way of doing this, especially since it is an element of all prayer with which he will be already familiar if you have taught him his morning and evening prayers in the manner which we have suggested elsewhere. Give him some simple examples of this type of prayer. Let him see that he can ask now for all those graces and blessings which he wants for himself and for others, especially for his own family circle. This idea appeals to the imagination of the child very easily, and he soon gets into the way of it.

You might also take the opportunity, during these little instructional talks, of getting home some of those lessons which are going to be very useful later on. Point out that Jesus Himself described this Holy Communion as the " food of the soul ". Expand that idea a little, and point out that therefore we should go to Holy Communion frequently, because, just as we eat our ordinary human food at regular times so as to keep up our strength, in the same way we have to be regular in the eating of our spiritual food as well. Keep to this regularity yourselves and thus you will give the child a good example which he will not forget. This food is also meant to be a help to us in all our difficulties, and so, if we receive Our Lord with Love we can expect Him to help us always. Lastly, do try to teach them that, after Holy Communion, we should all try to live as well as we can and be very good, because the life which we now live is the life of Jesus, in the sense that He has been with us and lived with us for a time.

You will find that all these ideas can be driven home very easily by repetition and especially by visits to the Blessed

Sacrament. There in church during those visits you will be able to practise, with the child, the acts of preparation and also those of thanksgiving. You will also be laying, at the same time, the foundations of a real love for the Real Presence which will last for the whole of the child's lifetime. Teach him a simple act of Spiritual Communion and make sure that he understands it and says it well, with care and attention.

After the first Holy Communion there are several things which need to be watched. We all know that Communion should make us better and transform the whole of our life. The real reason why it does not always succeed in doing this is because we ourselves put obstacles in the way by our coldness and indifference. This can be avoided, especially in childhood, by making the children always more and more conscious of what this great Sacrament really means. You can impress this on them in many simple ways. Keep the day of the First Communion of any of the children as a family feast day. All should go to Holy Communion on that day, and the *date* should be remembered, so that you can keep it every year in the same way. This is a very simple thing to do, and yet so many people do not bother at all about it, and the loss is very great. It has a very deep effect on the child and will remain a constant memory when many other things have been forgotten. These days should be kept as real feasts, with little presents given— they need not be worth much money, because it is the thought behind them that counts—to mark the occasion. You should also try to fix at least one day each month as the family communion day. This is not too much to ask, and it has a great effect on the unity of the family.

Do remember that, from now onwards, your example is going to mean at least as much, if not more, than all your teaching in mere words. This is especially true of anything which includes these great acts of religious worship. You will have to be very careful about them all in general, and in particular that you are always good-tempered and gentle with the children after morning Mass and Holy Communion. Many children are put off religion by their parents' conduct on Sunday mornings. It is a very common experience to find that at no time are parents so touchy and bad tempered as they are after

Mass on Sundays or Holidays of Obligation. There is really no excuse for this, even though the usual routine of the house is upset a little, and you should be careful to see to it that the contrary is true in your family circle. This can easily be done with a little care, and it does make a very big difference to the children, because it shows them that religion really means something to you. This, as you can see, is but an application of our old rule that you should be careful to avoid anything which might tend to make religion odious to the child in later life. This calls for self-sacrifice, it is true, but then if we are not prepared to exercise this virtue, as well as that of self-control, we cannot expect the children to do so. Teach them by your example that the Holy Communion you and they receive should colour the whole day. It is known as the Sacrament of Love, and in all our dealings with It this motive of love should be ever uppermost in our minds.

As the child gets older so your explanation of the Mass can go deeper. If the child concerned is a boy then you should be thinking very seriously at this point in his life of getting him to assist more closely in the ceremonies of the Mass by serving on the Sanctuary. Go along to see the priest about it and see what can be done. This will get him much nearer to the ceremonies, and so will do more than all your explanations can ever do to help him to understand them. However, make sure at the same time that your children never take the Mass for granted. Tell them stories of the English Martyrs during the days of persecution and so make them see that this Mass which we offer now in comparative ease and comfort is the same as that for which they gave their lives so cheerfully. A child is very easily impressed by ideals, and there can be no higher ideal outside that of Christ Himself, than that proposed to us by those great champions of the Faith and of the Mass. Once you can get this idea across then you will have given your child a motive for loving the Mass and for assisting at it with devotion which will last for a very long time.

You have also the task of developing the child's life of prayer. This needs a further word of explanation, because there are quite a number of parents who are quite content to let their children go on in the old ways without making any attempt to teach them either new prayers or new methods of prayer. Both of these are of great importance, and we should not leave this task to others, but undertake it ourselves. It is often neglected because it is almost taken for granted that the child will get on quite well with the prayers he says out of his prayer book or else with what he learns at school. This is by no means the case.

Prayer is, or at least should be, the mainspring of our lives, and we cannot afford to leave it to chance. Vocal prayer has to be watched, because children often become quite mechanical in their recitation of such prayers and so soon forget to pay much attention to what they are saying. Keep up your explanations of these vocal prayers and never teach a prayer without explaining its meaning and then going back over it again and again. New prayers have to be taught, too, little by little, so that the child will have some variety to choose from. Pick those which suit his age and temperament. Ejaculations are a very valuable form of vocal prayer for the child, especially because if they are not learnt and repeated frequently during childhood they will probably never be learnt at all. Devotion to the Holy Souls in purgatory—a devotion which every Catholic should take up seriously—can also be fostered by this method of ejaculations, especially those which carry indulgences with them and can thus be applied very fittingly to the Holy Souls.

But the life of prayer means so much more than just teaching new prayers—it implies new methods of prayer as well. Vocal prayer is very good and is necessary for all, but there are also other methods of prayer which are not to be ignored. One of these types of prayer is worth a little more explanation here because experience has shown that it has a great appeal for children, and that they can learn it much more easily than many people think. The great pity of it is that most parents do not take the trouble to teach it to their children and thus they never get a chance to practise it.

The whole idea of this method we are about to describe is to get the child to use his imagination as well as his intellect and will. Since examples in this matter of prayer can teach the whole method much quicker than long explanations, let us see, by a practical demonstration, in what this type of prayer

consists. Imagine that we want to say some prayers to Our
Blessed Lady. Instead of reading those prayers out of a book
we first of all imagine that we ourselves are present at one of
those familiar scenes from her life, let us say at the Crib. We
kneel down in imagination at her side with our joined hands on
her knee. Try to exclude everything else from the mind
except this picture of the three people concerned, Our Lady,
the Infant Jesus, and ourselves. Then we begin very simply
and in our own words to talk to her about all those things which
interest us. We thank her first for becoming the Mother of
Jesus and we worship her Son whom we know to be God made
man for us. We thank Him, too, for coming among us to love
us and to teach us. We talk to Him about our family, our
friends, our interests. We ask Mary and Jesus to bless all those
we love and to give them all those graces which they need to
get to heaven. We mix into these prayers in our own words
the simple acts of Faith, Hope, Charity and Contrition, saying
them very slowly and with attention. That is the whole
system of this type of prayer, and, as you can see, there is nothing
very difficult about it at all. The child can soon be trained to
pray in this way for five minutes during one of your visits to the
Blessed Sacrament together, and you will find that it is a method
of prayer which grows on him. It teaches more than any
other the familiar intercourse between the soul and Christ
which is the aim and the life of all good prayer. Naturally,
you will have to give him more than one example of the kind
of imagination pictures which will help this method of prayer,
but all those scenes can be made up quite easily from the
incidents in the Life of Our Lord. Concrete subjects lend
themselves to this type of imagination better than others.

Meanwhile you will still have to supervise the morning and
evening prayers for some little time yet, although you should
be giving more and more responsibility to the child in this
matter as time goes on, especially after his first Holy Communion.
I hope that, by this time, the Family Rosary has become a
habit with you all, and that you will keep that going whatever
happens. It is still possible, even during adolescence, as we
shall see later.

You must also foster in the child a deep personal devotion

to the Virgin Mary.   She was both a Virgin and a Mother, and
so she can understand all our difficulties, and also she has a very
personal interest in all of us as her children.   She works in all
things to lead us to her Son and to assure our eternal salvation.
She will be a real Mother to your children and they should
learn, through your example, to love her very deeply.   There
is no doubt at all about the attraction of this devotion for
children, but, like everything else, it depends to a great extent
for its success on your efforts during these formative years.   If
you do your share, then this devotion will grow with the child,
but if you are careless, then it will decline as time goes on.   The
months of May and October should be kept by all the family
with great devotion.   Also get the children into the habit of
saying three Hail Marys during the course of their night prayers
together with this invocation : " Mary, conceived without sin,
pray for us who have recourse to thee."

In developing the religious life and the life of prayer in your
children you must remember to go carefully and slowly.   Never
do anything to make religion odious to the child.   Think often
of the example of St. Monica, who had to pray and weep for
many long years before she won over her son, Augustine, to the
love and the service of God.   Your aim is to make your children
love God very much, and you will not succeed in doing that by
nagging at them or scolding them about religion.   You can
make religion very real and very beautiful to the child without
those hateful tactics, and you must do so, because you do not
want him to leave all those practices later with the excuse that
he was forced to go to church too much when he was a young
child and had religion " thrust down his throat."   It is necessary
to make a note of this objection here, because very many of
those who fall away from their faith give this as an excuse.
What they really mean is that they had religion put to them in
the wrong way, and that is often true.   Do not make this mistake
yourselves.   Love is the most important thing in all religion—
far more important than any amount of devotions as such.   They
have their place, too, but only in so far as they arise from love
almost spontaneously.   Never over-load your children, but think
of their age and their development, and then do the best you can.
You will succeed if you yourselves love God very deeply.

CHAPTER TWELVE

CHILDREN AND
SEX INSTRUCTION

T HE PROBLEM WHICH FORMS THE SUBJECT OF THIS CHAPTER
is one which bothers all parents at some time or another,
and so it should. At the very outset it is necessary to make
one or two general points quite clear.

In the first place, the obligation of giving such instruction
lies definitely with the child's parents. It is not primarily a
matter for the school authorities or for the priest, and that in
spite of the fact that most schools insist on sex instruction (for
the older children at least) more or less as if it were just another
lesson. Whether that is a good thing or not can be determined
better later on in this chapter. One thing is quite certain.
Because of this instruction by the school authorities many
parents tend to leave it all to them, and do nothing themselves.
They should remember that it is their obligation and their duty.

Secondly, the child has a *strict right* to be told such things in
accordance with its age and sex. Let us get it out of our heads
once and for all that ignorance is innocence in this matter.
Now, it is very easy to prove that these principles are not merely
the personal opinion of the author. The present Holy Father,
speaking to a gathering of Catholic mothers in Rome in the
year 1941, said, among other things :

" With the discretion of a mother and a teacher, and thanks
to that open-hearted confidence with which you have been able
to inspire your children, you will not fail to watch for and to
discern the moment in which certain unspoken questions have
occurred to their minds and are troubling their senses. It will
then be your duty to your daughters and the father's duty to
your sons, carefully and delicately to unveil the truth as far as
it appears necessary to give a prudent, true and Christian answer

131

10

to those questions, and to set their minds at rest.   If imparted
by the lips of Christian parents and at the proper time, in the
proper measure and with the proper precautions, the revelations
of the mysterious and marvellous laws of life will be received by
them with reverence and gratitude, and will enlighten their
minds with far less danger than if they learnt them haphazard,
from some unpleasant shock, from secret conversations, through
information received from over-sophisticated companions, or
from clandestine reading, the more dangerous and pernicious as
secrecy inflames the imagination and troubles the senses."

As you can see, these grave words of the Holy Father stress
several points which are of the greatest importance as an introduction to this discussion.   These main points may be summed
up as follows :—

1. The giving of this necessary instruction is a duty which falls
    directly on the parents, and the child has a strict right
    to it.

2. The mother should fulfil this obligation for her daughters
    and the father for the sons.   The task, as the Pope indicates,
    is one of the greatest importance.

3. When given by the parents and with the proper safeguards,
    there is no danger that such instruction may be a source of
    evil to the child, quite the opposite.   It will set the child's
    mind at rest with regard to those questions which are
    troubling him and will be received with love and with due
    reverence.

4. Parents should watch for and discern the moment when
    such instruction has become a necessity, and must also
    decide how much information should be given at that
    moment in accordance with the age, sex and development
    of the child.

Of these points there can be no doubt at all, and a careful
reading of them should serve to show parents quite clearly where
their duty lies, and also to kill once and for all the idea that the
longer we allow the child to remain in apparent ignorance of
these matters the better it will be for him.   That is a pernicious
opinion which, in spite of all the evidence to the contrary, still
continues to raise its head from time to time.

In order to make this point still more clear and definite in the minds of Catholic parents, let us see what happens only too often in actual practice when this instruction of the Pope is ignored. Investigation has shown that, even among Catholic children, over sixty per cent. get their information about sex from sources other than their parents. Further investigation has proved that, of all these sources, the most common in order of appearance are companions, books, magazines, the street, the newspapers and the films. Only about 18 per cent. get their first information on this delicate and most important subject from their parents. This state of affairs should make all Catholic parents sit up and think very hard. There is only one remedy for this. Catholic parents must watch for the moment and then must give this instruction themselves with courage. They cannot run the risk of allowing their children to pick up their information from any of those other sources, so often inaccurate, and certainly harmful to the child.

A normal child does not suddenly acquire a desire for full sexual knowledge. Certain questions occur to his mind and make him curious, and in all simplicity he puts those questions to his parents. This can happen, as experience proves, at a very early age. Instead of receiving as a reply a straightforward and clear answer which will settle his mind in accordance with his age and development the parents are often either evasive in their answers or else they give him a definitely ridiculous one which does much more harm than good. At times the child is put off by being told that he is too young to be told such things as yet, or that he must not ask such questions. He has been open and frank— and his parents have not. Nothing has been done to settle his mind on the question at issue, which he continues to turn over and over and perhaps discusses with his companions at school, who know as little as he does about it, or else—which is much more dangerous—they know just a little bit more.

Gradually his curiosity develops as he gets certain half-truths from his companions and from his general reading in books and magazines. At the same time, perhaps, he hears certain rather doubtful stories from his friends and companions. Puberty may be either upon him or at least approaching at this time. Soon an unhealthy attitude develops towards the whole question of sex,

which is so wrapped up in mystery that it excites his curiosity
still more as time goes on.   This attitude may persist for years
and sometimes even for his whole life.   By the time that his
parents pluck up the necessary courage to tell him some of the
real facts the harm has been done.   The knowledge has already
been acquired and by means which constitute a real danger to
the child's character.   The parents are to blame for anything
which follows.   The general result is an attitude towards sex
which is the very opposite of reverent.

This picture is no exaggeration—as most of us know from bitter
experience.   Parents should remember their own childhood, and
also the fact that things are much worse today than they were
some years ago.   They should then make up their minds that
this type of thing shall not happen in the case of their child
and through their own carelessness.   Now, the question which
interests us is how are we going to avoid it ?

First of all, by making quite sure that we ourselves have a right
attitude to the whole question and also towards our obligation in
this matter of sex instruction.   Our plain duty is to teach the
right attitude towards sex at the right moment, in accordance with
the age, sex and development of the child.   A brief examination
of the different elements of this statement will help us to clear
the ground for a more detailed discussion of methods to be used.

(a)   *The right attitude*

Mere knowledge of sex matters is not enough by any means,
in fact, it is often quite useless.   It is the attitude towards this
important life-function which is needed.   Consequently, in all
our answers to the children's questions and in all our instructions
on this matter we should be concerned, not so much with the
biological or the physiological details, as with the teaching of
a correct attitude towards sex.   Just what this attitude should
be and how it can best be taught we shall discuss later.

(b)   *The right moment*

In this connection there is a saying which has become common:
" Better a year too soon than a day too late ".   Naturally, this
teaching is best given gradually, but it should begin just as soon
as the parents see, either from the child's questions or from other

indications, that he is beginning to be puzzled about these matters or curious with regard to them. When in doubt, then, speak out without fear ; that is the only safe rule, and also the only one which can really prevent our Catholic children from learning about such things from dangerous or from unwholesome sources. We cannot afford to run that risk.

(c) *In accordance with the age, sex and development of a child*

All these different factors have to be taken into consideration in determining the correct moment and the method of our instruction, and also how much we shall have to impart at any given time. Of these factors the most important undoubtedly, and the one which, to a great extent at least, governs the others, is development. Not all children develop at the same rate, nor in accordance with mere physical age. In some cases a child of ten may be as fully developed mentally, and even physically, as another of eleven or twelve. Here parents will have to use their discretion and their judgment to a very large degree. By development we mean, therefore, not merely the purely physical, but also the mental and the psychological advance of the child's character.

Next in importance is the sex of the child, and this factor increases in importance as the child grows older. Naturally, girls and boys have a very different approach to this problem and so must be dealt with differently. In the following chapters we hope to deal somewhat more fully with this difference between adolescent boys and girls, but the main lines of the differences should be fairly obvious to most parents. It is, as we have said, the mother's task to deal with her daughters and the father's obligation to instruct his sons in this matter. The reasons for this are also very clear and so there will be no need to dwell on the subject. However, it must be remembered that the age factor also has an influence here, because small children will usually manifest their first signs of curiosity to their mother in the form of questions. She can deal with those herself, without putting them off.

Age cannot be considered as an important factor in sex instruction except in conjunction with the other two elements of sex and development, but it can help us to a certain degree in determining how much instruction will be necessary in any given case in order to settle the child's mind.   Some children show by their questions that they need instruction at a much earlier age than others.   This may be due to their advanced development or perhaps even more often to their environment or particular circumstances.   This happens more frequently in the case of boys than it does with girls, who tend to conform much more to type in this matter.   In judging age, then, as applied to sex instruction, take into consideration not merely the physical but also the mental age, the sex, the development of character already achieved, and above all, perhaps, the environment, which will include such things as companions, school, older children in the family, the type of home life, i.e., whether farm or town, and so on.

.   .   .   .   .   .

You should certainly have finished the whole of your sex instruction before adolescence definitely overtakes the child ; in fact, in most cases it will have been necessary to give fairly complete instruction a good while before this new factor is introduced to the scene.   The reason for this is something which will become clearer during the chapters on adolescence, but for the moment it should be enough merely to indicate that the child (that is up to the age of adolescence) has a fairly well defined character.   Once he is overtaken by adolescence, that character tends to become very fluid.   It has new problems of its own and very serious ones, which imply a change of attitude towards those around him.   Get your basic instruction in before that crisis and all will go much more smoothly.

It will be as well to discuss certain elements of this basic necessary instruction in greater detail.   To begin with, the first danger signals you will receive are almost sure to take the form of questions asked by the children, say between the ages of seven and eleven, although it is by no means unknown for such questions to appear even earlier on.   Now, such questions have to be answered truthfully, in accordance with the age, sex, development etc., of the child concerned, and in such a fashion as to satisfy his natural curiosity.   Once more let us stress the fact that it is no use putting the child off by saying that he is too young to know these things, or by turning to ridiculous answers which include such mythical beings as the stork and the black bag! That is worse than useless, because, although the child may accept that answer at the time, it is going to be a great shock to him to learn later on that his parents have lied to him. Your position in his eyes will naturally suffer.

Remember, in this connection, that the child's curiosity is perfectly natural, and that it is not normally connected with sex as such. What he wants to know is where beings come from. He is naturally curious about that and nothing else. Give him an answer which is at once true and satisfying and he will not only take it quite simply but also he will lose all morbid curiosity about such things. He now knows the answer, and that satisfies him completely.

Your frankness and your willingness to answer these first questions will impress upon his mind that he is able to come to you with all kinds of questions, and that you do not mind in the slightest. Thus, once your answers lead to further questions or doubts he will approach you once again on the subject. This second time may be occasioned by some chance remark of his companions—indeed it usually is. It will be a clear indication to you that the time has come for more detailed instruction, according to the child's age and sex. Give enough instruction to satisfy him, and meanwhile prepare yourselves for the final stage when you will have to give the complete instruction on these matters which is necessary before puberty. This means, in actual fact, that no boy should reach the stage when he has nocturnal pollutions without having been instructed fully in such matters, and that no girl should reach the stage of her first menstruation without such instruction. This is of more importance in the case of the girl, but they are both important.

Do not think that the advent of puberty will relieve you of all obligation in this matter of sex instruction by any means. There are many other problems connected with sex on which you will still have to give instruction, guidance and advice, but provided that, by the time adolescence arrives, you have given all that is necessary then you will find that there is much less difficulty in dealing with those dangers which come along later on. The important thing is to realize that this instruction must continue at odd times and at opportune moments until the boy or girl is perfectly prepared for the obligations of a married life. This is a knowledge that will grow gradually and beautifully under your guidance provided you have inspired your children with confidence in you from the very beginning.

We have said that mere knowledge is not what we are to aim at, but rather the imparting of a right attitude with regard to sex matters. Parents may well ask what that attitude should be and how they are to impart it.

As Catholics we are aware of the fact that marriage is a very sacred thing and a great Sacrament in the eyes of God and of His Church ; but there are still many people who do not seem to understand that the whole idea of sex is also something which, because of its connection with this Sacrament and with the idea of children who are born of it not merely as citizens of this world but also of the kingdom of God, is very sacred, too. It is just this idea of the sacred nature of sex which has to be imparted as an essential attitude of mind. It is because they have the wrong attitude towards it that many people regard sex as a rather doubtful subject, at best. There has been an attempt made to shroud the whole thing with the wrong kind of awe and mystery which has only served to give it an added appeal to the minds of the young. They tend to regard it as something which has to be discovered at all costs just because it is so hidden from their eyes. It is regarded as a subject for dark corners and shaded lights. Thus, the first efforts of parents to instruct their children must be directed towards removing any false notions they may get hold of in the future by implanting the correct attitude to begin with. This can be done quite easily by considering carefully the following points and then getting them across to your children when the time comes.

First of all, marriage is a very glorious thing, which implies the union of a man and a woman in real personal love. They live their lives together in companionship with a singleness of purpose which is truly wonderful. That purpose is love and mutual help, and is consecrated very often by the fact that it terminates in the birth of a new life—a baby who is part of the parents themselves, and who has an immortal soul which it is their duty to prepare for the glory and the happiness of heaven. It is just for this reason that God has given to all men and women the power in their bodies to have children, so that they can join with God in helping to bring new people into the world, and finally, into heaven, too.

The sanctity of married life really springs from this fact, and the wonder of it can be brought home to the child quite easily by dwelling a little on the idea that, in this whole matter of having children, God and the parents both work together. The parents form the body of the baby and God creates the soul. It is almost as though He had to wait for their co-operation before He could make new citizens for the kingdom of heaven. The action of the parents forms the preparation for a creative act on the part of God, and must be, therefore, a very holy and a very wonderful thing. Just because it is so very wonderful we do not talk about it very often. At this point you can indicate that it should not be made the subject of ordinary conversations between boys and girls, because that would be to make light of something which is very sacred, and of something by means of which they themselves are now in this world. If this power is used in marriage then the children are born happy and safe from harm. If, on the other hand, it is used selfishly or in a wrong way, then the children suffer, because they are born unhappily.

This power to bring babies into the world is entrusted to all men and women as something sacred, which they should keep and guard as sacred until they get married, when they can use it for the greater honour and glory of God. Then they can truly share it with someone else, and can also work with God in His plan for the world. It should, therefore, always be thought of and spoken of as a very sacred thing, and also protected as such.

You might then go on to point out that this is what we mean when we speak of the virtue of purity. It is simply the strong-minded effort to keep and guard by all the means in our power that wonderful thing which God has entrusted to us so that one day it may be used rightly in marriage to bring new children into the world for God. Thus your real positive teaching on purity begins.

Once more, with regard to this virtue of purity, there is a definite attitude which has to be taught, and it is intimately

connected with what has already been said about the origin of
new life. Too often parents tend to talk to their children not
about purity, but rather about impurity—i.e., they stress the
negative rather than the positive side. In the course of these
conversations the children come to the conclusion that purity
is a rather " weak-kneed " virtue, consisting mainly in not doing
those things which everyone would like to do were it not
forbidden. They thus think of the opposite vice as being
something rather manly. You can correct that impression
almost before it manages to take hold of the child's mind by
pointing out that purity is essentially a right use of this power,
and not a mere negative thing. This implies that the strong man
is the pure man, while the man who yields to these temptations
is the real weakling, who has no control over himself and follows
his passions wherever they may lead him. Stress the point that
purity means the guarding of this creative power that God has
given us. This, in its turn, means much sacrifice and much
hard fighting to overcome the temptations which are bound to
arise in us. This is not the act of a weakling, but a glorious
struggle. It also serves to give us a strong character—something
which makes us every inch a man or a woman. It also gives us
self-control and strength of will. In all ways, then, purity is
the strong element in our lives, while impurity means a weakness
which has to be overcome.

If you have timed these instructions on purity well, then they
should go home long before the crisis of adolescence comes upon
the child. In this way he will come to look on purity as something to be valued because it will carry him through to adult
manhood, and since it also implies a struggle for an ideal, he will
be all the more ready and willing to engage in that fight. It
will also help him to get his adolescent friendships into their
right perspective, which is very important.

Those are the attitudes which have to be taught. Both of
them, as you can see, stress the sacredness of this power which
is given us by God, and also both insist on the positive nature
of the struggle for purity. This is an ideal which can be made
to appeal very much to the youth, and which will make him
glory in the thought that he can do something *now*. It will also
make him understand that all smutty talk about sex is really

something which is an insult to his own parents and to the power
which God has given to him.   He will learn reverence for the
bodies of others as well as for his own.   In this way you will
have won half the battle before you really start on the task of
actual instruction as to the facts of life.   This right attitude is
a thing to be achieved at all costs, as you can see.

CHAPTER THIRTEEN

METHODS IN SEX INSTRUCTION

IN THE LAST CHAPTER WE EXPLAINED THE GENERAL PRINCIPLES
which should govern this question of sex instruction. Now
it will be necessary to explain those same principles with
an eye to actual practice and with advice as to the methods
which will be useful.

Experience shows that one of the greatest difficulties parents
have in this matter is that of vocabulary—they just do not know
how to explain these things in simple words which the child
will be able to understand. There are two ways in which this
difficulty may be overcome. It is perfectly true to say that,
provided you have the right attitude towards sex yourselves
and are trying to fulfil your duty of helping your children in
this matter, then the words will come. After all, the Sacrament
of Matrimony was instituted by Christ to give you all the graces
necessary for this state of life, and one of the greatest of those
graces is certainly the ability to deal with this matter. A
prayer will often do much more good than anything else. Be
natural, and above all, never show any surprise at the questions
or the confidences you may receive from your children. In
fact, you will have to be prepared for surprises!

The second way of meeting this difficulty is by reading books
which have been written by Catholics on the subject. They
will give you some idea of the methods you can use in order to
deal with it satisfactorily. In this connection there are several
pamphlets published by the Catholic Truth Society which will
be of help, and a short list of them and of other books will be
given at the end of this chapter. You should remember that
there is one fundamental difficulty about all books on this
subject, i.e., they are not capable of dealing in detail with every

individual case, and in this matter every child must be dealt with as an individual. That is where your prudent judgment as parents will be so very useful, and you should learn to know your children thoroughly.

We do not wish you to be talking to the child all the time about sex, nor is there any need for this, because it would only make him give to this subject an exaggerated importance. The golden rule is to perform this task whenever circumstances demand it, and also to do it thoroughly once the need does arise. Then there will be little need for a great deal of repetition. However, it cannot be done all at once, and hence the need for a clear summary of the main periods of this instruction and also of the methods which can be used with advantage during those periods and in various circumstances.

Without pretending to be too dogmatic about it we can divide the periods at which some instruction on this matter is usually necessary into four. First of all there is the childhood period, usually manifested by strange questions or by an obvious curiosity as to the origins of life. Next comes the pre-adolescent period, during which the child usually picks up little bits of information here and there, probably at school, and then comes along to his parents for a confirmation of them or for some explanation. Thirdly, there is the instruction which has to be given as a prelude to adolescence, and lastly that which has to be given to the boy or girl as a proximate preparation for marriage. We shall deal with these periods in turn, since both the difficulties and the methods of dealing with them differ very much in each case.

1. *The childhood period*

Once again, as a prelude to what we are about to say, it is necessary to stress the fact that the right attitude on your part to the whole matter of sex is of great importance, because, if you have accustomed yourselves to look on sex and marriage as something essentially holy, then you will have no difficulty in imparting that same attitude to your children. This is a holy thing, and not something which we have to be ashamed of or think of as partly immodest or anything like that. It is a holy function, created by God (who made nothing that was not good), for the purpose of bringing into this world citizens of the state and of the kingdom of heaven. Also, remember that we cannot deal with this function as though it were entirely animal. It is essentially a part of our whole make-up, and we must learn to think of it in that way. Stress the positive aspects of it rather than the negative.

During childhood proper the main difficulties you will have to face are caused by questions about the origins of life. To give a complete list of all the various forms these questions take would be impossible here, but we can indicate the main ones. In general these questions range round three topics, the origins of life, the purpose of the navel and the differences between little boys and girls.

The first question is usually put to the mother in some such way as this :—" Mummy, where do little babies come from ? " Or, alternatively, " Where did I come from ? " or perhaps, " Where do you get babies from ? " The second question usually has its origins in the bath or when the child is being undressed, when, pointing to the navel, the child asks quite simply, " What is this for, Mummy ? " The last question with regard to the difference between little boys and girls is often by no means a purely academic one, as are the others, because quite often there is a very definite worry behind it which normally develops more easily in the case of boys than in that of girls, and especially in those who have no little sisters. Large families do help a lot in this matter, because then the boys are so used to the sight of little girls that they take the differences in anatomy for granted in most cases. It is as well, therefore, to keep in mind the fact that there may be a reason for this question other than the mere physical differences which the boy has noticed, and that reason may be a fear that the little girl has been the victim of an unfortunate accident which has deprived her of something which she should normally have. The boy wonders if some such accident might not happen to him if he is naughty. This may seem rather far-fetched to our way of thinking, but experience shows that this worry or something very like it does exist in quite a few cases.

All these questions should be answered as soon as they manifest themselves, and that without any shame on the part of the parents. The first question about the origins of life is not usually connected with the sex-act as such, but is merely due to the child's natural curiosity with regard to the origins of things which he manifests in many ways. In any case, the question must be answered truthfully and not evaded by stupid replies which do not solve the child's difficulty or which may leave even greater difficulties behind them.

There are many methods you can use to give a completely satisfactory answer, and if you have not already thought one out for yourselves here are some suggestions.

In the first place, there are the analogies from Nature which are useful provided you realize that, just because the child knows what goes on in the case of birds or animals, it does not necessarily follow that he knows what happens in man. In his mind there is a very big gap between the animal kingdom as such and the human species. Usually, once you have explained the relationship, he will understand it well enough to be completely satisfied. The commonest analogy is that of the nest. You can point out that, just as the birds pair off at certain times, build their nests and then, from the eggs they lay there, produce a family of little birds, so in much the same way God has built a very special nest inside the mother for the little baby. She has to keep it there for quite a long time until it is strong enough to face the world. Then it is born.

You should not forget to stress, at the same time, how holy this all is, because by means of it we can help God to make new people who can know Him and love Him. If you are fortunate to have animals near where you live then there are other analogies to hand. Point out that these animals keep their babies under their hearts in order to keep them warm for a time, because they love them so much and because they must be strong enough to face the world before being born.

The process of actual birth does not usually worry the young child at this time, because he is not so much interested in biological details as he is in the origins of life. Once that question has been answered to his satisfaction he is usually content. However, a question on the actual method of birth may follow, and that too will need an answer. In the case of the little girl you can show her quite simply, during the bath, where the baby comes out of the mother, while in the case of the boy it will be necessary first of all to point out to him that God has thought of that difficulty, and that therefore He has made little girls in a different way from little boys so that they can be mothers. Tell him quite simply what this difference is and then point out the right answer to the question. Don't be ashamed or afraid, because the child does not feel any shame at asking the question and you should have none in answering it.

The question on the purpose of the navel need not detain us long, because all you have to do is to point out that it is what is left of the little tube which joined the baby to his mother when he was too small to be born and was still being kept warm inside her.

The third type of question concerning the difference between little boys and girls need not worry you unduly, although it may seem a little more tricky at first than the others. Remember the possible reason behind the question and direct your reply more to this unspoken difficulty than to the biology of the sexes and you will have no difficulty. Usually it is enough to point out that the main reason for the difference is that God made boys and girls in a different way. It can also be pointed out that these differences which the child has noticed are not the only ones. For example, little girls dress differently, play different games, wear their hair done in a different fashion— and all those things too come from the fact that God made them different. Sometimes all these questions come together, and then it is best to answer this last question first, then explain the origin of life, and then finish with the reason for the navel. That is usually quite enough to satisfy the child's curiosity for some time to come.

So far we have dealt only with the direct questions put to you by the child. However, it may be necessary for you to tackle this matter because you notice, from certain indications, that the questions are troubling the child even though he does not come out with them directly. Thus, it sometimes happens that he notices the mother's increased size owing to advanced pregnancy and either by questions or by his attitude shows that he is thinking about it. Then the form of reply we have indicated above could be used to explain to him what is about to happen. This is usually best done by the mother during this stage, and it is normally to her that the first questions are addressed.

In general, then, we can sum up the duty of parents at this stage by saying that they should answer all questions, no matter how delicate or peculiar they may seem, without fear and quite simply and truthfully. Satisfy the child's normal curiosity and you will have done all you need to do. Warn him at the same time that it is just because this is such a holy thing that we do not talk about it to others apart from our parents. Let him see at the same time that you welcome his questions, and that will give him confidence for the future. If you want time to think over the form of any particular answer you may be called on to give, then say quite simply, " That will have to wait until tomorrow ", then make quite sure that you do deal with it on the following day. Don't put the child off in the hope that he will have forgotten all about it by then and that you will have no need to give him an answer. If you have reason to think that some of his questions are prompted by things he has heard from other children then question him gently and he will soon tell you what it is all about. Be matter-of-fact, and don't make a mystery of the whole affair.

2. *The pre-adolescent stage*

Puberty ushers in the stage of adolescence, but these two terms do not mean the same thing, because adolescence lasts for a fairly long time while puberty is one single fact. It implies that stage of development when a person becomes capable of parenthood. There is no very fixed rule as to when this change is liable to take place and the age differs very much in individual boys and girls. Generally it may be said that the normal age for the advent of puberty in the case of boys is between the ages of 14 and 16, while in girls it varies between 13 and 15. In the special chapters on adolescence we shall have more to say about this, but for the moment it is enough to point out that there are fairly frequent exceptions to this general rule and that the individual case has to be taken into consideration. This is not too difficult in actual practice, because puberty is usually preceded by certain well-defined physical signs and bodily changes which are useful in determining whether in any particular case this development is liable to take place sooner or later. However, it should not be imagined that merely physical development is the only factor which we have to take into consideration, because there are others which should determine both when to give this necessary instruction and also how much is needed. We have already mentioned some of them, i.e., the child's mental as well as physical development, its age and also its sex, as well as the whole family and school environment.

Therefore no general rule can be given as to when you should undertake this pre-puberty instruction except this very definite one, i.e., no boy should be allowed to reach the age of puberty without the necessary sex instruction. There should be no need to point out that this is even more true of girls, and in this matter parents should remember the warning already given, " Better a year too soon than a day too late."

Up to this point it has been possible to give the same practical advice for boys and girls, because there has been little real difference between their problems and the methods of dealing with them. From now on, however, we shall have to divide the sexes, because both the methods of teaching and the matter to be taught is different in both cases. So too is the attitude you will have to inculcate, and so we shall attempt that separation here, dealing first of all with the instruction to be given to the boys, and bearing in mind that it is the father who has the obligation of giving it, although, of course, if he fails in his duty, then the mother must step in. So far as the boys are concerned, however, he is easily the best qualified to tackle this problem, and should do so without fear.

The first elements in your instruction to the boy should be the right attitude towards sex in general, because this is going to become increasingly important, and also because he is on the verge of that very fluid period of life we call adolescence, when there are going to be many factors pulling him in different directions. It is the right attitude towards sex matters which is going to pull him through and enable him to reach manhood unscathed.

There is one danger which needs mentioning. Sometimes parents, in dealing with such things as sex and marriage, tend to reflect in their instructions their own personal marriage problems, especially at this stage. This should never happen. Just because your own marriage has not been the success you would like it to have been, that does not give you the right to reflect that in the life of your son. Give him all the benefit of your experience in an impersonal manner and it will do much more good. Teach the ideal rather than the imperfect imitations of that ideal.

As a preliminary to the methods of instruction to be employed at this stage let us indicate exactly how far your instructions should go.

First of all your main duty is the teaching of a right attitude towards sex and marriage, and no amount of knowledge will compensate for the lack of that right attitude. Therefore read through what we have already said about it and make sure that you understand what that right attitude should be.

So far as the actual amount of instruction is concerned, it may be laid down as a general rule that the earlier problems which were indicated by the childish questions of a few years ago will now have to be discussed in more detail and must include some description of the sex-act itself. Still, there will be no need for you to deal with all the different problems which can arise in married life, because there will be time for that later on. Keep in mind the particular problems which the boy is going to have to face during adolescence and take into consideration his age and mental development as well as his whole environment.

Remember too that these instructions can seldom be given with real profit in one session and yet we do not want to be always talking about sex matters, otherwise they will occupy the boy's mind too much and he will tend to give them too much importance. Consequently, make your preparations and space out the information to be given into three or at the most four talks. This will have the added advantage of giving the boy a chance to think over what you have said and ask questions if he needs to do so. Open out well to him and let him see that you are ready and willing to give him all the help he needs. The more matter-of-fact your approach the better for all concerned. Do not be nervous, because there is no need, and be definite and clear.

Now, as to methods! Here Nature herself comes to our help, because there are certain physical changes about to take place in the boy's body, in particular the fact of nocturnal pollutions, sometimes called " wet dreams ", which give you a good starting point. It is all-important to get your instructions in *before* that experience overtakes him, and thus your first approach to this subject might take some such form as the following.

Point out, first of all, the sanctity of marriage, which has been raised by God to the dignity of a Sacrament in order to help married people to fulfil their obligations. One of those obligations is that of having their children in the right way in union with the creative act of God, who alone can make a human soul. This will lead you quite naturally to the question of the origin of children. Since you are dealing with the boy, you can approach this subject from his angle. The power to have children is enclosed in the bodies of the parents and is itself a very sacred and holy thing. Men and women are the custodians of this great power and they have to guard it for the one purpose for which God made it, i.e., for bringing other souls into this world who will one day reach heaven. Some people make up their minds that they are not going to use this power at all ; instead they consecrate it to God who gave it to them just because they understand how wonderful it is. These are the priests, nuns and religious. Others, on the other hand, decide that they are going to use this power, and they are perfectly free to do so, because God does not demand that anyone should give up the right to use it—that must be a free act of the individual.

Those who choose to use this power get married and, having promised God that they will love each other all the days of their life together, they also resolve to use this power which God has entrusted to them in order to bring children into this world who will be able to love and to serve Him. (Here you have an excellent opportunity to stress once more the great sanctity of married life which comes from the fact that the parents actually help God to bring a new person into the world. They co-operate with God in the production of new life, and that is a very holy thing.)

From all this it is a very simple step to instruction about this power which God has given us. Children (i.e., before a certain age) have not yet received this power, because their bodies have not yet developed fully. That only comes with the approach of full manhood and womanhood. Point out to your son that he is growing up very fast now and that the day is not far distant when God will entrust this great power to him. Once it is granted, it must be guarded and preserved until such time as he may use it with God's consent and help. Here it is a useful thing to point out that God gives us this power some years before the actual time when we can use it in accordance with His will. There is a good reason for that, namely, so that we can get so accustomed to it, and guard it so carefully that, when the time does come for us to use it, we shall do so in full accordance with the will of God. Then you can continue with your instructions.

God has been very good to us in this matter because He has given us a sign so that we shall know when that power has been entrusted into our keeping. All boys have a similar experience and they should know exactly what it means before it happens so that, rather than being frightened or suspicious of it, they should thank God for yet one more of His great gifts and promise Him that they will look after it for Him as good Catholics.

One of these days—probably quite soon—he will experience a peculiar kind of dream, generally very vivid and most times in the early morning, just before waking up or in a half-waking state. This dream will be accompanied by a sense of physical pleasure and the passing of a small quantity of liquid. That is the sign which God has fashioned to let us know that our body is now sufficiently developed to receive this power from the hands of God. When that day comes he will know that God has actually given him this power which needs guarding against such things as evil talk or jokes just because it is a holy thing. This is a good place to break off the instruction for the time being.

In your next talk you will have to point out that, although girls are not made in quite the same way as boys, still they too receive their half of this power. They have to guard it just as carefully as the boy does, and only use it for their future husbands. There is no need to go into greater details yet.

When boys and girls grow up into men and women they feel an attraction towards others of the opposite sex. That attraction is very natural and is a good thing because it is the prelude to real love and reverence. If they love each other enough, then they feel that they want to use with each other that power which God has given to them. In other words, they want to get married. That too is a very great and wonderful thing, so much so that God has made a special Sacrament for them to receive in order that they may have all the graces they need to use that power in a holy way, in accordance with the laws of God. Once they have been married, then, just because of the great love which exists between them, they unite in one act of love the two halves of that power. It is from the loving embrace of those two people that the union takes place.

If your approach so far has been through the sanctity of this act of love then it will not come as a shock to the boy to learn that it is a question of the union between the ovum in the body of the woman and the semen of the man. The easiest way to get this idea across is to compare the power which the woman has to a seed, which cannot produce a baby until it has been surrounded by the liquid which comes from the body of the man. The two are necessary, and have to be fused into one by an act of love and union. This should be quite enough, but you may have to answer a few questions afterwards. This should be simple after this preparation.

The result of this union of love is often a little baby, which grows inside the mother for some time before it is born into the world. There, close to the mother's heart, it is fed with her blood and kept warm and safe so that nothing shall come near to harm it. When it is big enough and strong enough it is born into the world, and becomes the great sign of the love between this man and this woman. That is just why parents love their children so much, because they have co-operated with God to bring them into the world and they are really and truly a part of their parents. The parents make the body and God creates the soul.

In your last instruction go back to the original idea of the sanctity of marriage and of this power which God has given us ; also stress the great love which this supposes on the part of God and also on that of the parents. Because it is so good and holy we do not talk about it or listen to talk about it either from companions or friends. Tell the boy how to deal with these situations when companions start to talk in a nasty way about such things. The best thing to do is to walk away and leave them, because such talk is only bringing down to a very low level something which has been the cause and the reason for their being in this world. It is almost an insult to their own parents to talk like that. You might also point out that we try to keep this power intact until we get married so that we have something very great to offer our future partner whom we love so much. It is thus a great offering as a proof of our love.

Such a right use of this power is what we call the virtue of purity, and this is your great chance to stress the positive side of this great virtue, and to point out that it is a very manly thing, and not for a weakling. It is only a very strong character which can overcome the difficulties which lie in the way, and we can have that strong character through the grace of God and the Sacraments of His Church.

This should be enough information for the moment, although you must give the boy the chance to ask questions and also you must be prepared to answer such questions simply and truthfully. After these talks you will find that the air has been cleared very much and that from now onwards the going will be much easier.

Now you should both make a special effort with regard to the religious education of your sons, especially in the matter of prayer and also that of frequent reception of the Sacraments. The testimony of the Fathers of the Church shows us quite clearly the importance of the reception of Holy Communion. Our Lord Himself is certainly the best Person to deal with all the difficulties experienced by the growing boy.

Confession, if properly used, can also be of very great help, and is a great source of inspiration and grace, but it must be used properly. In this connection it is as well to repeat what you have already told your children, namely, that if there is anything worrying them or something which they do not quite know how to confess, then all they have to do is to mention it to the priest and he will help them and put them at rest. It is much better to get the children to go to confession because they themselves want to go, if possible. That does not imply that you should not suggest the idea to them if they show any signs of becoming slack, but it does mean that you should use tact and example rather than words. If you have kept up the custom of family confession and Communion you should have much less difficulty. We shall have more to say later about the religious life of the adolescent.

3. *The adolescent period*

Your next occasion for serious instruction will arrive during the period of adolescence, when your son begins to show signs of being interested in the opposite sex and perhaps to go out with girls. If you have dealt with the other periods in the manner suggested here then you should not have a great deal of difficulty in applying those general principles now. The problems you will probably have to deal with arise mainly through the temptations which come to the boy through his companions, especially if they are not Catholics. Repeat what you have said before about the sanctity of this life-force which is given to us. Stress the point that, if we love someone, then we do all that we can to keep her from harm, and above all, we respect her. All love must be based on reverence if it is to be regarded as true love and not just selfishness. If we really love someone, then we shall respect her purity and do all that we can to help her to keep that great virtue intact.

To help you to give your boy the advice which will enable him to deal with this kind of temptation it is well that you should know the difference which exists between girls and boys in this matter of affection and the demonstrations of it. A boy's nature, being more passionate, is more easily moved and tempted to sin by these demonstrations of affection than is the girl's, at least in most cases. She seeks to be the object of someone's love and affection, and frequently she does not realize the harm she is doing by being too affectionate. The boy should think of this, and help her, not merely to keep pure in her relations with him, but also not to do anything which might hurt him.

Always encourage him to bring his friends home, and supervise such friendships without seeming to do so. When necessary, step in with a word of warning if you think that things are going a little too far.

But the temptations do not all come from such friendships, and you should remember that such things as books, newspapers and films have been proved to have a great influence on the attitude of the growing boy towards sin. If you want to keep your son mentally and morally healthy then do what you can to see to it that he has plenty of good activities which will help to distract him from those other sources of temptation. You will not be able to prevent him from going to the films altogether, but you may be able to direct his social activities in such a way that film-going is kept within reasonable limits. In this matter the chapters which follow on adolescence will help you to understand at least some of his problems and will also give you some suggestions as to the possible solutions to them.

4. The period before marriage

We hope to be able to give more direct advice later as to the kind of things which you will need to tell your sons and your daughters before they enter upon the state of matrimony, and so here we shall confine ourselves to mentioning the main element of your sex instruction to the boy before he marries. In general, give him the full benefit of your own experience without in any way damping his enthusiasm. It is only too easy to pass on a pessimistic or a cynical attitude towards the whole idea of marriage, especially if your own married life has not been very successful. Avoid doing that, because you have an obligation to the very enthusiasm of youth, which does not allow itself to be put off by difficulties. This does not mean that you should go to the other extreme and paint marriage as a bed of roses, but merely that you should not allow your personal unhappiness to influence your judgment of the ideal and the teaching of it. You will probably be able to warn him of many of those pitfalls which can only be avoided by the guidance which comes from experience, and he will be very grateful for that later. In general, too, you should open out to him very freely, making sure that he knows perfectly well what marriage implies from the sexual point of view. If he has the confidence in you which he should have by this time then he will be only too willing to ask you questions about such things, and it should be your privilege to answer them, safe in the knowledge that you are the best person to get this information across in the right way. If you do not do it, he will have to ask someone else or get his information from books, and perhaps they are not written by

Catholics and so will tend to give him the wrong slant on many marriage problems. The mother should also take her share in these pre-marriage instructions, because she is in the very favourable position of being able to give him at first hand the woman's view point on these same problems.

Before we close this chapter there are one or two things which still remain to be said. Since this book is being written mainly for parents we have not mentioned anything so far about those children who are in the unfortunate position of not having any parents, and so are in the care of some institution—we presume, since we are dealing with Catholics, that this will be a Catholic institution of some kind. Obviously, their problems in this matter of sex will be, in general, much the same as those of children who are living at home with their parents, but the question has often been asked, " Who should give such children their necessary instruction ? " Since no one seems to have the definite obligation of doing this, the problem is often shelved, and so not dealt with in the proper way. First of all, let us make it quite clear that it does not matter much whether such an obligation is assumed by the teachers or directors of the institution concerned or by the priest in charge of it, but perhaps the best solution is for the directors to deal with the preliminary questions which children ask, and the priest to assume the obligation of giving the necessary pre-adolescent instruction. Such a system seems to work well in actual practice, because the older boys take such things much better from the priest. If it is a question of girls, it seems best to leave the whole thing in the hands of the nuns who are running the institution, because a woman can deal with her own sex much better than anyone else.

Also we have been asked frequently what action parents should take if they find out that their children have already acquired some knowledge of these matters either from their companions, their readings or from some other source. Obviously, the first thing to do is to find out, by discreet questions, exactly how much the child has heard and what kind of things he has learnt. Most of the knowledge acquired in this way is not accurate, and so you should first of all do all that you can to put that right. If the child has received a great shock by what has been told him through the medium of companions then you must be prepared to go to any lengths to correct that, and you will generally find that, once you have supplied the correct information, the danger passes very quickly and the shock, in most cases, is rendered harmless. The main difficulty you will have is to extract the necessary information from the child, because they very quickly pick up the impression from outsiders that such things are just a little " dirty," and they are ashamed to talk about them to their parents. You will find that, of course, the right attitude towards the whole matter of sex has not been taught at all, and that is your main duty, so supply that as well as you can. Once you can succeed in doing this you may rest assured that the false information or the harm done by the fact that the true information has come from outside will have been repaired or at least minimized to a very large extent. It also means that you have not been quick enough to get in first and also, most probably, that you have not done all that you could have done in the matter of looking out for suitable friends for your child. However, sometimes this situation does develop even where the parents are very careful, and if you follow out these general rules you should be able to deal with it successfully in the vast majority of cases.

Lastly, a word of warning to any priest who may happen to read this book. There is a great temptation at times, especially when we discover that children have not received the necessary instruction in these matters, to do something about it ourselves. This is a good thing, provided we go the right way about it. First of all, you should consult the parents, and indicate that you feel the child needs a certain amount of basic instruction on sex matters. If the parents ask you to help them to give it, then the best thing you can do is to indicate the general lines of such instruction, and let them handle it themselves. It comes much better from them than it does from anyone else, however well instructed that other person may be. If you stay in the background and give your advice you will feel much happier about the whole thing. We should not give such instruction ourselves where that can be avoided, and in any case, not without consulting the parents first.

The case of adolescent boys is a little more difficult, because on some occasions they come to us deliberately because they cannot or will not go to their parents with such questions. In those cases we can give a certain amount of advice, and indeed we must do so if we are asked questions which concern the morality of certain actions in the confessional. Even in these cases it is much better to get the child to have confidence in his parents and to go to them with his difficulties, because they are the best people to deal with them.

Note :—

Parents may find the following books and pamphlets useful in helping them to deal successfully with these problems of sex instruction.

The Sex Instruction of Children. (C.T.S. No. S.208).

Child Guidance, by Sister Mary Hilda, S.N.D., B.A. (C.T.S. No. S.186).

Preparing our Daughters for Life. (C.T.S. No. S.165).

Preparing for Manhood, by Fr. Adrian Chapple. (C.T.S. No. S.179).

For Boys and Men. (C.T.S. DO.163).

The Daughter of Today, What can her Mother do? (C.T.S. No. DO.187).

Into their Company. A book for the modern girl on courtship and marriage. (Burns Oates and Washbourne).

Purity, by Bede Jarrett, O.P. (C.T.S. No. S.93).

Training in Purity, by Canon E. J. Mahoney, D.D. (C.T.S. No. S.134).

In general, for the right attitude towards sex and marriage:—

The Holiness of Married Life, by Archbishop Godfrey. (C.T.S. No. DO.207).

Courtship for Girls and Instruction for those about to be Married. (C.T.S. No. S.129).

The Catholic Mother, by Bede Jarrett, O.P. (C.T.S. No. S.115).

The Pope speaks to Mothers, by Pope Pius XII. (C.T.S. No. S.168).

CHAPTER FOURTEEN

MOTHER AND DAUGHTER

OWING TO THE PECULIAR DIFFICULTIES INVOLVED IT HAS been decided to devote this separate chapter to a brief discussion of the method of sex instruction which has to be employed in the case of girls. The title of the chapter is explained by the words of Pope Pius XII, which we have already quoted, in which he insists that it is the mother's duty to give this instruction to her daughters.

Like the father, she should not be caught by situations which she cannot control, and therefore she should prepare herself beforehand. The questions which bother the child in early childhood will usually be brought to her, by the girls and also by the boys, partly because the children spend more time in her company during the pre-school years and partly because very young children are still a little in awe of their father, especially where it is a question of these problems. The general rules for answering these questions have already been given. However, it might be as well to point out once more that when questions concerning the difference between the sexes come from the little girl they have a slightly different meaning than when they come from the boy. The girl is more interested, by her very nature, in the origins of life, and this fact should be kept in mind. It is not very usual for the girl to have the worry that she may have lost something which the little boy has. Therefore the general answer to this question which has already been given in the previous chapter will usually be quite sufficient. The same applies to the questions about the origin of babies, but you may find that the girl tends to ask more questions arising from your answers than the boy. These, too, should be answered quite simply and truthfully.

It is when the pre-adolescent stage is reached that the difference between the nature of the girl and that of the boy has to be taken into consideration seriously and for the first time. In preparing for the instruction which she will have to give at this stage of her daughter's life it would be as well for the mother to begin by reading carefully what has been written in the last chapter about sex instruction to boys. There she will find the outline of the general attitude which has to be taught and which is the same for boys and girls.

However, there are two big differences in the method of approach to this instruction in the case of the girl. In the first place, her character has to be trained for a double rôle. In our modern civilization she has to be trained to take her part in the world as a wage-earner, at least for a time before she gets married. But, whereas in the case of the boy this element of his character has to endure for a long time and is a permanent feature, in that of the girl it is not so. When she becomes a wife and a mother the usual thing will be for her to cease to earn her own living. She will then enter into what we may call her true vocation in life, that of a good wife and mother. Consequently, it is not enough to train her to be a good wage-earner. She must receive, first and foremost, the necessary training to enable her to be a good wife and mother. Later on we shall have much more to say about this training, but at the moment it has been mentioned because of the influence it has on the type of instruction to be given in sex matters, especially in this pre-adolescent stage of the girl's development.

The second factor which shows very clearly the great difference between boys and girls is their different approach to the whole question of sex. The boy is naturally the active agent, while the girl is more passive. This is determined in its turn by their different reaction to the question of sex in general. The girl's approach is through the line of affection. She longs to be loved, and so to be the object of affection on the part of someone of the opposite sex. The physical side of such affection does not worry her very much at first. The boy, on the other hand, soon finds that, although he, too, wants to be the object of affection, his physical make-up submits him to a much greater strain and tends to take the upper hand. These two differences must be kept in mind when we are instructing girls in the necessary details of sex life.

So far as the actual method of instruction is concerned we shall make the same general divisions as we did in the last chapter for the boys, namely, the pre-adolescent stage, the adolescent period of life and the pre-marriage stage.

1. *The pre-adolescent stage*

We can take it for granted that you have already learnt one thing which is of the greatest importance, namely, that it would be absolutely criminal—no less—to allow any girl under your charge to reach adolescence and to have her first menstruation without due explanation and warning given beforehand. This should be sufficiently obvious when we consider the great shock it must be for a girl to go through this experience without any previous knowledge of it—a shock which is so great that it may quite easily affect the whole of her future mental attitude to such matters. Consequently, the mother must make quite sure that she gets in all the necessary instruction before that time does arrive. The normal age for the onset of puberty in girls is usually between 13 and 15, but again, as in the case of the boys, these dates are only rough estimates, based on the average, and in the individual case the physical development must be taken into due consideration, since some develop earlier and others later. Remember that the principle on which you must work is " better a year too soon than a day too late," and that this is even more important in the case of the girl. In the boy there is not such a great shock in nocturnal pollutions which mark the outset of puberty as there is in the girl's first menstruation.

As in the case of the boy, so in that of the girl, nature will give you your best clue as to the method of instruction which should be used. With the boy, we approached the whole thing from the point of view of those nocturnal pollutions which demonstrate the existence of the life force in his body. With the girl, the approach will be through her periods, as a demonstration of the same fundamental thing.

Begin by recalling past questions on the origins of new life, and point out that the time has come when the girl must know a little more about such things. That is a good enough introduction to the whole question. You should then deal with the attitude to marriage, namely, that it is a sacred union between a man and a woman which has as its normal term and completion a baby.

Then you will have to describe the life force as it is found in the body of the woman. Here, the actual examples and analogies which you can use are many and varied, and you will have to choose one which is simple and also known to your daughter. Perhaps of all such examples the easiest in many ways is that of the plant. As we know, a plant goes through a whole series of changes until it reaches maturity, and when it does reach that stage, then it produces the seeds from which further plants can be grown. Those seeds contain the germ of the future plants which can be grown from them. In much the same way, once the body of the woman has matured sufficiently it produces the seed from which, under certain circumstances, the life of the future baby can be produced. This is God's way of producing in the woman that part of the material which belongs to her sex. Through it, with God's co-operation, we can produce a citizen of the kingdom of God, both in this world and in the next. It is one of the most magnificent and wonderful designs of the Creator, and we can see His hand in every step of its development. Stress this point a good deal, because you want to get out of the child's mind any idea that this is a degrading thing or in any way nasty or dirty. On the contrary, it is something very holy indeed, and so must be treated as such.

From this point onwards your teaching can develop along two different lines, and in actual practice it does not matter which one you choose, provided that both are included by the time you reach the end of your instruction. In this outline we have decided to continue by developing the idea of the seed, but you could continue, if you wish, on the line of the difference between the sexes.

About once every month, in the grown woman, this seed, by a slow process of nature, reaches its full maturity. In itself it is a tiny, microscopic cell, containing, as a plant's seed does, nearly all that is necessary to give full bodily organization to a baby. Only one thing is missing, as we shall see. If this one missing element is not supplied then the seed is not developed beyond this stage. Like all other parts of the body it has to be renewed from time to time, and so it cannot remain indefinitely. God in His wonderful wisdom has provided for that. By means of a flow of blood it detaches itself from its resting place and passes out of the body. This happens to every grown woman at a certain time in the course of a month, and once it happens it is a sign that the life-force is present and that the girl is approaching full womanhood.

This is a good point to break off your first instruction and give time for questions which may arise from it. These should be answered simply and straightforwardly. You might also describe the bodily changes and the symptoms which indicate the onset of these periods. In your next talk you will have to deal with the element which was, as we said in the last instruction, missing for the full and perfect development of the cell into a child.

The best approach to this idea is certainly that which follows out the working of the Divine Plan. God, in His wisdom and love for us, decided that He would divide this life-force into two halves. One of these halves would be entrusted to the man and the other to the woman. Until they are joined into one no new life is possible. It is God's divine plan that they should be so joined in the loving embrace of man and wife in the Sacrament of Matrimony. Here you can discuss once again, from this point of view, the dignity of the Sacrament. This union of the two halves of the life force is something which God intends to be the great proof of the love of husband and wife. The child which results from that love and union is therefore peculiarly the product of the parents so far as its body is concerned, while God plays His part by creating the soul out of nothing. Thus, the parents co-operate with God in the production of this new life, because part of it comes from them and part fron God. This is the real key to the sanctity of marriage, and therefore to the reverence we should have for this life force which is entrusted to us.

This is your chance to deal more in detail with that attitude towards marriage and sex of which we have already spoken. The girl has to be taught to think of this force as a great gift from God, entrusted to her some years before she will actually use it so that she can get used to the idea of guarding it properly for her future husband as a proof of her love for him. Here you can also point out that some people make a very great sacrifice, because they consecrate this power to God who gave it to them, and never use it in this world at all. These people we call religious women or nuns. Others prefer to use it, and they are quite free to do so, provided that they recognize God's plan and follow it, namely that the use of this force must take place only once it has been sanctioned by God through the Sacrament of Matrimony. So far as our bodies are concerned it is the most wonderful thing we possess, because through it we can, if we so choose, use it one day in co-operation with God and with our husband to produce new life in the form of our children, who are really, thus, living parts of our two selves. God intends us to guard this life-force against all misuse. However much we may love someone we must on no account use that life force with him until we have received the Sacrament of Matrimony, which gives, as it were, God's consent to our love. The preservation of this great gift is the best offering we can make both to our husband and to God in marriage, and that is what is meant by the virtue of purity. Here you should stress the fact that purity is a very strong virtue, because it means a fight and a victory over our lower nature which inclines us at times towards the pleasures of this life without consulting our reason or our religion.

Point out, too, that this is such a holy thing that we do not talk about it to our friends and companions. We can, whenever we like, ask our parents about it, because they have already used it on our behalf, and also because God has appointed them to teach us all that is necessary for us to be good servants of His Majesty. To discuss it with others, especially in any nasty way, would be an insult to God who has given us this gift, and also to our own parents who have brought us into this world for God by the right use of it.

In the course of your next talk you will need to tell the girl what happens when these two halves of the life-force are joined together in matrimony in such a way that they give rise to a new life. Here, as always, you should describe these effects with relation to God who, in His wisdom, arranged them in one unified plan. God has made the woman in such a way that within her body she has a special place where the future baby can develop without coming to any harm until it is big enough and strong enough to take its place in the world. Thus it develops, hidden within the mother for nine months, growing stronger and more perfectly formed every day, until at last it is brought into the world. This explains, to a very great extent, the love and the union between a mother and her children.

Point out that the responsibility of the parents for their children at every stage of their lives also derives from this fact, since the child is a gift from God, who allowed them to have it. This also explains why parents are so careful about every department of the child's life, her habits, her companions, and so on. It is the basic reason for punishment, and also for the present talks, because God has said that parents must tell their children all that is necessary for them to know Him and love Him and serve Him in this world so that they may be happy with Him for ever in the next. It also supplies the reason for the love of the children for their parents, and their respect and obedience to them. They should have great confidence in their parents because they should know that what the parents have to do is to look after them in every way. They are responsible to God for their children. In this way you will do much to increase the girl's respect and confidence at this important stage when she is about to enter upon adolescence, and when she will need all your good advice to help her. When that advice happens to run contrary to what she herself wants to do, then she will remember what you have told her in these talks and will be much more ready to take heed of what you say. It is only by means of this open and frank exchange of confidences that you can hope to keep up with her physical and mental development during the next few years. The modern girl leads a life which is, in general, much more free from controls than before, and she will need, therefore, much stronger motives for action on the right lines than you ever did. Remember that. Your hope is to win her love and confidence by the obvious love which pervades your treatment of her during these years.

Finally, you can ask for and expect questions with regard to what you have told her in these talks, perhaps especially with regard to the actual physical method of the birth of the baby. Answer those questions simply, as usual, but without stressing too much the pain which goes with it. This is important, because sometimes mothers put their daughters against the whole idea of children by their very vivid descriptions of the pains of childbirth. They do this, frequently, from what they think to be a good motive, i.e., to make their daughters grateful to them for bringing them into the world, but they are liable to produce quite a different effect. Stress rather that the mother no longer thinks of the pain because of the joy she has in her newborn son or daughter. Remember that your main duty is to teach a right attitude towards the whole question of sex and marriage, and you can only do that by following God's wonderful plan in all its details.

2. *The adolescent stage*

When dealing with this period in the lives of their daughters it will be well for mothers to take into consideration all that follows in this book with regard to the problems of adolescent girls, many of which will be discussed at length in other chapters. As in the case of the boys, these difficulties, at least in so far as they are connected with this question of sex instruction, will normally arise from the girl's social contacts and their environment. Consequently, during this stage you must be rather careful to watch those contacts and also the effects of that environment.

As soon as your daughter begins to go out with boys and to dances, etc., then you will have to point out the dangers which have to be avoided, and also the positive things which have to be done in order to preserve intact the grace of God and in particular the gift of purity. As usual, stress the positive side rather more than the purely negative. These are some of the things on which you will have to insist. The love of a man for a woman is a very holy thing provided that it is connected with the Sacrament of Matrimony. Teach her the great difference between physical attraction and that real affection which borders on love. Remember that respect—one might go so far as to say reverence—is the only true foundation for love, and anyone who respects and reverences another will not do anything to harm the object of his reverence either in soul or in body.

Point out that boys are far more easily roused as far as their passionate nature is concerned than are girls, and therefore girls should be very careful what they do and also what they allow in the way of demonstrations of affection. They may not think that they are doing anything wrong, while at the same time it is easy to be the cause of the sin of another. That is not part of God's plan for mankind.

You should tell your daughter quite simply and yet clearly what is allowed when out with boys and what is not. This information is received with great thankfulness by adolescents, because most of them are in dire need of it and yet do not know where they can get it. They are much too shy during this stage to ask many questions about it, and they welcome your advice on these matters if they have full confidence in you. At the same time, of course, it is not wise to be always harping on the same subject. Do it once and for all, unless some special danger warns you that you will have to repeat some of the things which you have already said. They do not forget what you say to them on these subjects very easily.

Don't be afraid to keep open house for your daughter's friends. This will provide you with a ready method of keeping some check on them, and will thus serve very frequently to indicate to you which friendships are useful and healthy and which are not. Many parents fail in this duty, and more easily in the case of their daughters than in that of their sons. This may be very natural in its way, but it is not a good thing at all. If they are afraid to bring someone home although you have always shown them that they may do so without fear, then you may be quite sure that there is something radically wrong with that particular friendship. We shall have other opportunities of talking about this whole question of friendships during adolescence later on.

Your religious instruction and help during this period is very important. It should stress the importance of the sacramental life, especially with regard to confession and Holy Communion. You will find that your own good example in this respect is worth much more than any words.

3. *Pre-marriage instruction*

This is of very great importance, too, because the modern girl has one big fault ; she will insist on thinking that she knows practically all there is to be known about such things as marriage and home life, when, in fact, she knows less than one would imagine. So far as her sex knowledge is concerned, there is now no use or sense in being reticent, and you should make quite sure before her marriage that she is fully aware of all that such a state of life implies. Here you will be able to draw on your own experience, but once again, do not colour your descriptions of marriage with any of your own unhappy experiences unless that is absolutely necessary. This does not mean that you should describe it as a bed of roses, or hide from your daughter the true facts with regard to it, but it does mean that you should not damp her ideals and her youthful enthusiasm by harrowing stories of broken marriages unless in her particular case you feel that there is real need.

If you have followed out these simple instructions you will find that you have laid the foundations for a life-long friendship between you and your daughter, and one that will stand both of you in good stead during the very difficult times which follow her marriage. You will still retain her confidence, and she will come to you with her difficulties. You will also be able to advise her with regard to her own children much more easily because you will have passed through the experience yourself.

CHAPTER FIFTEEN

ADOLESCENCE

O F ALL THE PERIODS OF THEIR CHILDREN'S LIVES THIS IS THE one which parents usually find most difficult, and for that reason a whole chapter has been dedicated to it, so that parents may be helped towards a clearer understanding of the main problems which it presents to the average boy and girl. It is only by understanding these difficulties from the children's point of view that parents can hope to help them through this crisis—because that is exactly what it is. Also any book such as this, which intends to provide for parents some methods of education which will enable them to deal with their children in a proper way must, necessarily, take into consideration the problems which arise at different periods of the children's lives in order to give some kind of solution for them. Any other way of working would deprive parents of that deep understanding of their children which is often the key to the methods which have to be applied in education as well as to many and varied problems. Therefore, in this chapter, we shall study adolescence in general, while in those that follow, some attempt will be made to give parents advice as to how they should deal with their children during this period. It is hoped that this chapter, which is the key to much that follows, will be read carefully more than once.

As we have already indicated, adolescence is ushered in by what we call puberty. Certain very definite changes take place in the child's body during that time, changes which have a great effect on mental development, and indeed on the whole of the future mature character. Forces hitherto unknown and undreamt of begin to exercise their influences on his intellect and will, with the result that the fairly clearly defined character of the childhood days tends to become fluid and unstable. This character will harden and crystallize once again at the end of this period of crisis, and as it forms then so it is liable to remain, at least in its main outlines. New and vital sensations are perceived, some of them connected with the physical changes which we have just mentioned, and some connected with the outside world, which takes on a new and a strange aspect to the growing child.

We should try very hard to understand these facts, because they are very important. Childhood is essentially a happy time ; perhaps it is true to say that it is in reality the happiest time of our lives here on earth, because at the most it contains very few real problems. A child takes reality for granted, and so finds little or no difficulty in adapting himself to it, and in any case it makes few demands on him. He feels quite secure and sure of himself, and as a last ditch he can always run to his parents for help and for consolation. He does not have to think very much for himself, because that is done for him by his parents, nor does he have any inclination to think of himself as a person with any definite problems to solve. We have already indicated that the problems of childhood are rather problems of the parents than of the child himself. The new situations with which he has to deal nearly all come from outside himself, for example, going to school for the first time, and they tend to remain outside him, without causing very much trouble within his mind, even though they do contribute to the formation of his character. But, with the advent of puberty, and consequently of adolescence, a very great change takes place.

This period is essentially one of trouble and unrest and therefore of uncertainty. Indeed, it may be said with truth that the basic feature of adolescence, in the light of which every-thing else has to be judged, is this uncertainty.

Seen from the outsider's point of view adolescence is the period of transition between childhood on the one hand and mature manhood or womanhood on the other. It begins at puberty, that is, between the ages of 13-15 in the case of girls and 14-16 in the case of boys. It lasts much longer than puberty, however, and generally comes to an end at about the age of 21 in the case of girls and 23-24 in that of boys. Naturally, these estimates are only the general average, and the individual has to be taken into consideration in every case, because, just as puberty itself can be delayed or can take place earlier, so adolescence can last either for a shorter or for a longer time, according to circumstances.

To the outsider the physical changes which take place during adolescence are by far the most obvious feature in this stage. In the case of boys, for instance, the whole physical aspect changes in a very short time from that of a child to that of a youth. There is very rapid growth, changes in the blood system which often lead to skin blemishes or troubles with the circulation, a change in the voice, and many others which can be summed up by saying that the grace and the beauty of childhood are replaced by awkwardness and clumsiness of movement. The whole body seems to be out of proportion. In girls, the physical changes are no less obvious. The girl at the advent of puberty often outstrips the boy of the same age in height and weight. She, too, becomes awkward in her movements, and tends to assume that "gawky" look which is so characteristic of this stage of development. But this is merely the outsider's point of view. What of the inner character of the adolescent? Here the changes are even more marked to the eye of the careful observer, and far more important in every way. Above all else it is necessary to see these changes from the adolescent's point of view and to judge them, not as the outsider sees them, but as they appear to the boy or girl.

The root of all these changes in character is *uncertainty*, which causes internal struggles to arise in the mind of the adolescent. On the one hand, he desires more than ever before in his life the friendship and the understanding of others and he longs for their respect. He is always (perhaps unconsciously) looking for a guide and an adviser. On the other hand, there is the contrary urge, which, if anything, is even stronger, and that inclines him to stand on his own feet and to make his own decisions, even though his character does not feel secure and safe enough as yet to do that satisfactorily. That is just the whole trouble. At every step he is brought up against this "self" and against his own character, and he finds that this element on which he has to rely is uncertain in every way and changes from day to day. The things he likes today may quite easily be hated tomorrow. As a result of this, his central "self" is being put under the microscope for the first time in his life.

The aim of all education at this period will be to give its final formation to that inner self, and it is this formation which is the main preoccupation of the adolescent. Everything else that happens at this stage is only a manifestation of this central problem, and is also, in a certain degree, a means towards its final solution.

On the other hand, the period of adolescence is marked by a growth in the intellectual sphere and also in the moral order. As we shall see, the adolescent is only too ready to take up any ideal so long as it appeals to him, and this factor contains great possibilities. During this period of final formation there are also great possibilities in the religious sphere, which accounts for the fact that most vocations to the religious life manifest themselves for the first time in adolescence. The most important aspect of this change which is now taking place is undoubtedly in the emotional sphere, because these emotions are now acquiring a new force for the adolescent, his experiences are richer in meaning and his sensitivity is increased. This factor must always be kept in mind, because from the educational viewpoint it has great advantages and also great dangers.

As you will see, from this very brief summary of the main elements in the life of the growing boy and girl, it would be altogether wrong to think that sex and preoccupation with sex matters form the basic problem of adolescence, as so many people seem to think. To give to everything that the adolescent does a definite sex bias is not only a great mistake, it also leads to faulty education. On the other hand, if we consider these same actions and reactions from the point of view of the uncertainty and the fluidity of character which, to our way of thinking, is the main feature of this stage in the child's development, then we shall be much nearer the solution to the problems which go with it, and also much nearer to the true understanding of what goes on under that exterior shell, which is often so deceptive. It is really because of this uncertainty of his character that the adolescent is so hard to understand. He is torn between doubts and fears, between attractions and repulsions, curiosity and fear of a rebuke or rebuff, so much so that he does not know which way to turn and, consequently, never reacts in the same way twice to what may seem to the casual observer to be the same situation. Whenever he is misunderstood—which to him happens often—he tends to withdraw into his inner self, where no one can enter to do him harm or to laugh at him. One day he may act as a child, and the next day as an adult. In a word, his conduct is almost always unpredictable, and we must expect just that.

At the same time, understanding is very necessary if we are to lay down any rules, even general ones, for his guidance during this period of his life. To understand means quite literally what it says, namely, " to stand under " someone, to support them and to help them to bear their burdens. But, before we can share in the burdens and the trials of another, we must know quite clearly what those trials and burdens are. The easiest method of getting to know the adolescent problems of your children will be to observe their actions carefully. It is what a person does rather than what he says which really tells us what he is and what he is experiencing at any given moment, especially if we are able to get behind the mask which most people put on and see the motives behind their actions. You will thus also be able to detect the character and the stability behind these actions.

This observation of the actions of the adolescent is very important, but, of course, it must not be too obvious, because if it is then you will not get very far. At the same time, it must be total, i.e., not confined to one aspect of his life, but covering as far as possible the whole field of his activity. Thus, it should take into consideration the way of acting at school as well as at home, on the playground, at work, with companions, and so on, because no one single department taken by itself will serve to give us the clear insight we need if we are to guide these adolescents correctly. Individuals differ too much, especially at this stage, for us to be able to make any general deductions from single, isolated actions.

It is even more important not to confine your observations to the mere surface actions. Get right down to the motives for those actions whenever possible. For example, a preliminary surface observation may tend to show us a youth who is boastful, over-bearing with others, especially with his companions ;

indeed, in general, far too confident of himself. Yet the truth may be very different, because the underlying motive for such actions could be a feeling of inferiority, and anxiety which may never show itself on the surface at all. Again, we may find an adolescent who always seems critical of the opinions of others and far too set on his own. This is again very natural, demonstrating, as it does, not so much a desire to criticize as the urge to find real solid reasons for holding the opinions which others propose to him. He needs the reasons why instead of mere authority. Remember that, changing and even absurd as their ideas may be, adolescents take them very seriously while they last. This is partly because they look on them as something new which has never been thought of before, and thus a great discovery of their own. This tendency to regard oneself, one's difficulties and problems as altogether unique is common, in a certain measure, to all adolescents, and is one of the main things which we shall have to break down gently but firmly.

Apart from this method of observation, one of the best ways of getting to know the adolescent's problems is, of course, by getting him to confide in us. Now, it may seem to parents that their sons and their daughters will confide in them quite naturally and as a matter of course. After all, they have always looked after them and loved them. But it does not necessarily follow that such will, in fact, be the case. Very much more than we are prepared to admit will depend on the past, i.e., on the parents' way of dealing with the children during the years of early childhood. Only too often those early years have seen the sowing of the seeds of a future rift, perhaps through some injustice in the matter of punishment, through the parents' lack of confidence in their children, through their selfishness or harshness, or indeed, from any of a dozen different causes. The parents may hardly have noticed any reaction at the time on the part of the child, but now one of those things which then seemed so insignificant may easily bar the way to that complete confidence which should exist between parents and child. That is one of the reasons why we have stressed so often, in the course of these chapters, that there is always need for real love and understanding on the part of the parents, as well as full respect for the rights of the child. We cannot be too careful how we deal with our children during those early years of their childhood. Education is one whole, and one part of that life will necessarily affect all the others.

There is yet another reason for the lack of full confidence between the adolescent and the parents. Youth always tends to look on the last generation as " old fashioned ", and therefore unable to understand fully modern needs. Sometimes this is true of only one of the parents, and sometimes it is not true at all, but it appears so to the eyes of youth, and that is enough. Therefore, in our approach to youth with all its problems we should always show a sympathy and understanding which will break down these barriers and will establish full confidence. This method of approach is slow and gradual, but in any case all education needs great patience, and it is only by constant exercise of this virtue that we shall succeed in the end. Often we have to learn to bide our time and not to be in too much of a hurry—to wait for the right moment and the right opportunity. We must also learn to make opportunities for the adolescent to confide in us and to let us examine his problems with him. When you are given one of these opportunities never let it slip from your grasp, but seize it at once, because if he is put off at this first attempt, then the youth may never approach you again. Thus, when a youth comes to his father and says, " May I talk to you, Dad ? " or even when he manifests such a desire without using any words, then the reply, " Later on, son ; I'm busy just now " is not good enough. It must be here and now, as he wishes. The same is, of course, true of the girl's approach to her mother. Never put them off, never let them see that you are impatient with them and that some other time will do as well, instead of just now when you are rather busy. This is your prime obligation, and you must attend to it at once, because you may not get another chance.

Another very normal manifestation during this period is a radical change in the adolescent's attitude towards all authority. Up to this time he has been quite willing, especially if he has been brought up on the right lines, to accept authority and to take its dictates more or less for granted. But now he often refuses to do so, and we can witness in many adolescents a gradual revolt against all constituted authority, whether it be that of the home, the school, or in politics and religion. This is, as we have hinted, a normal manifestation of his generally unsettled condition of mind, but in a way it is rather more than that. It is an implicit demand once again for reasons. The correct attitude to authority has to be built up gradually, and this construction should follow a unified line through adolescence until full maturity is reached. The method of educating the child to this full sense of what is meant by authority will vary at the different stages of his life. During childhood authority is imposed, and there is little or no need for reasons or arguments to support that imposition, whether the authority be that of the teachers, the parents, or others who have care of the children. But during the period of adolescence a change in the method becomes necessary if the youth is to reach full maturity with a right attitude towards authority. Even though it may seem to succeed at first, mere imposition of authority during adolescence will always fail in the end and may easily be contrary to the rights of the child. Reasoned and sensible motives have to be presented to youth, together with a chance to talk those reasons over with others, and if this is not done then there is every chance of at least a mental revolt against authority. Once and for all let it be said here that the bad habit some parents have of appealing to their own deeper experience as the ultimate justification for their advice or their commands carries little or no weight with the adolescent. He wants arguments and reasons which will convince his mind, and the argument from mere experience does not do that successfully. Length of life means very little, and we could cite many cases of people who have both lived a long time and had many experiences and yet seem to have learnt practically nothing from those experiences. Parents should avoid this argument, while at the same time using their experience as a basis for their advice. How often the uselessness of this so-called argument from experience has been proved in actual practice, and yet how slow parents are to realize it!

One final word of encouragement to parents is necessary. You may find this general picture of adolescence very dark and frightening. It is not really quite as bad as that, because, in spite of all the difficulties, there are other factors present in adolescence which serve to make the general picture much more cheerful than it appears at first sight.

This stage of development may be one of troubles and problems ; but it is also one of very high ideals, especially in the religious sphere. If he is handled properly and well guided then the youth goes through what might almost be termed a religious conversion during adolescence. These ideals are very precious things, and you will soon find out from experience how deep and lasting they can be. Therefore you should never despair during this stage of your children's education. The consolation of seeing your boy or girl winning through to final success and also that of watching their characters form under your very eyes will encourage you to still greater efforts. There is also the satisfaction which comes from the deeper understanding and confidence between parents and child which should be the normal outcome of this period of your lives together. Your aim should be so to attract your children to you by your sympathy and understanding of their problems that, by the time they reach full maturity, you will have set up a new relation between you, i.e., that of real friendship. How many children have been heard to complain that they wished their father or mother had been more of a friend to them! Once you have established this relation, you are very fortunate, because you will have completed your parenthood with the subsequent friendship which will endure for life.

Remember, too, in all your difficulties, that you have received the great Sacrament of Matrimony, and that the graces which flow from it are always at your disposal for the asking. Therefore there is never any need to despair when you are confronted with difficulties in this matter of bringing up your children in the love of God. All that is required is a willingness to guide them with love and sympathy, a deep and true grasp of the problems which have to be faced, together with confident prayer to God for His grace to perform this task worthily.

When all your words seem to fail and produce no effect on your children then there is still one final argument left which will have its effect in the end, and that is the great argument from your own constant example, which is always worth much more than mere words.

CHAPTER SIXTEEN

PHYSICAL EDUCATION
IN ADOLESCENCE

FIRST OF ALL LET US SAY A WORD OR TWO ABOUT THE SUBJECT matter of this chapter. Having discussed briefly the general characteristics of adolescence so that parents may have a clearer view of the problems which this stage presents, we shall go on to discuss the three main branches of all education, namely, the physical, the mental and the religious, as they are applied to the adolescent. It will be unnecessary to remark that by the term " physical " we do not mean merely such things as sport, although we shall have something to say about that. Also, in the course of this present chapter we shall be given yet further proof in support of something which we have already said, i.e., that all education is one whole, because we shall see that many of the things which are discussed here under their physical aspect will also need to be dealt with in the following chapters under their mental and religious aspects. In the present chapter, then, we shall deal with the guidance which has to be given by parents owing to the physical changes which accompany this stage in their children's development. Parents will have to take it for granted that the rules and suggestions given here are based on experience and experiment, because it would take too long for us to give reasons for them in every case. However, when it seems important and when space permits we shall try to give at least a summary of the main reasons behind the suggestions.

If the general health of the small child is necessary for good character development this is even more true in the case of the adolescent, although in general it may be said that he is relatively free from many of the ailments which attack the child and normally enjoys good health. The following points should be noticed in particular.

1. *Sleep*

Owing to the very great bodily changes which are taking place during this period, and more especially during its initial stages, it can be taken as a general rule that all adolescents need plenty of sleep. They should have regular hours for going to bed at night and for getting up in the morning. In fact, it is necessary to stress the need for this regularity more now since parents as a whole are inclined to be rather careless about it. In some cases girls during the time of puberty and until their bodies become adjusted to the changes which are taking place in them should be given a day in bed once every month on the advent of their periods.

It is obvious that the adolescent is going to expect much greater freedom than he enjoyed during the years of childhood proper, but that does not mean that parents should allow their adolescent children to come in at night at any hour they choose. A reasonable time should be fixed, one which takes into consideration the convenience of both child and parents, and also the adolescent need for sleep, and that time should be observed as far as possible, without many exceptions.

Homework is liable to be a great nuisance during this period, because often it is increased beyond all bounds, and the adolescent has to stay up later than usual to finish it. In this connection it would be a good thing if parents and teachers could work together more than they usually do, and exchange views on such matters from time to time. Regularity in hours and methods of working should help you to see to it that the whole of the evening is not taken up with homework, and that there is a certain time free during which the youth can get either exercise or relaxation. This will also help sleep.

Cases of disturbed rest during adolescence are not by any means as common as some people would have us imagine. However, they can and do occur, and the cause for this is often obscure. Occasionally sleep walking manifests itself during this period, much to the worry and disturbance of the parents. Now, the causes of this disturbance are not very well known at present, but in general parents can take hope from the knowledge that, in the vast majority of cases, this comes to an end before adolescence is over, not to appear again. It can often be helped by strict attention to diet, exercise, and by avoiding all over-excitement just before going to bed. This excitement may come from a certain type of reading which tends to stimulate the imagination too much, or sometimes from too many visits to the cinema late at night. Normally it is not caused by worry, but if you should think that there is something on your child's mind which is at the back of it then the best thing for you to do is to consult a doctor.

Nightmares are quite common, however, but respond more easily to treatment. Take care to see to it that the evening meal is not too heavy and that there is plenty of time to digest it before bed-time. Excitement can also be a cause of this trouble.

2. *Diet*

Next in importance after the question of sleep is that of food. During adolescence the bones, muscles and the nerves are all developing at an almost alarming rate, especially during the early years of this period. The demands made on the whole bodily system are very great, and consequently, good, nourishing food is very necessary. You should make a special effort to provide those foods which are most important for the growth and development of the bones and muscles. Also remember that it is very important to see to it that the meals are carefully and attractively prepared. There is nothing so conducive to lack of appetite and consequently of nourishment as badly cooked or unattractively presented dishes. See to it that the growing boy and girl have plenty of fresh fruit, green vegetables, in salad form where possible, and also fresh milk, where you can get it. These are all-important for regulating the blood conditions which appear so frequently in the adolescent, and they should easily be obtained by those who make the small effort necessary. If parents were more careful in this matter the growing youth would have much less trouble with such things as constipation—a frequent thing in adolescence, and one which often passes undetected. In this connection you should see to it that the good habits which you started to teach during early childhood are brought now to full maturity and become second nature. You will have to obtain your knowledge by means of carefully worded questions, because usually the adolescent is rather afraid of mentioning such things, even to his parents.

At this stage, as in childhood, it is inadvisable to get the youth into the habit of taking laxatives regularly, and by laxatives here we mean any kind of drug. It is far better to continue with the idea of orange juice or fruit juices, and leave Nature to work things out on that basis. Remember that quite often constipation is due to the fact that the child has not been trained to attend to the wants of Nature at definite times, but instead leaves it to chance. This is all wrong, and your early training should have removed this possibility altogether. This is not merely a physical ailment, but also, and in the main, it is a psychological one, depending to a very great extent on the mental attitude.

3. Sports and games

Exercise is necessary for the adolescent, not merely to help in regulating the circulation, which is frequently bad, but also because sport, and games in particular, help in the development of character. Consequently, there is a double element to be considered here, the merely physical, from which point of view sport is necessary for the development of the body, especially the long muscles and the long bones ; and also from the integral point of view, in so far as sport tends to bring out the full maturity of character. However, exercise is one of those things which can easily be overdone, or even given too much importance. The growing boy or girl is normally full of energy and the desire to " let off steam ". They think that they are capable of any physical effort, no matter how great, and so are not sufficiently careful to use their strength within the proper limits. It is very easy to put too much strain on the heart during adolescence, and so parents would be well advised to keep an eye on such things as their children's sport and games in order to keep them within the proper limits. On the other hand, there is no need to go to extremes, but merely to remember the tendencies of youth to overdo things and to keep your eyes open for signs of strain. Where girls are concerned, although a certain amount of exercise is necessary, they should never be allowed to go in for very strenuous sports during the years which mark the outset of adolescence.

We have mentioned the fact that regular and gentle exercise is a very good thing for the development of character. The real reason is that such things teach the adolescent, as nothing else can, self-control, the team spirit, unselfishness towards others, and also a general attitude of give and take. It also serves to determine better the whole approach to authority, because in their games they learn that some rules and regulations are very necessary if life is to be lived in community as it should be lived, i.e., for the benefit of the whole and not for the parts.

Occasionally, however, we do come across the strange case of the adolescent who manifests no interest whatever in sport and games. He prefers to bury himself in a book during spare time or the time devoted normally to recreation. Now, such a tendency is not at all natural and should be watched, because it may come from a badly developed social sense, from an inferiority either real or imagined, or perhaps even from some other physical or mental cause. Perhaps the youth is not so good as his companions at sports, and so tends to withdraw from them so as not to be put in the shade by others, especially by those who are younger than he is. Perhaps it may be due to the fact that he does not like submitting to direction by others. Seldom is it due to nothing but laziness. If this tendency is allied to other symptoms, then parents should not hesitate to consult a doctor at once. Such symptoms are inability to concentrate as he did before, impulsive, odd or unusual behaviour, and emotional indifference and sluggishness.

In general you must do all that you can to correct this false attitude on the part of your child, but do not think that this can be done just by making him play games. Some less direct method of approach has to be found. Sometimes this can be done by encouraging other forms of exercise which at first do not seem to lead into the field of what we may call " combat " sports. Such forms of exercise as walking, cycling, nature hobbies and so on lend themselves to this approach very easily. Naturally it is advisable that such exercise should be taken in the company of others, because if the youth is allowed to be alone all the time then the fundamental cause of the attitude is not corrected, but may grow more strong in spite of our efforts to prevent it. This companionship in his recreation is the thing which is going to count most, by bringing the adolescent into contact with others through his periods of relaxation. For this reason, too, these companions should, as far as possible, be of the same age as the adolescent. The walks or the excursions should be made as attractive and interesting as possible, and this can best be accomplished if the parents themselves are interested in such things, or even if they can find a companion who is interested in things like nature study ; then their children will be interested too, as like as not, and thus the exercise will lead to the beginnings of a hobby which will stand them in good stead later on in life.

However, where possible, this type of exercise should never be allowed to replace games altogether, because games have the added advantage of forming one definite side of the character, namely, the combat side, with all that it implies, such as learning to give in to rules, and to join with others in a general common effort. Mere walking and so forth can never supply this.

Reading can also be included here, although it has its proper place in the next section, which will deal with mental development of the adolescent. There is a sinister sound for most young people in the phrase " good books." They have the idea that this means a namby-pamby type of literature which is contrary to all their natural tastes at this age. Now, this need not be true at all. We are not trying to suggest that parents should exclude altogether from their children's reading matter everything which falls under the heading of light novels, nor is it our intention to suggest the direction of *all* their reading in an obvious manner. But parents could do much more than they generally do to see to it that their children's taste in reading develops gradually during this period. The taste for good literature is something which stamps a character as nothing else can, because on the one hand it gives the child a good vocabulary and on the other a fluent expression of his own thoughts, which in its turn breeds self-confidence. Apart from this, it also helps to give him some companions for life. Anyone who has no taste

for reading is very often lost for things to do, and thus turns to
other diversions which are by no means as healthy. Don't
discourage your son or daughter if you find that they like reading.
Very often the books they start with are not literature, by any
means, but you can change that by being a little helpful and by
putting interesting books into their hands which really are
literature. We shall have more to say about this matter later
when we talk about the mental development of the adolescent.
It has been mentioned here because of its obvious connection
with lack of interest in games as such.

This is the time in the life of the boy and girl when their parents
should help in the formation of some hobby which will be of
lasting interest. This matter is of very great importance, and
yet so many parents ignore it altogether. If our lives on this
earth are to be reasonably happy and full then we need some
absorbing interest outside our ordinary work. Just as the
person who has no interest in reading is very often at a loss for
something to do in order to pass the time, so, in the case of
those who have no hobby, their spare time is apt to become a
demon of boredom. This is quite unnecessary. If they had
been guided during the period of their youth towards the formation of a definite hobby then they would have something which
would interest them and which would distract them from their
worries or from the ordinary work which they have to do in
order to earn their living. Although it is not ordinarily a bad
thing for the hobby to have some connection with a man's work,
it is very much better if it takes him into a different sphere of
interests altogether. Parents have to be rather careful in this
matter, because they are too inclined to think in terms of the
future wage-earning and work, and thus attempt to put a stop to
all hobbies which they consider are not useful. The hobby is
useful in direct proportion to its ability to distract from ordinary
affairs and also to interest and absorb. Remember that, and
act accordingly. Wherever possible it is as well to have
two such interests, one which can be of use indoors and the
other which is essentially an outdoor occupation. There are
several hobbies which can be suggested, such as nature study,
which is an absorbing interest to those who take to it, departments of drawing or painting, walking, cycling, music, all types

of carpentry, pets, needlework, dressmaking, and a whole series of others.

In order to foster these hobbies it is necessary to go slowly and to watch the youth for some indication of interest in such things. That interest must then be fostered by every means in your power. Girls can be encouraged to take up some such hobby as dressmaking by being started on small things first, and then led up to larger and more ambitious efforts by being promised that you will give them materials, etc., for their clothes if they are prepared to go to the trouble of making them up. They are usually only too glad to co-operate and you will have fostered an interest which will be of the greatest use to them later on. If you see that your son is interested in the things of nature then you can always provide books which deal with that subject and also take some interest in it yourselves. This may be rather boring for you at first, but it is a great encouragement to them. Remember that the hobby has to interest *them*, not you.

We have dealt with this matter under the heading of physical education because it is of such great help in the co-ordination of the muscles and the nerves of the whole body, which usually cause such trouble to the adolescent. It is hoped that more parents will make an effort in this matter of hobbies for their children. The expense is not very great and the benefits which ensue are out of all proportion to the outlay. It is in no sense a waste of time.

4. General health

Whatever you do, never be over-anxious about your children's health at this stage without very good reason. So many parents are worried to death about all kinds of imaginary ills that they give to their children the same kind of pre-occupation. This fear is often present without any encouragement from the parents but if they, too, are over-anxious then this fear is liable to develop into something abnormal in the children. Rather you should develop the positive side of health during this stage. Teach them, in other words, how they can keep themselves fit and well, and do not always harp on illness, and if you see that they are developing any undue fears for their health then try to encourage them and reassure them. If the fear persists, and is about some serious thing like tuberculosis or cancer, then it may be necessary to have them examined by a doctor to whom you can explain the whole circumstances beforehand, so that this fear may be finished once and for all. It is surprising how many children at this age do in fact worry about health, but this is usually due to over-preoccupation on the part of the parents.

In this connection there is one thing which often worries adolescents but which the parents seem to notice and yet pass by without being of much use to the growing boy or girl in quieting fears and worries. The senses at this age are very acute, perhaps more so than at any other time during life. We need not bother about whether this acuteness is due to an actual fact or rather to the power of a very vivid imagination ; the important thing is that it is present in all adolescents to a certain degree. They become very conscious of smells, of dirt, of the danger of infection and so on. This leads them to take what often amount to unnecessary and even absurd precautions to avoid these things of which they are secretly so afraid. It may even account very often for their fear of meeting certain persons or shaking hands with them, and of going to certain places. Parents should be on the watch for these manifestations and should do all that they can to help their children to acquire a right attitude towards such things. It can be pointed out that we all go through some such experience at some time or another, that contact with infection is not so harmful as all that in the majority of cases, because man builds up resistance to germs and to illness by keeping himself fit and especially by not allowing the thought of such things to become an obsession with him. Often the fear of a thing is more dangerous than the thing itself, and so on. Above all, give them some practical help in the matter of cleanliness and you will have done much to take the worry off their minds. The adolescent is not helped by the various newspaper and magazine advertisements which take advantage of these fears. You can help a great deal if you learn to encourage and also not to laugh at such things, because to the youth they are very serious and a source of much worry.

5. *Speech defects*

It is not usual for speech defects to show themselves for the first time during adolescence, but it is by no means unusual for defects which have manifested themselves in childhood and have then been overcome to reappear during this period. If we think of the nervous strain of adolescence and also of the fact that during this period there is much more fear of making a fool of oneself than there is in childhood, the reason for this appears quite clearly. In some cases this reappearance of speech defects is due to the voice changes which are such a painful element of this stage of development. It would take us altogether out of our field if we were to attempt to go deeply into this very intricate subject, which is definitely a matter for a specialist in speech defects. However, it must be pointed out that no speech defect which manifests itself during adolescence should be allowed to go on without expert treatment, and so advice should be sought in every case from a doctor who is competent to deal with such cases. If they are allowed to go on too long then the evil becomes almost impossible to eradicate. As a preliminary you can suggest deep breathing, slower speech and also practice, which is one of the best methods of overcoming these defects when they are slight and in the early stages. Try getting the youth to repeat voluntarily the sound he makes when stuttering over a word. This has been mentioned once before in the section on habits and the methods of curing bad ones and of acquiring good ones. This tends to bring the habit under voluntary control, thus making it easier to overcome. If you see that these methods do not succeed within a very short time then you must consult a specialist.

The care of the teeth comes under consideration at this period of life more, perhaps, than at any other. Regular habits of cleanliness have to be established, and the youth should go to the dentist for inspection every six months. This should have become a regular habit by the end of adolescence, and it should be impressed on the minds of the youths by their parents that this routine inspection is very important, at least while they still have their own teeth. You can point out that in this way they will keep their teeth much longer and avoid many defects which cannot be remedied later on in life.

The eyes are very important, too, because so many adolescents who have severe headaches are really suffering from some defect in their sight and will not complain of it because they have a horror of wearing glasses. This is especially true of girls, because they think that such things ruin their beauty. The danger signals of eye strain are fairly obvious, and you will have to watch out for them yourselves, because the youth is almost certain to hide it as far as possible. Headaches which persist and for which there seems no other cause, irritation of the eyelids, screwing up the eyes when reading, holding the book either too near or too far from the eyes for comfort, trouble with objects at a distance—all these signs should warn you of some defect in the sight, which may be cured altogether now if it is taken in time. Do not hesitate to consult a doctor, because he does not prescribe glasses without necessity.

Here we can also deal briefly with certain other physical things which influence the conduct of the adolescent or which tend to worry him unduly. The bodily changes which are now taking place can and usually do produce effects which are very disturbing to the youth and which he takes very seriously. The body is normally growing out of all proportion at this stage, and owing to glandular disturbances or irregularities, it is not unusual for some features to outdistance the others. Thus, a boy may seem to have hands or feet which are out of all proportion to the rest of his body, or perhaps it is the nose or the ears which are the cause of the trouble. These defects are usually only transitory, and will pass like all other defects of adolescence, but that does not mean that we should laugh at him because of them or make fun of him. He will have to suffer quite enough of that at the hands of his companions. These things do worry the growing youth out of all proportion to their real importance, and thus, parents should be careful to point out that, in a very short time, these defects will right themselves. This reassurance is very necessary, because only too often the youth has the idea that such things are permanent. A word in time will prevent a good deal of this unnecessary worry.

Another frequent cause of trouble is blushing, which has, however, a very simple explanation which usually serves to put the adolescent more at ease about it in time. This is a thing which will not last. The heart is a very powerful muscle, and is in process of development at this stage. Often it is too large, or too powerful for the veins and the arteries, which tend to develop more slowly. This is the main physical cause for those sudden blushes which are so embarrassing a feature of youth. Often the very fact of knowing the reason for the blushing will serve to put the youth much more at ease about the whole thing, together with the fact that it will pass one day. Parents can do much to ease this situation by not making fun of their sons and daughters when they blush, by not calling attention to it, and also by helping to pass it off satisfactorily when in company. Such help is much appreciated by the children and will give them new confidence in their parents and in their desire to help.

Those blood conditions which so often give rise to skin blemishes worry adolescents, too. This can be helped by getting them into good habits and also by keeping a watchful eye on their diet ; in particular by seeing to it that they get sufficient exercise in the fresh air together with plenty of fresh fruit, vegetables and so on. Adolescent girls especially should be warned that any attempt to disguise these ills by the use of creams and powders, etc., is only liable to make things worse, because such things clog the pores and thus literally choke the skin, which is unable to breathe. It is, indeed, a very great pity that parents are not careful to point this fact out to their daughters, and to warn them that their passion for " make-up " is liable to ruin their skin very early in life. But do go gently with this advice, or else they will think you old-fashioned. Of course, the very best thing would be for the adolescent girl to use no make-up until she has to, and then only very little. There is no beauty like the human skin as God made it. Once they have made up their minds that they will have to use such things, then you can step in by showing them how to do so in moderation and gracefully. Your advice, especially if you are careful to become something of an expert, will be much appreciated, and you should be able to attain to some moderation in the use of this modern fashion. Unfortunately, it has become impossible to root it out altogether, much as one would like to do so in the case of adolescents.

Allied to these defects are such things as chilblains, which are normally the result of bad circulation. Exercise will help, and so will food rich in protein.

Perhaps the most common of all the physical manifestations of adolescence is awkwardness. This is due, in the main, to the bodily changes which are taking place at this time, although a small part of it is, of course, due to nerves. It will show itself in many ways, such as dropping things, knocking things over, tripping up, ungainly movements, slouching postures and so on. Now, parents must remember that it is no use getting angry with the youth for such things, because they are a natural defect of the age, and harsh words are not going to do any good. You will have to be patient and very understanding. Certain things, such as slouching, can be put right by a word of good advice at the right moment, delivered in the right frame of mind on both sides. Don't hold other boys or girls up as examples (what a horrid habit that is!), but just correct the fault gently. Awkwardness, as such, is a thing that will pass when maturity takes the place of adolescence, but you can do something at this stage by encouragement, especially by suggesting exercises such as games which tend to develop control over the muscles, by being patient and by making excuses. Help the adolescent to understand that all these silly things will pass one day, and that he can do a great deal to make that day come a little sooner by not paying too much attention to them. If you do the same, then it will help a good deal.

From all that we have said so far it will be clear to parents that their main rôle in this matter of physical education is that of one who can advise and also sympathize. There is nothing so difficult and yet nothing so very helpful to the growing boy and girl as this. They will always remember your efforts with grateful thanks because these little things are just those which make you a real father and mother to them. Do all that you can to keep your temper at this stage, and remember the days of your own youth, if you can, when you, too, went through this trying experience.

CHAPTER SEVENTEEN

MENTAL EDUCATION
IN ADOLESCENCE

I F THIS PERIOD OF THE CHILD'S LIFE HAS ITS PROBLEMS AND
its difficulties, it also has great and even glorious opportunities. This is nowhere more apparent than in the
spheres of mental and religious education. We are not directly
concerned here with the tasks and the obligations of teachers,
although a good deal of what is said here for the parents might
be studied with advantage by teachers and applied to the school
life. Before we can hope to make use of the opportunities which
are provided for us during these receptive years we shall have to
know a little more about the changes which are taking place
in the mental processes of the youth. The following is no
more than a very brief summary, but it will give us sufficient
to work on.

We have already mentioned the basic mental problem of
adolescence, namely, the uncertainty which bothers the youth
in all that he undertakes. There is, on the one hand, a strong
desire to stand on one's own feet and make one's own decisions,
yet on the other hand there is the knowledge which is slowly
impressed deeper during the first few years of adolescence that
the character which has to take the decisions is fluid and
unstable. This leads to much searching of heart, combined
with a seeking of support from others, which is partly concealed
beneath an exterior attitude of indifference to or contempt for
the opinions of others.

From this fundamental difficulty arise many of the other
changes in the adolescent which we can notice if we are careful
to observe him as we should. Perhaps the most obvious of all
these is that which affects his attitude towards those things
which *have* to be done. No longer is the adolescent satisfied

with the old motives of authority and of command ; he is on the lookout for others which will serve to convince his reason of the necessity for this course of action. This reaction often puzzles parents not a little, since they do not see the reason for it, and consequently they often react against it in a way which only serves to estrange the youth from them, tending as it does to make him all the more convinced in his own mind that there is no real reason for the things commanded beyond the personal will of authority. Yet, if the truth were known, he is only too willing to be convinced, even though he may frequently give us the opposite impression. It is not enough for us to put off these demands for reasons, or to think of them as a revolt against the whole structure of our parental authority. The change is a very natural one from every point of view and should be met with understanding and kindness. Those old motives (let us understand this once and for all) are no longer sufficient. It is no use our replying that such things have to be done " because mother says so," that is only to fall back on childhood motives which no longer satisfy. Reasons must be given where possible, at least the general reason. What is even more important in the long run, the general attitude towards such necessary laws must be taught. This will be a slow job, but it has to be done. The parents are in every way the best people to do this well, and it should not be left to the school authorities. Nor is it sufficient to provide reasons where possible ; they must also be reasons which convince. It is no use quoting your own experience to the adolescent, hoping that such a statement will convince him and finish the whole thing once for all. It will not. For one thing, he wants general principles which he can apply, not merely in this case but also in others, and you must remember that in many ways he is still a child, and therefore sees no reason why what was good twenty or thirty years ago should also be good now. You have to teach him that. Many of the mistakes of later life come from the fact that as a young man or woman in the 'teens no real motives for right action were ever provided. Their place was taken by mere authority, or at the worst, by sentiment. Let us give some examples of this, because it is of the greatest importance.

Perhaps you have heard the story of the boy who came to the table for meals with dirty hands and was met by his father in this fashion. " You never see me coming to the table with dirty hands, do you ? " The son's reply was, " But I didn't know you when you were twelve ". There is a basic element of truth in that statement which should have let the father see that the old motives would no longer do, and that reason has to be tried in their place.

Again, the quoting of adult experiences will not provide a sufficient motive either, because the youth does not really believe that his parents understand his difficulties, and he is convinced, by such an appeal to experience, that they are living in a past generation and are really old-fashioned. Experience does not count with the adolescent unless it is expressed in such a way that his mind sees and appreciates the reason behind it. He can grasp and respect that kind of argument.

Sentiment is, of course, worse than useless, and the youth feels that it is really an unfair approach to the whole question, as indeed it is. There is also nothing he hates with quite such a deep resentment. If parents only knew how much their children do detest this appeal through sentiment, and how unfair they know it to be, perhaps they would not be so free with it. Yet it is very common indeed to hear such appeals as this :—" How ever could you do such a thing when you know that we (that is the parents) have done all that we could for you all your life, have looked after you, etc., etc." I once remember hearing a reply to such an argument which was at once truthful and crushing. The boy looked up and said, " But, after all, I didn't ask to be born, did I ? " That answer may sound disrespectful, but it does contain an element of truth which the parents have obviously not appreciated. They have had the children, and it is their obligation to do those things for them, no more and no less ! There is, of course, a corresponding obligation on the part of the children to love and to respect their parents, but such a silly sentimental way of putting this to them does not deserve to meet with any success. The best method is to take their love and their respect for granted, and then to point out in gentle language both the duties and obligations of parents and children. That will teach them more than all the sentimental nonsense in the world would ever teach.   Once the children know that their parents regard all that they do for their children as their duty and their obligation then they will respond naturally once they come to realize that, and they will soon do so if your approach has been a good one.

Consequently, it can be said that, as a general rule, the main element in the mental education of the adolescent is to provide real sound motives for action which will cover most of those difficulties which arise from this attitude towards authority.

During the period of adolescence another big change takes place, this time in the will. This, too, is a perfectly natural thing to happen, because the will is being assailed from all sides by many new appeals of the senses and the emotions which are in themselves very attractive and yet the youth is still not too sure how to deal with them.   The will has to be still further trained, and yet voluntarily ; which means that the adolescent must see the need for that training and must co-operate in it, otherwise it will be a complete waste of our time as educators. This, in its turn, brings us back to what we have just said about motives, and their importance. You have to convince the growing boy or girl that this strength of will is the best sign of full maturity.   Adults are distinguished from adolescents because they know what they want and set out to get it without all that changing of mind and hesitation which is so common in the case of the latter.   That cannot be acquired at once, but needs training. Point out, also, and with examples, that provided the reason for doing something is strong enough, then it will get done, at least in those things which do lie under the control of the will.

This will-training needs exercise in small things, and frequent exercise, at that.   It is the only way to get the motives in line with the actions which should follow from them.   You will have to provide many, if not all, of those aims for the youth.   Don't forget that he is still in the stage when rewards must be fairly near at hand and not too difficult to obtain in order to succeed. Thus, small acts of self-denial, of unselfishness, of courtesy and consideration for others, should be both practised and also rewarded in some way or other, at least at the beginning of this period of training.   Remember, too, that we are not out to crush the will and to make the adolescent obey just because he has been given an order or to save himself from future punishment. That motive is not one which will last, and tends to form an adult who cannot stand on his own feet at all, but is constantly leaning on others for support when important decisions have to be made. Our obligation is to train and to guide in such a way that we end up by making the adolescent independent of us and dependent upon the motives for right action which we have helped to inculcate. This fact is of growing importance as the years go by. He has to be taught that the man or woman who has full control over the will is fully mature, a strong character and the master of all, or nearly all, of the difficulties which can confront us in this life. We learn in this way to rule our emotions and not to let them rule us. That is the ideal, which has to be achieved by you, the parents, after years of small efforts. The great importance of the early training given to the small child as outlined in the opening chapters of this book will now be apparent to you. If you have been careful then not to give in to all the whims and fancies of the young child, then you can be sure that your path will now be comparatively easy, and that your present efforts will be crowned with success.

There are changes in the memory and the imagination, too, during these years. Images are much more vivid and things are stored up very easily in the memory. This faculty, too, will need a certain amount of training; and to make that training as easy as possible, it should be made quite clear to the adolescent that now is the time to make sure that the memory learns all those things which are necessary for it, and in particular, that he must cultivate the habit of remembering when and where he wishes to do so. Thus, learning things by heart at this stage in life has a deep reason behind it which goes far beyond the small piece of poetry which is actually being memorized. Memory depends very much on attention, and this, too, has to be taught. As we shall see, there is one difficulty which always has to be overcome if we are to train the adolescent to attend well.

This difficulty is of such importance that it merits special treatment. We know that the young child tends naturally, at least on certain occasions, to day-dream, and to live and to play in a little world of his own which is very vivid to him. This is perfectly natural, but he should grow out of it in time, as he comes more into contact with the world of reality. However, this tendency to day-dream is sometimes, if not always, present in adolescents, and it can be a source of great dangers if it goes unchecked. At the same time, we must avoid the extreme of over-exaggerating this danger, as some writers have done, because we all indulge in a certain amount of day-dreaming, even as adults, and it is out of those day-dreams that some of the greatest inventions have finally appeared. The danger really comes from another source. Adolescence is a time of very high ideals, some of which are never realized. Those ideals are often the subject matter, at least in general, of the adolescent's day-dreams. He sees himself holding the centre of the stage, popular with others, one who has achieved success in many and varied undertakings, both in the realm of sport and also in the more serious departments of life. Later on, these day-dreams will almost certainly centre round some member of the opposite sex, and will frequently be the source of temptations against purity if they are not checked. The danger lies precisely in this element of *dreamed* success in opposition to success which is actually achieved in the world of reality. If the youth gets discouraged, or feels unable to cope with real-life problems, he may quite easily tend to retreat into this world of the day-dream, where he can succeed every time and overcome all opposition. If this is allowed to go on without a word of good advice then he will tend to fly to it more and more as a means of relief, and thus the danger will be very real. Such an individual rarely develops properly from adolescence to manhood, but remains a moral coward, who will fly to such relief as his imagination can offer him whenever the opposition of life seems too great.

Now, the question naturally arises, how are parents to deal with this situation when they see that it is getting out of hand ? Perhaps here once again the old saying that prevention is better than cure has a direct application. We can make sure that the growing boy and girl find real things in life in which they can achieve success. Encourage the children to tackle small problems and see to it that they manage to succeed and that they are made aware of that success and you are well on the way to preventing this day-dreaming from ever doing very much harm. They should also be warned of it more directly when they are ready to listen to conversations about such things. Once they see the danger they will usually be quite ready to co-operate with you in setting it aside quickly, because the shadow world of the day-dream cannot really compare with the hard facts of the world of reality when it comes to the real test.

One of the very common features of adolescence which has already been mentioned is the development in the power and in the desire for reasoning. This is a very good thing, and an opportunity for education which should not be let slip through any fault on our part. The most useful thing which parents can do for their children at this stage is to help them and guide them to reason things out for themselves. Thus, parents must be ready to discuss things freely with their adolescent children, and more so as they grow older. In this way the boy and girl acquire the motives for action, and also the necessary arguments are assimilated by the intellect in preparation for future occasions when they may have to discuss these same things with others. It is also important to see to it that they have the right mental attitude towards the truth. Truth is not merely speculative, but is essentially a motive for action. That means to say that, if this particular thing is proved to be the right thing to do, then it must be done, no matter what opposition stands in the way. Now is the time to fix this idea firmly in the minds of your children, because it is so badly interpreted and understood by the present generation. Only too often truth is separated from action. Any code of action needs reasons behind it if it is to be what we call " reasonable ", and those reasons are called the motives or the truth of the action. If they are true then the action will be good, while if they are false it will be bad in the moral sense. In this way, and especially by application of this teaching through examples taken from the daily lives of the children themselves, you will help their reasoning power very much indeed, and also prepare the way for your religious education. You can do adolescents no better service than this.

Discuss things reasonably with them, remembering that they have a point of view, and that your task is to find out what that point of view is. Don't condemn them out of hand just because their point of view seems to you to be silly or even stupid. They have a right to think for themselves, and owing to their age the process of their reasoning is not going to be so perfect or so mature as your own. We cannot expect to put old heads on young shoulders all at once. This desire to reason, which often amounts to a desire to argue, grows with age, until maturity brings with it the ability to argue correctly and from the right principles. You must be patient with them and try all the time to understand them. The natural idealism of youth will lead the adolescent to adopt many " lost causes " of which you may not approve, but don't ridicule or condemn too soon. Have your reasons and arguments ready and discuss the whole matter calmly with him ; you will get much further that way.

The present generation is characterized by its emotionalism, and, during this period, the adolescent will feel things more deeply himself and also will be swayed by the general atmosphere around him. It is your task to help the boy or girl to bring those emotions under efficient control. In themselves, these emotions are not bad things—indeed we would not go very far in any line without them—but they need the guiding hand of reason. The balance has to be maintained. You see that, once again, the power of reason has to get to work here, as in other fields. Point out the social implications of unbalanced emotions. Youth is very easily influenced by the thought of popularity or its opposite, and once get the adolescent to see that a certain course of action will make him socially unpopular and he will be willing to drop it at once. This is very often the case with uncontrolled emotions, and you can illustrate your teaching in this matter with simple examples, some of the most effective coming from the field of sport.

These very same emotions will make themselves felt in yet another way. You will soon notice that the adolescent is constantly changing in his attitude to things and to people. One day he will be full of enthusiasm for a certain thing or a certain person, and the very next day quite indifferent. Such rapid changes are to be expected and should not take you by surprise. Remember that, at this age, the youth is an emotional paradox, and that almost anything can be expected of him. Therefore you should be on your guard against any show of anger because of such changes of attitude. Sympathy is our very best weapon very often, and you will find that, provided you are not soft with it, the boy or girl will respect you, and you will never have cause to complain that he or she is abusing your kindness.

Since we have already mentioned the changing attitude towards authority during these years, there will be no need to do more here than repeat briefly some of the main points which parents have to keep in mind. This change in attitude is not in itself a bad thing or abnormal, but an integral part of those other changes which we have already noticed. If you look at it in that light and remember that the youth has no intention of being rude or contemptuous of authority as such, but quite the opposite, then you will not go far wrong in your attempts to deal with him. He needs to be convinced that his submission is a rational act, that is all. Above all, he needs new motives especially ones which appeal to the idealist in him, and once he is provided with those motives and they become a part of his general character, then you will soon find that, quite naturally, he falls into line with authority. Deal with him reasonably and you can expect reasonable service in return. On the other hand, if you use authority unwisely, then you may get lip service, but that will be all, and you will find that, once the parental bonds are loosened as they have to be sooner or later, there will be no response to your appeals. You will have only yourselves to blame if that happens. Remember, too, that the adolescent is trying hard to attain independence, and it has to be proved to him that he can only do that satisfactorily through submission to authority, and not by rebellion against it. He is also in the process of asserting himself, and that is always a painful thing both to the one who is doing it and also to those who are on the receiving end! If you can only bear patiently with his first trials and errors, then you will soon find that your authority is more respected and obeyed than it ever was before.

There are certain factors which have a very great influence on these various changes in the mental development of the adolescent. They are so important, and as parents make so many mistakes in the handling of this material, it has been decided to say something about them here under various headings, to make it easier for the reader to follow.

Reading

We have already discussed one aspect of reading in the last chapter, and now we shall have to consider it from yet another angle, which is even more important. There are two kinds of adolescents, those who are interested in reading and those who are not; but it has been proved beyond all shadow of doubt that all adolescents without exception are profoundly affected for good or for evil by what they read. Naturally, those who are more interested in reading will be more affected than those who are not. In general, therefore, the type of reading done by the adolescent should be very closely watched. You will be able to notice a very definite change in the type of books read as he grows older. He usually starts off with some kind of boys' paper or magazine together with some type of novel, usually of the " blood-and-thunder " type, and works up by easy stages to the novel as such. Unless we are rather careful, the vast majority of reading done by the growing boy may be classified as trash, and that is why we have insisted that the reading matter should be supervised by the parents at the very beginning of adolescence, then it will become a thing to which the youth is so accustomed that he will not object to it later on. Of course, it has to be done with tact and sympathy, and you might as well be prepared for an occasional objection. However, provided that you are ready to give your reasons why a certain type of book or magazine is not suitable for him to read, then you will soon find that your advice is sought freely.

You can do a great deal by introducing him to books which you know to be suitable and yet interesting to him at the same time. For example, the youth who is interested in adventure stories can find just as much to please him in *Treasure Island* and similar books, as he can in the trash which is usually served up to the youth of today. Such literature has the added advantage that it provides a good vocabulary and literary style. Find the right kind of literature to suit him and the youth will soon cease to be interested in the other type at all. Here again you must be prepared to discuss the questions involved with the adolescent, and it is always a good thing to note, as example to illustrate your arguments, that some of Nature's most deadly poisons are displayed to the world in the most attractive colours possible.

The same thing often happens in the case of books, where frequently, fine descriptions hide evil ideas which poison the mind. A healthy attitude is what is needed here, as in other matters. You will have to allow a certain number of what Chesterton has called " penny-dreadfuls ", but you will usually find that the wild-west novel, for instance, does not do any harm. Rather the danger lies in the trashy novel and the slushy magazine. Also you will have to be rather careful what kind of newspaper you allow to come into the house. Lending libraries have to be watched too, because most of the present-day novels are definitely not fit things to be read by anyone, never mind an adolescent! Point out to the children when the need arises that there is a definite attempt being made in certain quarters to pervert good morals in the youth of the country by such filth. They will naturally resent that attempt and you will have gained a great victory if you set about your task with tact.

Just as a lie, however attractively told or artistic, still remains a lie, so, too, art or literature which presents a false standard of morality, no matter how attractive the dress, still remains bad literature and bad art. That point has been lost sight of by so many people today that it has to be mentioned here. It is no argument to say that " everyone " is reading a certain book. Keep a good reading list for your children and they will come to thank you later on for it, because it is one of the finest things parents can do for their children.

Films

Another thing which has a very great influence on the mental development of the adolescent is the cinema. This is very natural, because there they will see and hear things which affect some at least of the problems with which they themselves are concerned. The danger of the films is not confined to one single aspect of them, but is manifold. In the first place, grown-up motives are provided for actions which are not, as yet, within the capacity of the adolescent mind to grasp fully. They all tend to imitate, to some extent at least, what they see there. We have all observed this tendency in adolescents and so there is no need to stress it any more by examples. Also the films tend to present an ideal type of existence which we, as adults, may know to be a mere figment of the imagination, but which the adolescent is far more likely to take seriously. He gets a false impression of life, and so tends perhaps to become discontented with his home life and longs for other things which he can never have. Again, there is no doubt about the fact that many, indeed the vast majority, of the films which are shown today contain as their basic theme something to do with sex, usually presented under the aspect of the " eternal triangle ", tending to glorify such things as divorce and to glamorize a lust which passes for love. All these things are presented in such attractive dress that they may even deceive " the elect ". All these factors constitute a danger which it is almost impossible to exaggerate. It may be true that the adolescent does not understand fully all that he hears or sees on the films, but that is not the point. The danger lies just there, because in such a way motives for action enter into his mind almost without his being aware of it. If you need any proof of this, just think how easy it is for the adolescent to remember things that he has seen or heard in films, perhaps a long time ago. Thus we need not be very surprised to find that adolescents often admit that they frequently attempt to solve their own personal problems with the aid of what they have seen or heard on the films. This is especially true of nervous and easily excited children, and you will notice that the films influence this type far more easily than the others. Much of the modern adolescent's attitude towards the opposite sex and towards such things as love and marriage is gleaned from the films, where such things are certainly not presented in a way which we Catholics can accept. All these things make the problem of the films a pressing one for parents. Nowadays, to make matters worse, there is a tendency for the children to go to the films much more frequently than in former days. As parents you will have to keep a very close watch on all this. The ideal would be, of course, to limit their visits to the cinema as much as possible, and also to provide them with other interests which will occupy them to the exclusion of the cinema. This can be done, with a little care on the part of the parents, and it is a pity that more of them do not realize their obligation in this matter. This danger is a very real one, and you cannot afford to have all your efforts at a good and moral education of your children frustrated by something which can be controlled at first, but which becomes more difficult if you allow the habit to creep in without any real effort to control it. A right attitude towards these things is once more the really important thing, and that you can and must produce in your children.

Friends

There should be no need to stress the obvious importance of this factor in the character formation of the children, but it is always strange to see that parents who are usually so careful about other things should show such little interest, very often, in the friends their children make. Naturally, this is a very delicate matter, and you will have need of all the graces which the Sacrament of Matrimony can give you in order to handle it with the tact and the understanding which it demands. Some general principles will be useful first of all.

If you learn to observe your children without seeming to do so, and also if you practise patience with them when they first go to school, then you will soon find that they are quite open with you about their friendships. The boy or girl, just after going to school, is very liable to come in when you are busy getting the dinner ready and start talking about friends and things like that. You must learn to listen then, and not put the discussion off to some other time. That is the only way in which you will be able to show your children, from the very first, that you are always interested in them and their doings. It is by means of such simple little conversations that you will pick up a vast amount of most useful information with regard to the companions with whom your child is now beginning to associate. Some you will no doubt pass as quite satisfactory, once you have had a look at them ; others you will soon judge to be unsuitable. What are you going to do about these ? At the beginning of your child's school life this problem will not be too difficult, because you can just point out quietly but firmly that you wish them not to go with so-and-so, and that will be that. Later on in life, and especially during the last few years of adolescence, you will need much more tact and sympathy than before, and your methods will have to change. Any violent opposition to the adolescent's wishes is very liable to drive him to the opposite extreme. As a first principle you will have to learn to keep open house for your children's friends, and you should always encourage them to bring their friends home, so that you can see them. However much you may dislike some of them, never show it openly. Bide your time, until an opportunity presents itself, and then tackle the subject delicately and from a reasonable point of view. Sometimes it is enough for the adolescent to see his or her friends in the home atmosphere to know that they do not fit in, and so begin to cool off them sooner or later. Try to discover good Catholic friends for your children, and then you will feel much safer about the whole thing. However, there are times when a firm stand may be necessary. This usually occurs later on in adolescence, when your children are beginning to be much more interested in persons of the opposite sex and are going out with them. Then you may find that they are seeing far too much of an undesirable character. Perhaps it may even be that the person they are becoming far too friendly with is even divorced, or something like that. Now, to allow such friendships to continue has proved tragic in so many cases that a word of warning must be given about it.

Don't imagine that you are going to be able to allow it to continue for a time without any danger, because in the vast majority of cases you are not. Once you find out about it, then it is time to have a straight talk with the boy or girl with regard to it. In the course of this talk you should begin by pointing out the danger quite clearly, namely that, if we allow such things to go on, then a time will come when what is now mere friendship will develop into something which it will be extremely difficult to break off. There is only one course open to us, and that is to remove the danger once and for all and at once. Point out that such a friendship constitutes a dangerous occasion of sin, and that, as such, it should be mentioned in confession—but do not leave it all to the priest. Remember that, if anything should come of such friendships later on, then *you and you alone*, as the parents, are to be held responsible in the vast majority of cases. Consequently, your action must be firm, decided and effective. You can make it so in many ways, but perhaps the most important thing of all is the sympathy and understanding between you and your children, which has been mentioned so many times before, and which should never be allowed to reach the point of sentimentality or weakness.

Reasons and arguments might be tried first, to see if they will do the trick. Follow that up with the religious arguments presented as strongly as you know how. Ask advice of a priest if you are uncertain how to deal with this side of the matter. When and if all else fails then you will have to exert your full power of authority as parents, both on your child, and also on the other party to the dangerous friendship. Point out that it is a course which you never desired to take and never expected to have to take either, but that it is now inevitable. Then see to it that your commands are obeyed to the letter. Remember that a person who has been divorced is not only older in years than your adolescent boy or girl, but also knows all the tricks of the trade. You cannot afford to take any risks. Forbid the whole thing once and for all, when your arguments and reasons fail, and do so firmly and with conviction that you are acting in the right way. There is no other course open to you, and you need not fear that you may lose the confidence and the love of your child, because any temporary estrangement will soon pass and you will find that your final position will be much stronger. There is no such thing as love at first sight, remember, except in novels or on the films—what can exist in real life is physical attraction at first sight, and that has to be prevented in such cases from becoming a real danger if you are to preserve your child's soul from the ultimate menace of an eternity in hell. Compared with that danger nothing else matters; and remember, too, that those who marry outside the Church in such circumstances as these run a very great risk indeed of ending up in hell, because there is no way in which such marriages between a Catholic and one who has been divorced can be put right, except by the death of the real wife or husband, and that often refuses to come at the right moment! Also much bitterness often enters into the Catholic's attitude towards religion and the Church, and that closes the gate to final repentance very much more often than you may like to think. It is therefore your task and your obligation to break up this miserable association before it can become anything more dangerous than a mere attraction.

Experience has taught us that most, if not all, of the cases of Catholics marrying divorced persons or others in a registrar's office or outside the Church, could have been prevented by the parents with a little tact and firmness at *one* stage of the whole miserable business. Those parents will have much to answer for when they stand before their God to be judged. The fault may lie in early childhood, either because you have shown yourselves unsympathetic towards your children, or because you have not been firm enough in your methods of education. If you have given in to your children too much when they were young then it frequently becomes quite impossible to reverse the process later on in life when it is most needed. Education is one whole, and must be considered as such. Start right from the very beginning and you will find that you have less difficulty when dealing with these matters in adolescence.

The desire for independence

One of the commonest complaints which most adolescents give voice to from time to time is that their parents do not give them sufficient freedom. Now, a word about this difficulty is very necessary, because it is so easy for parents to fall into one of two extremes in the matter. The adolescent's desire for freedom is, in itself, a natural thing and also a good sign, because it shows that he is getting more accustomed to standing on his own feet, with the corresponding desire to meet life as he finds it. However, that does not mean that we can or should allow the adolescent all the freedom which he desires. Nor— at the other extreme now—does it imply that we should look on him as still a child. Greater freedom must be allowed during this stage of his life, and also much more personal responsibility, but all within the framework of the good running and the discipline of the family. Thus, for example, a reasonable hour should be fixed for the children to be in at night, and that hour should be kept, within reasonable limits for an extension of grace in certain circumstances. Ten o'clock is quite late enough during the later period of adolescence, but, of course, at the beginning it should not be as late as that by any means.

There should not be any need for many restrictions with regard to this, because if you have encouraged them to bring their friends home then they will not want to be out at all hours very often. If you make these easy conditions depend on their observance by the adolescents then you will find that, normally at least, they respond with equal generosity. It is the feeling of independence they really want at the beginning, and not the freedom itself, and thus you can usually combine the one with the other in your ruling. Whatever you do, never allow them complete freedom, because from the point of view of education alone that is a bad thing. They must learn that rules will have to be obeyed all during life, the difference being that, whereas in childhood such rules have to be kept from the motive of obedience, in later life they have to be observed out of respect for the authority and the wishes of others, who can be seriously inconvenienced by selfishness in this matter. If you have been careful, during childhood, to give your children an ever-increasing sense of responsibility by giving them charge over their toys, books, clothes, pocket money and so on, you will find that they take your ruling easily in such things as the number of times they can go to the films per week or month, the dances they attend, the time for being in at night, and so forth. Be gentle but firm in this matter, and never be afraid of discussing it quite openly with them if they show that they are beginning to question your decisions.

Dances

That brings us quite naturally to a question which has increased in importance nowadays, that of dances. In general we may say that, although in itself dancing is not evil, still it has dangers for adolescents which cannot be denied. We must look at it from their point of view, and not from our own. It is, in a sense, a drug, especially to the imagination and the emotions ; and so, if it is to do no harm it must be used as other drugs are, in the right circumstances and in the correct doses. The dangers of it arise from the fact that, apart from any other evils to which it may lead, the modern dances are conducted in an atmosphere of sensuality which is apparent from the very tunes themselves, and this, in its turn, tends to sap the moral fibre almost without our being aware of it. It may do it very slowly, but it is no less effective for all that. To the over-sensitive adolescent such emotions are pleasing, and therein lies the chief danger. However, given the right circumstances and surroundings, dancing *in moderation* is not always evil. What is definitely evil, both in itself and also in its consequences, is the pre-occupation with dancing which can reach the level of a real craze.

So far as the parents are concerned, our advice is this. Do not allow your children to attend dances at too early an age. See to it that they always have a fitting companion, and that they attend Catholic dances run by Catholic clubs. If this is not indulged in too frequently, then there is a lessening of the very real dangers which attend it, and without any loss to the adolescent.

In this connection it is a good thing to see that our Catholic clubs are running all-Catholic dances in many parishes. This does not mean that parents can afford to relax their watchfulness, or cease to take the necessary precautions, but it does help to do two things which are very important. In the first place, it serves to lessen the dangers, and also it helps to develop friendships between our Catholic boys and girls which may lead to Catholic marriages. However, more could be done to see to it that there are also inter-parish dances at times, so as to increase the possibility of such Catholic friendships a little.

CHAPTER EIGHTEEN

RELIGIOUS EDUCATION
IN ADOLESCENCE

FROM THE VERY BEGINNING WE HAVE INSISTED THAT THE whole of education must be directed towards one single end, the salvation of those souls which God has entrusted to our care as parents. If this is either neglected or thrust into the background then nothing else that we may do, however good for the children, can be said to count. Therefore it will be no surprise to you to discover that many of the things which have already been mentioned in the former chapters on physical and mental education have a direct application here, in this chapter, when we are discussing the religious development of the adolescent.

In general it may be said that the child's life is ruled by a simple trust in his parents. His religious life—which is a very real thing to him—takes on the same aspect. He believes quite simply what he is told by his parents and school teachers he has to believe. He performs religious duties according to his age and capacity, such as his prayers and going to Mass, because he is trained to do that by his parents. This does not mean that his religious life is mechanical—far from it, but it is most certainly of a very different type from that of the adolescent. This childlike faith and practice is the foundation on which the religious life of the adolescent and also of the adult has to be built, and the more solid that foundation, so much the more firm and secure will be the final edifice. However, just as the laying of a foundation for a house requires one method and the actual building of the house another, so it is quite true to say that the methods of religious training during adolescence cannot be the same as those used during the early years of childhood. If we take into consideration the physical and the mental changes which take place at this period, we shall see clearly enough that such a change in methods is absolutely necessary. This does not imply that we are at all in favour of the opinion which seems quite common nowadays that during adolescence, a period of religious doubt almost amounting to scepticism is bound to show itself in the vast majority of cases. Investigations have proved that, at least in the case of our Catholic youth, this opinion does not hold water, especially if their religious education is developed along the right lines. Naturally, a certain amount of this training in their religion will be acquired at school—or at least it should be acquired there—which is one more reason why it is important that they should attend a Catholic school. The main part of their religious education, however, will still depend on you, as it always does, because you alone can give them that real love for their Faith which will hold them all their lives.

It is also worth while to mention, at the very outset, that this period of adolescence is one of golden opportunities where religion is concerned. This is a period of life when high ideals are regarded as almost a commonplace. Indeed, youth, by reason of its energy and activity, has a right to expect that such high ideals should always be kept before it. Now, there is nothing else on this earth which holds up such a high ideal as the Catholic Faith. We have only to consider for a moment the life of its Founder, Christ, as that life is portrayed for us in the Gospels, to see just how great and attractive that Faith can be for the adolescent. Here is what seems at first sight to be a lost cause which, through the courage of Jesus and His disciples, develops into a glorious triumph. This same struggle is going on at the present day, and we, as followers of Christ, are expected to follow in His footsteps and champion the very same cause. There is the same possibility of apparent failure, as the lives of the martyrs bear witness, and there is the same triumph, if not always in this world, at least in the world to come. Christ's teaching is hard to put into actual deeds, and requires heroic courage at times. All this appeals to youth, and there is no reason why our Catholic young men and women should not be fired with a burning zeal for the cause of Christ—no reason except apathy and carelessness on the part of those whose duty it is to inculcate these ideals. During this period you can bring the religious life of the adolescent to a very high level indeed, but to achieve that you must first of all know at what you are aiming, and also how to succeed in reaching that goal.

The ultimate aim of all our religious training has already been outlined. It is to bring those souls entrusted to us to eternal life as easily and as securely as possible. That aim should have been constantly before your minds during the whole course of the children's lives ; but now its demands become even more urgent, because once the adolescent leaves your hands a fully matured man or woman, there should be nothing wanting which is necessary to attain that end perfectly. However high a standard of material and secular education we may have provided for our children, that is all counted as nothing compared with this final end, towards which the whole of our efforts have to be directed.

To make quite sure that, so far as our duty lies, our children have all that they need to achieve eternal salvation we must do three things :—

1. We must make sure that they know their Faith, and in the right way.
2. We must get them to practise that Faith from the right motives.
3. And lastly, we must be ready and able to help them with their religious difficulties.

The knowledge of the Faith

While it is quite true to say that mere knowledge, of itself, will not assure salvation, it is also true that love is born of knowledge. We cannot love someone we do not know, and what is even more important, we shall never be able to serve someone with loving obedience unless we both know and love that person. For this reason the Catechism tells us that we have to know, love and serve God in this world in order that we may live together with Him in the glory of heaven. Those three things are intimately connected. However, the knowledge which we are aiming at during this period of the children's lives is rather different from that which we have been trying to form in them up to now. Perhaps it would be better to say that our present aim is rather intimate realization than knowledge. Let us illustrate this by an example. As Catholics we all know and believe that Jesus Christ died on the Cross for our salvation; but have we ever penetrated that doctrine to the point of seeing clearly what it means to us as individuals ? If not, then let us do so now for a moment.

Christ was the Son of God, and therefore He knew all things even during His life on earth. He knew *me*, by name ; all about me including the most minute details of my life, such as the identity of my parents, where I was going to go to school, all my good actions and also my bad ones—all this was an open book to Christ. The sacrifice of His death was made and offered for *me as an individual*, and the merits of that sacrifice are applied to me, again as an individual, through the Sacraments of His Church. Such a personal attitude towards the Redemption should make a very great difference to my life. It should give me a great and a living faith in my Redeemer. It should make me have confidence in Him as my Brother, who died that I might live. This is the element of knowledge which has to be stressed when we are dealing with the religious education of the adolescent, because it is only this personal realization of the implications of the truths which he believes which will give him that strong, driving spirit of Christ as an ideal to live up to.

There are many ways of achieving this attitude in the youth, and many methods of teaching which bring it out. Here we shall mention only some of them which may be of use to parents and also to teachers. First, and by far the best method of all, is the study of the life of Christ as revealed to us in the Gospels. There are several good books on this subject, written by experts especially for the adolescents, which will help them to study those Gospels with relish and profit. Make sure that such books find their way into your children's hands and encourage them to read them carefully. Once they have become sufficiently interested then you can rely on their own natural enthusiasm to carry them much further in this study.*

The adolescent is interested in the truths of Faith if these are presented in an attractive fashion. Above all, he is looking

* A short list will be given at the end of this chapter.

for the reasons behind those things which he has already been taught in childhood and which he already believes. It is not so much more knowledge of them which he requires, but rather the reasons and the arguments which can demonstrate to him that such things are really true and that there are valid and cogent reasons why we should believe them. In other words, the youth needs a course of apologetics in the basic truths of the Faith. Here we can see quite clearly the change in the method of approach. Before, in childhood, it was merely a question of learning the Catechism by heart, and of understanding something about what he learnt. Now, that method cannot be retained altogether or alone. There must be much more recourse to arguments, explanations and reasons. This has many obvious advantages. It flatters the adolescent to be treated as a grown-up person and to be given the reasons for things, and no longer to be considered as a child. In consequence, he takes a deeper interest in those teachings, and this helps him to remember them better and also to act up to their demands. Also, doubts are removed by reasons, and seldom by mere authority. In fact it is true to say that mere authority never settled any doubt, it was and is the reason behind the authority which achieves that end. For this reason the element of authority in the teaching of the Church should be stressed at this period, but from the right angle, i.e., the reasons for trusting in that authority should be given. Then it will be much easier to obey that authority, because the youth will know that, although the reason for a certain decree of the Church may not be in itself obvious to him, still she alone has the divine authority to teach entrusted to her by Christ, and since she cannot make a mistake in teaching the whole Church in matters of Faith and Morals, we are quite safe in giving our ready obedience to her laws and commands. In this sense, as you can see, it is the *truth* of the Faith which should be stressed rather than its truths.

Once the youth has good and valid reasons for knowing that the Faith which he professes is the truth and that anything contrary to it is error and false, then he no longer worries about many of those doubts and difficulties which are bound to be presented to him by the world in which he has to live. He may forget many of the arguments for the truth of the Faith later on, but he will always remember with gratitude that there is an answer somewhere and, indeed, that once upon a time he himself knew that answer. Then, if necessary, he can always fall back on authority, and also on the fact that a simple enquiry will once more give him the right answer to the difficulty. That is a very great standby.

In this way a Catholic attitude will become second nature to him. This is more than ever important today, when so many of the " modern " ideas are in direct conflict with the teachings of the Church. This conflict could give rise to many doubts and difficulties, because we cannot all be trained theologians and know all the answers, at least, not in such a short lifetime as that granted to most of us. For this reason God, in His great wisdom, gave us the infallible Church to save us from undue worry and doubt. Once that attitude of thinking *with* and *in* the Church of Christ becomes second nature, then such doubts are conquered once and for all, and can do no harm. On the other hand, if that attitude is not present, then the mere knowledge will never make up for it. Indeed, then the knowledge may prove to be a dangerous thing, because, instead of leading to a deep pride in the Faith and in the Church, our Mother, it will lead to a pride in ourselves which is so often fatal.

It is, of course, natural that this method of reasoning cannot be developed fully at once. The change over has to be gradual. With regard to this we can give one or two hints which may be of use to parents and to teachers alike.

During the early years of puberty the old method of the Catechism can be continued and developed slowly. The doctrine already taught briefly can be repeated, this time with greater detail in the answers and the explanations given. Parents cannot hope to do this in quite the same way as the teachers, nor is that necessary. Much of their teaching will be in the form of talks and general discussion with their growing children about the truths of the Faith, such as the one example we have already given of the Redemption. However, towards the later years of adolescence another method should have replaced the old one. There should be a growing stress placed on the Gospel stories and the life of Christ, who is set up as our Model and our ideal. Although not all are agreed as to the form this new method should take, nevertheless all are in full agreement with the following general principles.

(a). The method should be an interesting one, which will hold the attention and also make the facts easy to assimilate. In other words, the truths of Faith must be made to live. We are not dealing with something which was preached for the Jews of Palestine over nineteen hundred years ago, and for them alone. We are dealing with a Faith which was intended for all men and women at all periods of the world's history since Christ.

(b). It becomes more and more necessary to give practical examples of the applications of this Faith to the world as we know it today, with its social problems and its moral side-steppings. These examples will be easily come by through your own general reading, especially of the daily newspapers, and you can and should discuss such things with your children from time to time. You will find that they are very interested, especially if you make your examples live for them by seeing to it that they are topical and apply to the real world in which the adolescents live and move.

(c). Some kind of course in apologetics is necessary for the senior classes in our Catholic schools, so that they can see for themselves on what a firm basis their Faith rests.

(d). They can and should be encouraged to read up certain things for themselves, and also to join in Catholic activities such as the Young Christian Workers movement, the local Catholic club, and so on. In this way they will be kept in touch with Catholic thought in its practical applications to their own district or parish. A Catholic newspaper should be in every Catholic home in the country. The benefits of this are obvious, and yet we know from bitter experience that there are still many Catholic homes where the Catholic press makes few and rare appearances. That is all wrong, because in many modern problems we need guidance if we are to acquire the correct attitude towards them, and also the correct principles of the solution proposed for them by our Faith.

(e). It would also be a very good thing if our Catholic youth could be given a reasonable opportunity of self-expression with regard to these matters of Faith, especially as applied to the social problems. This could be done by means of discussion groups, either in the last few years of their school life or else in the Catholic clubs, by means of study circles or debates. In any case, it can be done to a certain extent in the home if the parents will only take an interest in such matters themselves, and also encourage the youth to talk about them in friendly discussion with the parents. There are many things which can only be known thoroughly through this method of question, answer and discussion.

(f). Above all, of course, we must do all we can to bring them up in a strong spirit of loyalty to Christ and to His Church. This, too, is not difficult if you, as parents, have this same attitude towards your religion. It is very difficult if you are indifferent. We shall have a little more to say about this personal loyalty towards religion in the next section when dealing with the moral difficulties of the adolescent.

(g). The high ideal of Christian perfection should be explained to them in detail, especially the basic struggle between the natural man, burdened with the effects of original sin, and the supernatural life of grace. This struggle is at the root of all our difficulties, and the adolescent is only just beginning to feel the power of the waves on that stormy sea. Now is the time to teach him what this struggle means and the methods which have to be used to win through. That means that you, as parents, by your teaching and by your example, must show the youth what part the sacramental life of the Church really plays in the fight.

Now let us attempt briefly to bring this general doctrine down to the practical level.

We know, from experience, that the fight against temptation is in reality a fight against self in all its expressions. It is ourselves, with those strong passions which are so useful if they are used rightly, but so very harmful if they are misused, that constitute the main enemy. That self has to be beaten in a straight fight in order that we may be real men and women and not something a little lower than the brutes. To accomplish this effectively means in practice that we have to control ourselves in such a way that the revolt against the rule of the mind aided by grace is hardly noticed. This is a very high ideal, but one which it is by no means impossible to achieve if we use the right

methods from the very beginning.   The call to sanctity, which
is given in some measure to us all, is very attractive to the adolescent once he knows about it.   What you will have to do, as
parents, is to prepare the soul for action during the years of
childhood, and then help even more actively during the years
of adolescence.

In actual practice we must learn to put first things first.   The
great commandment of the New Law is that of love—the love
of God first of all, and then love of our neighbour.   It is there
that the real fight must take place, because such love implies
a breaking down of all the claims of self and a surrender to those
of God.

We have already said that it is very important to train small
children not to be selfish, and the reason for that early training
will now be apparent.   Once the child has learnt that he must
be prepared, at least at times, to give in to the wishes of others
it will soon become second nature to him, at least in so far as
the mental attitude is concerned, to recognize that such a
surrender of his rights is the highest form of love.   When the
time of adolescence arrives, new efforts must be made to see to
it that this surrender is complete, both in so far as God is concerned and also our neighbour.   Let us begin with God.

Motives for the love of God must be stressed, because without
them love is impossible, since we cannot love someone we do
not really know.   The easiest way of doing this is through the
life of Christ as revealed for us in the Gospels.   He is not merely
our Redeemer, to whom we owe a vast supernatural debt of
gratitude, but also our Model.   His life, His sayings, His actions
—all had a double purpose, being intended not merely for the
salvation of the human race, but also to serve as a model for our
own activities in the world.   If we can only get adolescents to
study the life of Christ with this idea in mind, then we shall have
done much to ensure that they love Him.   This love which we
hope to foster in them must not be a weak and puny thing, but
a burning enthusiasm for the cause of Christ in the world.   There
is no danger that they will be bored by this life-story, because
in all the literature of the whole world there is nothing so
appealing or so moving.   Once they get used to reading the
Gospels for themselves then they will soon catch fire with the

enthusiasm which that story arouses. Parents are often responsible for not fostering this interest as they should. There is no real reason why a chapter of the Gospels should not be read every day in every Catholic home. The practical applications of that life to our own problems could be pointed out, especially from the Parables and the actions of the Saviour. Is this too much to ask of Catholic parents, when it is the all-important thing in the lives of the children?

They must also be taught to put those motives into actual practice. This is done through prayer and through the Sacraments. Prayer is a duty which we all owe to God, but that does not mean to say that it must necessarily be a boring duty. There is so much that we have to say to Him if we only examine our lives a little. Still, we have to remember that prayer is not a thing which comes easily and naturally to man after the Fall. He is so much more interested in the tangible things of this life with its attractions and pleasures. This duty of prayer has to be learnt in the hard school of experience. If parents have taught their children to pray while still young then it should not be very difficult to make this prayer a very real thing to the adolescent, but it has to be handled in the right way. First of all, the basis of all prayer must be there, i.e., the right idea of exactly what prayer means.

In actual fact our prayer should be based on the friendship which exists between man and God, as without that basis there will never be any real interest in prayer. We love our friends; we love to be with them, to hear their voices, to exchange confidences with them, to help them or to seek help from them in times of trouble and distress. All these sentiments have to be translated to the supernatural life of prayer. God is our Divine Friend, who loves us so much that He has not hesitated to send His Son to take our nature and also to give His life for us. All the words and actions of Christ during His life on this earth speak to us of this love and friendship. But friendship cannot be a one-sided affair ; there must be a corresponding love and affection on our part and a desire to be with Him as there is on His part to be with us. Those affectionate meetings between God and the soul take place during the times of prayer. Then it is that we thank Him for all that He has done for us. We tell

Him that we believe in Him, even though the world rejects Him ; that we hope in Him for eternal life, and for all those things which He knows to be for our good. It is then, above all, that we tell Him of our love for Him, and also make up to Him for the sin and the ingratitude of the world. We learn to go to Him in time of trouble and temptation, when it seems that the whole power of evil is working against us. We lean on Him as did St. John the Evangelist, and from Him we gain all our strength to continue the fight in His name and with His power. You can put these ideas to the youth and you will find that he responds easily and naturally to them.

So far we have not said anything about method because the most important thing is this spirit of prayer, and the method will follow. The finest method of all is undoubtedly the Eucharistic Prayer. Let us therefore examine this a little more closely.

The centre of all our religious life is the Mass, and it is of the greatest importance to see to it that your children learn to have a great love for and devotion to the Mass. Once again, they will never learn to love it until they know just what it means. As children you should have taught them to follow Mass in some way or another, and now that method should be perfected and completed. They should be taught to use the Missal and to follow the Mass in its liturgical form as far as possible. In this way they will learn to come into real contact with the Mass as their own prayer together with the priest. This will mean a little time and effort on the part of the parents, but it is well worth it.

The Sunday Mass should be made the centre of the family life of prayer. If possible the whole family should attend Mass together, and if this is not practicable every week, an effort should be made to make it so at least one Sunday in every month, when all should go to Communion together. There is nothing which will give your children a better example and also nothing which is so effective to draw the family together. Remember, however, what we have said before about not making religious life hateful to your children. This can be done so very easily if we are not careful, either by giving them too much of it or else by doing it in the wrong way. Make sure that Sunday is not merely a day of prayer but also a day of real joy. There is no need for us, as Catholics, to whom Sunday is the " Lord's Day ", to make it a day of puritanical gloom! With a little effort and understanding on the part of the parents it can so easily be made a holy day and a joyous one at the same time. This will help a very great deal to get the children to appreciate the feast days of the Church, not to dread them.

The Sunday Mass is not the only part of this Eucharistic Prayer, because Our Lord has given Himself to us in the Blessed Sacrament to be the life and the food of our souls. We have to make the most of that gift, and at no time is this more important than during the period of adolescence. If the children have been trained correctly during their earlier life then they will already have the habit of going to Holy Communion frequently, and not merely once or twice a year. This habit must now be safeguarded and increased little by little, a thing which will need both care and patience on the part of the parents.

Once again, the motive is important. Our children must have a clear idea of the Holy Eucharist as the food of the soul. This analogy is very obvious and also well known to us all, and you should make full use of it in explaining to your children what this great Sacrament means to us. When we receive Holy Communion, Christ comes into our souls and sanctifies them with His Presence, and this sanctification brings with it, as a natural consequence, a much closer union between Christ and the soul. There will be a greater likeness now between us and our Model. There is an interchange of ideas and of gifts. The gifts which He gives us are a growing strength in virtue, power to fight against the dangers and the temptations of the world, a hunger and thirst after spiritual things and a promise of our eternal salvation. Read to them the story of the promise of this Sacrament as it is to be found in the sixth chapter of St. John's Gospel, and then follow that up by reading the prayer of Christ before His Passion, which you will find in the seventeenth chapter of the same Gospel. That will do more than mere words can to make them see and appreciate the value of their frequent Communions.

Make opportunities for them to receive Communion. Thus, the anniversary of your wedding can be made a day of special prayer and of joy, including Mass and the reception of Holy Communion. The children's birthdays can be treated in the same way, special feast days can be kept, such as those of the Patron Saints of the members of the family, the feast of the Guardian Angels, and all the greater feasts of the Church. We can put before the children special intentions which will also provide motives for receiving Holy Communion, such as the sick and dying, success in work or examinations, the Holy Souls, and so on. Any means, in fact, should be used which will give a motive for the more frequent reception of this Sacrament.

Insist from the very beginning on a good preparation and thanksgiving. See to it that the children have some prayers which they can say during those times. Instil into them the idea that the very best preparation for tomorrow's Holy Communion is today's, and that the best thanksgiving for the Holy Communion we have received today is tomorrow's. Get them accustomed, from very small children, to thinking of Communion as something which should make us live better lives, which means in actual practice that we should live with more consideration for others, unselfishness, good temper and so on. Good example from you is everything here!

In general a great devotion to the Presence of Our Lord in this Sacrament should be your aim. This can be fostered by visits to the Blessed Sacrament, and these should be a normal part of the family life, according to the circumstances and opportunities which you have. Encourage such visits, explain what this Presence means to us and why it should be used to develop the friendship between the soul and Christ. Link this idea up with the other ideas on prayer which have already been explained in this chapter.

Another important factor of the religious life during this period of adolescence is the attitude to and the reception of the great Sacrament of Penance. Here parents have to be rather careful, because during the early years of childhood it is easy to get the child to go to confession, but sometimes the special difficulties of the years of adolescence with its temptations make him a little diffident about approaching this Sacrament. It is not a wise thing, perhaps, for parents to show their children that this worries them or that they are constantly on the watch to see if their children go to confession or not. Much more freedom must be allowed for the personal element during these years, especially as maturity approaches. However, a good deal can be done indirectly to see to it that your growing children come to look on this Sacrament in the right way, namely as something which is of very great help to the living of a life in conformity with the ideals of Christ.

In the first place, it might be pointed out to the youth that there is nothing shameful in having to confess our sins ; everyone has to do it, even the priests and the Pope himself. In fact, the priests and the Pope probably go to confession more often than lay people do. If we have not been ashamed to commit the sin, then we should not be ashamed to tell it in order to get it forgiven. The priest is there in the person of Christ, and Christ never dealt harshly with sinners. On the contrary, He loved them to come to Him because He alone could heal them and so render their sins harmless.

Secondly, it is as well to point out that the Sacrament was instituted by Christ to get rid of grave sins. We have got into the habit—and it is a good one—of confessing even when we have nothing but venial sins on our souls, but the main purpose of this Sacrament is for the forgiving of mortal sin. It is a comparatively easy way of doing this when we think of the great insult given to God by such sins. Therefore, when we have anything serious on our minds, we should go to confession as soon as possible and with great confidence, because that is what this Sacrament is for.

Your example will do much more than your words, and it is a good thing to let your children see that you receive this Sacrament frequently; then it will not be anything unusual for you to suggest that they come with you. Leave it to their free choice whether they do so or not, and also how often they confess, but point out to them that it is a Sacrament which we should all receive frequently, because it not only means the forgiveness of mortal sin, but also gives us the graces we need to avoid such sin.

See to it that your children know how to confess well, and that they are helped from time to time by your advice in a general way. Thus, you should be able to bring it home to them that we are all troubled from time to time as to whether such-and-such a thing is a sin or not, or sometimes how to confess certain things which we do know to be sins. In those circumstances the only thing to do is to tell the priest quite simply that we do not know, and then ask his advice.   He will do the rest.   Tell your children just how to put this to the priest in confession.   A word is all that is needed, because the priest is quite used to such difficulties, and so will be able to develop what the youth says in his own way, and thus give him that complete confidence which is such a necessary part of confession.

Make sure, too, that you continue with the family Rosary during the period of adolescence.   You may find that there are more difficulties than there were before, owing to the times at which people come in at night, but those can all be overcome by means of a little patience and good will on your part.

When in any doubt or difficulty, don't hesitate to consult a priest, either inside or outside of confession.   In the long run you will find by experience that sometimes the only thing you can do to help the adolescent girl and boy is to go on saying your prayers and give them good example.   You have a model in St. Monica, the mother of St. Augustine, who won such a marvellous victory in the end simply because she retained the confidence and the love of her son, and thus was enabled to give to the Church one of her greatest saints.

Note :—

The following books are recommended for the purpose of teaching the children to love the Story of Christ :

The Christ, the Son of God, by Abbé Fouard.   (Longmans).

Scripture Manuals for Catholic Schools and Colleges, by Sidney Smith, S.J.   (Burns Oates & Washbourne).

In the Footsteps of the Master, by H. V. Morton.   (Methuen).

Most of these books can be obtained through a good library, but no book should be allowed to take the place of the actual Gospel text itself.   You can obtain the Four Gospels in separate volumes from the C.T.S. or Burns Oates & Washbourne very cheaply.

CHAPTER NINETEEN

SPECIAL PROBLEMS
OF ADOLESCENCE

W E HAVE RESERVED FOR THIS CHAPTER THE DISCUSSION OF
some of the special problems which arise during
adolescence with a view to making the parents' task a
little easier in handling them. Many, if not all, of these
problems have a moral aspect, and so here we shall try to do
two things at one and the same time, namely, trace the origins
of the difficulties themselves, and also, in their solution, outline
the general principles of moral training during this period in
so far as that training concerns the parents.

During adolescence the temptations from without are
increasing in violence, while those strong supports from within
which should win through in the end are proving to be weaker
than was thought possible. The very atmosphere in which we
live has a great deal to do with this, since modern life goes on
in a materialistic world, believing only in success and in all
those methods which can lead to it, whether good or bad. In
general the only thought is for the pleasure which life can bring
to the individual. To live in such an atmosphere and not to
be contaminated by it needs heroic virtue, which is not usually
found in the majority of adolescents, because it is something
which has to be developed in the hard school of experience, and
by the constant teaching of priest and parents. Now, obviously,
this atmosphere, in which God is forgotten in self, creates many
problems for those who are trying to serve God in the world.
This is even more true of the adolescent, who is not yet fully
able to distinguish between the false attractions of all those
things which the world includes under the term " liberty," and
the true attraction of a reasoned submission to a code of laws
which God and the Church have promulgated throughout the

centuries. It is one of the many duties of parents, and perhaps their special obligation, to help their children through this difficult period, and the advice which is given in this chapter has for its object to help them in that task. Since these problems have many ramifications and angles, these brief notes will not take into consideration the task of either the priest or the teachers, but only that of the parents.

One of the first problems we come up against is that of the right attitude to matters which pertain to the virtue of purity. This is not the main problem of adolescence, although it is frequently regarded as such, and we have placed it first on our list simply because it gives us a line on other problems and on the best ways of dealing with them. It would be fair comment to say that, in our generation particularly, this problem has increased out of all proportion owing to the circumstances of our daily lives. However careful parents may be, they are not going to be able to prevent their children coming up against the modern attitude to some of these questions. Nowadays " sex " is considered to be the very hinge on which the whole of life turns. The damage to youth is done in such an insidious way that it is hard for us to avoid the conclusion that there is an organized attempt being made to corrupt our youth. The modern novel, the newspapers, magazines, films—even the advertisements—all tend to give too much importance to this matter of sex. One example will be sufficient to illustrate this. We are taught, by the laws of God, that adultery is a grave sin, and that to marry a person who has been divorced while the former partner still lives is equivalent in all things to adultery. Yet in how many cases, in the literature and the films provided for the recreation of this modern generation, is divorce made the main topic, and of course, everything comes out right in the end and true love is vindicated—usually at the expense of the Sacrament of Matrimony. It is only natural that some of this should penetrate into the receptive minds of our adolescents. and it is our duty as parents to rectify this evil so far as we can.

There is a tendency on the part of some parents to pass the responsibility for dealing with this subject of sex on to the priest in the confessional ; which is not altogether fair, because he has to be very careful what questions he asks in the Sacrament of

Penance, and also he usually gets the cases when they have gone much too far to respond easily to treatment. The best remedy lies in the home teaching, and you must see to it that your children receive that guidance which is necessary before it is too late. It should be made a very definite part of your duty as parents, and should not be left to others. But, naturally, you will ask, " How are we to set about it ? "

Well, if you have observed the rules already given for your guidance in the chapters devoted to the question of sex education then you have broken the back of the difficulty, because you will have established a bond of real unity and confidence between yourselves and your children which will result in their coming to you with their difficulties, rather than discussing them with other people who are by no means as qualified as you are to deal with them. That bond of union and confidence is very important and nothing must be allowed to break it down. Your children will also know that you do not mind questions, in fact, you welcome them, and what is more, answer them with the truth and not with some fable thought up on the spur of the moment to put the children off.

Even so, it is not sufficient to wait until you are asked questions. You have to do all that you can to see to it that those difficulties which are sure to arise sooner or later, or which you suspect have arisen already, are provided with a solution. This means a certain amount of thought and careful preparation on your part, but that is all part of your duty as parents, and the grace will always be there to help you to fulfil that obligation safely and well. You cannot have too much trust in that grace which is given you as parents from God, because He will never let you down, since the salvation of souls is at stake. This means, too, that your education of the children is bound to be a slow process, extending over the whole of their lives, through childhood and adolescence, until they reach maturity, and also that, in this matter of sex, it has to be proportioned to the age, sex and special needs of the child concerned. That is, perhaps, the most difficult part of the whole affair, because individuals differ so much that what will suit one may not suit another.

During these years of adolescence much clearer rules are needed on sex matters than those which are usually given, as also is a more detailed explanation of the two commandments dealing with sins against purity. It is not enough to say that the children will get all they need from their classes in religion at school, because they will not. In the first place, this is not a subject which is easily adapted for class work, especially in mixed classes, and secondly, the questions and the answers in the Catechism are formulated in such a way that they teach us what we should avoid rather than what we should do. Your children need to know what they should do in order to cultivate the virtue of purity, which is no negative thing, but rather one of the strongest and most virile of all the moral virtues. It is this positive teaching which falls to your lot. Suppose you start off with thoughts—often a great bother to adolescents.

Teach them exactly what is meant by an " impure thought," and what makes it a sin. In this connection you might point out that it is not so much the mere thinking such thoughts or the pictures which are formed in the imagination which make a sin against purity, but rather the will to think such things. There are some simple rules which govern this kind of thinking, and which can be taught with great profit. " Did you put the thought in your mind deliberately, knowing full well that what you were going to think about was something sinful? " " If it came all by itself, so to speak, did you keep it there deliberately once you knew that to continue thinking about it would be sinful? " Those are the test questions with regard to thoughts against this virtue, and if they are answered in the affirmative then there is serious sin there. The will to sin by thinking such things deliberately is necessary before there can be any mortal sin. Remember that.

You might pass on from thoughts to words, and speak about the morality of " smutty " stories and talk. It should be easy for you to point out when and why such things are sinful, especially if you keep in mind the advice which has already been given with regard to the sanctity of marriage and of all that marriage implies. Point out the difference between the ' vulgar " story and the sinful one, and indicate the fact that even the vulgar story, although it may not be gravely sinful, does much harm because it weakens our defences and also means that we are in company which will not hesitate to pass on to other stories which are not so harmless.

Once relations with the opposite sex have started, as they are bound to do sooner or later in the case of every adolescent, then special rules for conduct are necessary, and those rules should be given by the parents. It is not enough to give our children the right motives for doing good and avoiding evil ; we must also give them hard and fast rules which they can follow and which will safeguard them in their difficulties. Youth is highly inflammable material, and unless we understand that clearly, we are liable to put our children into danger almost without realizing that we are doing so. Tell them quite simply, but in general terms what they can do and what they must not do when out with persons of the opposite sex. Give them positive rules which will govern such things as kissing, for example. Tell them when it is sinful and when it is not, and above all, teach them never to cheapen either themselves or their companions. Teach them that it is a bad thing from every point of view to allow oneself to be kissed and fondled, because it weakens all our defences and also it means that we are giving up something which should mean so much if done properly, in circumstances which make it furtive and mean in every way. They will thank you for clear directions on these matters, because the adolescents of today, in spite of giving the appearance of knowing a great deal, are really not so well up in these matters as they would have us think.

If you have been careful to keep open house for your children's friends then you will soon know what kind of company they are keeping, and that will often give you a clue to some further development of these instructions which may be necessary. In this connection there are some books which can be put in the hands of the growing boy or girl with profit, but do not leave it all to books, because very often it is the personal touch which matters, and you are the only ones who really know the personal needs of your own children.

Teach them how to meet and deal with the ordinary temptations of everyday life, especially when they reach the age when they start to go out to work. That is a time when those outside influences of which we have already spoken come into their own. While the children were still at school the parents could do a very great deal to shelter and protect them, but now the world is going to try very hard to claim them for its own, and you will have to put up a hard fight to maintain your position and your influence. Much will depend on how much confidence they have in you and in your judgment. Now is the time for you to insist on those clear moral principles which govern our relations with others, and you must make quite sure that they understand both the principles themselves and the reasons behind them. Thus, for instance, it is not enough merely to point out that divorce is wrong ; you must go on to tell them that they must not get into the habit of mixing with married men or women or with those who have been divorced, and you must also tell them why such things are wrong, and why it is that there can be no exceptions to this rule. Perhaps this may mean that you yourselves will have to do a little healthy study of the Catholic position with regard to divorce, but that will not do you any harm. Here is a brief summary of some of the points which you might raise.

1. Begin with the authority of Christ and with His teaching on the matter as outlined for us in the Gospels. He allows no exception to this rule of the indissolubility of marriage, and He is the Son of God who came on this earth to teach us how we must live if we wish to get to heaven. It is also useful to add that He is the kindest of teachers, who would not have imposed such a grave obligation unless there was a real necessity for it. Consequently, apart from the authority of Christ, there must also be a real and a grave reason for this law.

2. Go on to the authority of the Church, which is the divinely appointed interpreter of the teachings of Christ. She has no power to make any exceptions in the matter simply because it is the teachings of her Master.

3. There are many reasons from the natural law why this rule should be so strict. In the first place, the very nature of marriage requires such a precaution, since the education of the children demands a permanent union, not a mere transitory one, and the principal object of marriage is the procreation and the education of the children. The woman's position in the home is thus safeguarded, too, because it is she who gives up most in marriage, especially her own security, and she is not going to

do that with such a glad heart or so entirely if she knows that the union into which she is entering may not stand the test of time. Point out, as well, that there is no need to rush into marriage, and that those who enter into this state do so of their own free will, knowing full well the conditions on which they make that contract. Therefore they would be well advised to take time and care to choose a partner with whom they can live for life, and that is what they are expected to do. If some exceptions were, in fact, made, then the security of the whole community would be threatened, as it is in fact threatened in those countries where divorce is allowed. It is not without significance that in the Soviet Union, where divorce used to be so easy, things are now being steadily tightened up to make it almost impossible.

Open discussion of such points as these will give your children much greater confidence when they have to face up to the arguments of others who are not Catholics, and who believe that there is nothing wrong in divorce. You will soon find occasions and opportunities for this discussion in modern literature, plays or films. Remember that not only is this firm doctrine of the Church the object of special attack today, but also that experience has shown that the number of our Catholic adolescents who marry divorced persons is increasing. For one thing, there are many more divorces! In this connection there is only one really safe rule we can give them, and that is to drop like a hot coal any person of the opposite sex with whom they may come into contact and who happens to be married or divorced. It has been proved that all protestations about the innocence of such friendships mean nothing, except the miserable state of self-deception which usually accompanies such affairs in Catholics. If you allow these friendships to go on then you may easily be faced with a situation which has gone too far to be remedied because you have been too weak and vacillating in the years when your authority might have turned the scales. Make a very strict rule with yourselves in this matter, and then you can rest in peace as far as your obligation in conscience is concerned.

In this connection it might be pointed out that a frank discussion on such matters with a priest will sometimes help to get the whole thing cleared up to the boy's or girl's satisfaction. Since the confessional does not give sufficient time for such a discussion, you should get in touch with the priest and ask him for his help. He will be only too ready to do all that he can, and will be able to put you on the right lines in dealing with it.

There is another problem which sometimes arises in connection with this matter of purity, and that is the difficulty of masturbation. A word or two about that in so far as it concerns the parents will not be at all out of place. The origin of the problem is simple. One of the first manifestations of the approach of puberty and adolescence is the fact of nocturnal emissions. If the boy—because this occurs more frequently in boys than in girls—if the boy has not been prepared beforehand for such an event then it is only too easy for him to be led by his own curiosity and by the physical pleasure attached to such emissions, and thus try to reproduce those sensations for himself and by his own movements. Now it is possible, and happens not infrequently, for this to go on for a long time, sometimes for a matter of years, before the boy happens to find out that such things are serious sins. By this time the habit has been formed and it may take a long time to cure. Many parents are careless about this matter and so fail to fulfil their obligations.

In general, if you have done all that you can to instruct your boy in these sex matters then you will have done something to prevent this habit from beginning. In this connection be careful about the following points which are sometimes overlooked. In the first place, start your instruction from the positive rather than from the negative angle, i.e., indicate the sanctity of the power which God has given us to transmit life, and also that He has given us this power years before we are to use it in marriage in order that we may train ourselves to use it properly and with control. It is a sacred trust which must not be abused. You should also point out the moral harmlessness of such things as these nocturnal emissions, which are nature's way of relieving tension, and also the need for being absolutely frank with our confessor on matters of purity. You should be able to work into your talks some general advice on the way to confess such things as this, and also all sins whether of thought, word or deed.

Over and above this, you can take certain precautions. You should insist on personal cleanliness, sufficient exercise and the avoiding of very heavy meals just before going to bed. Supervision of reading matter is important, and in this connection you should not allow the boy to become what is usually called a "book-worm." If, in spite of all your precautions, you find that the boy is beginning to contract the habit, what should you do? Obviously, you will have to move with caution, and my advice to you is not to leave it all to the priest in confession, because it is not at all certain that the boy is actually confessing this particular thing, or getting the advice which he needs. You will have to act, remembering that the longer you leave it the worse it is going to get. Obviously, it is the father's obligation to deal with this matter, and the boy himself will feel much better about it if it comes from the father.

Choose your time and opportunity, and then launch straight into the subject. There is no need to point out that you have reason to believe that the boy is contracting this habit. Begin by indicating that it is a common thing for boys to be troubled by such temptations and that you want to prevent any harm from coming to your son because of them. That is as good an introduction as any. Then keep the following points in mind :—

(a). The age you have to watch is normally between 12-14. Most boys think that there is something peculiar about them because they have these temptations, and seem to think that others escape without having them at all. Correct that first of all, by pointing out that the feelings which give rise to these temptations are so normal that if we did not have them then there *might* be something wrong with us.

(b). Some boys may not even know that this is a serious sin. This may come from lack of the preliminary sex instructions which you should have given before puberty, or it may be through the influence and the teaching of older companions. Point out the truth, i.e., that if this temptation is consented to fully then it is a serious sin and as such it has to be confessed. You can use this opportunity for pointing out once more the sanctity of this power which God has given us for the purpose of producing new life. Give the boy all the motives you can for resisting these temptations, and don't forget to mention that control over this urge is the thing which develops character most of all, because it means that our minds have reached a stage of great maturity and power over our bodies. Teach a positive formula for confessing these sins, such as " I accuse myself of having committed impure actions by myself so many times, causing pollution."

(c). Some people still seem to have the old-fashioned idea that if this habit takes a hold on the boy it will bring with it some physical damage to health or that he will end up in a mental institution. Indeed, it is not unknown for parents to teach these things to their children in the hope of breaking down this habit. Such a thing is very wrong, and only serves to increase the boy's mental conflict. The truth is that this action has its root in a perfectly normal and natural inclination which God has placed in the body of man for the benefit of the human race. Consent to it outside marriage is a sin, because we are misusing a power which God has destined for a definite purpose. We are human beings, and as such are expected to control this urge and keep it in its proper paths.

This urge is just another appetite of the human body, and has to be thought of as such. Remember that, in the long run, this habit—if not the isolated acts—has its root in some kind of rebellion, either against our circumstances, our lives or perhaps against our weakness in competition with others. This is so true that sometimes the cure comes through encouragement and success in small matters. This is important, because you can do a great deal to see to it that the boy does manage to succeed in these small things, and you can praise him for those minor triumphs. Also, once you can get him to have a right attitude with regard to this then you are more than half way to overcoming it.

Depression can sometimes lead to sins of this kind in adolescents, and you should deal with this by pointing out that there is never any need for despair in the life of a Catholic, because God is always with us and will never let us be tempted more than our strength can stand. In a way, this trial is a good thing, because it is by overcoming it that we finally reach the full perfection of manhood. It is only when we have this control that we can be said to be men in the fullest sense of the word.   Failures need not worry us, because this control is not won in a day, but once it is acquired then it is just as hard to lose as it was to attain.   Every time we resist makes it much easier to resist the next time.   It is this constant struggle that God demands of us, and provided we give Him our loyal co-operation then we can safely leave it to Him to decide when we shall actually gain the complete victory.   He alone knows just how much of a trial we need in order to fit us for the tasks which He has for us in the future.

(d).   Stress the need for complete frankness in confession, and also the fact that, in order to overcome this habit and this temptation, we have need of the Sacraments, especially Confession and Holy Communion.   We receive Our Lord in Communion because we have need of this life-giving food, which alone can give us the strength to fight hard and to win through.

(e).   Together with the mental attitude to this struggle one of the best methods of attacking the actual temptations is to resist always for a day, and not to think of what has happened in the past or of what is to come tomorrow.   The reason why this helps a good deal is because of the mental make-up of the adolescent.   He finds it very difficult, as does the child, to realize that time does not really matter.   A month may seem fairly short to us as adults, but it seems an age to the child and also to the adolescent, who still retains many of the traits of childhood.   On the contrary, anyone can resist for a day, provided that he does not look back on the number of days he has already resisted, or forward to the length of time he has still to fight.   The secret of success in this matter is to fight from day to day, without thought of tomorrow, which may, after all, never come.

(f).   With regard to the physical advice which we can give, here are some things which do help.   Cleanliness of body we have already stressed, together with a certain amount of physical exercise which will help the adolescent to get to sleep quickly.   If the force of the temptation is more noticed in the early morning, when he first wakes up, that may easily be due to a full bladder which tends to press on certain nerve centres and thus cause sensations and sometimes erections.   The solution to that is simple.   Normally it is a very bad thing for the boy to be allowed to stay in bed for any length of time after waking up. He should be trained to get up at once and dress himself. If you have been careful to fix a reasonable hour for this morning rising then you will not have to worry too much about this angle of it, but do watch things during holiday periods, when parents are inclined to encourage their children to stay in bed and have a rest. That may not be a good thing in every case.

Apart from this, mental training will help a good deal, and especially the rejecting at once of certain thoughts which may be quite harmless in themselves but which have a remote connection with this action. Such thoughts need not be sensual ones at all ; they may be thoughts of despondency, feelings of discouragement or doubt of one's own ability to meet certain situations, but in the adolescent they can have a very bad effect and a great influence in this matter of sex. The reason is obvious. It is because this action is not only a source of pleasure, but has the added spice of being forbidden. It is hidden from all eyes, except those of God, and so constitutes a rebellion which does not pass into the world of reality. It does not bring the boy into conflict with the external world at all until much later, when there is question of his having to confess it. It is very important for us to understand this aspect of the question, because it lies at the root of this habit in very many adolescents, and until it is tackled then all our attempts to deal with this temptation successfully will fail.

For the same reason it is dangerous to allow the adolescent to indulge in much day-dreaming, because sooner or later those dreams will take on a sexual aspect which may easily be a cause of the persisting of this habit against all efforts to overcome it. There is only one thing to be done in such cases, and that is to train the mind to reject those day-dreams and come back into the world of strict reality. The weakest spot of this habit is at the same time the thing which makes it persist, namely, the selfishness which is behind it, and here we are using that word selfish in its widest meaning, i.e., the love of and the concentration on self to the exclusion of other things which are more important.

We should be ever sympathetic and helpful about this matter, because it does worry the adolescent a great deal more than we might think. He wants to overcome it, and yet the habit is perhaps very strongly rooted and the fight seems endless. We must do all that we can to give him our full support and also our constant love and encouragement. Those things are very precious to him and he knows that they help.

We have discussed this habit from the viewpoint of the boy, but that does not mean to say that it cannot occur also in girls at this age of puberty and later. However, normally it is not so prevalent in girls as it is in boys, and the usual precautions, especially the physical ones, are much more effective. The girl may feel the same type of urge, but usually it is later on in adolescence and is normally due to the fact that she has allowed herself to be unduly stimulated in her senses by the company she keeps. You can do a great deal to help to prevent this by keeping a close watch over your children's friends, especially as they grow older. There will be no need to say more about this here, because the same rules apply as before. The chief thing is always the mental attitude. However, one thing may be noted in passing. Girls do not usually know how to confess such things, and therein lies a danger that the habit may go on for a long time without any effective check from the priest in the Sacrament of Penance, for the simple reason that he does not know anything about it. The mother should have confidence enough in her children to be able to talk about this to the growing girl sufficiently clearly to make her realize that it is a sin, and also how it has to be confessed.

If we have dwelt at some length on this matter in this chapter it is only because experience has proved that parents do not take sufficient notice of it, and also that they are sometimes afraid to deal with it because they do not know how. Also some people seem to have the idea that this could never happen to one of their children—they have been too well brought up. That is a snare and a delusion, as experience has proved.

It is your duty, as parents, to see to it that your children receive from you all the help they need in order to save their souls, and this matter is of great importance. You should not shirk your responsibilities, but shoulder them bravely, because the grace will never be wanting. Your words have a special efficacy simply because you *are* the parents.

CHAPTER TWENTY

FURTHER PROBLEMS

ANOTHER PROBLEM WHICH MAY COME YOUR WAY CONCERNS both the boys and the girls, but in this case more particularly the latter. It is a well known fact that nearly all adolescents tend to be hero-worshippers, and this is not at all a bad thing, because it springs from their natural high ideals. This trait can be of very great use to us in the teaching of religion to the adolescent, because, if we go about it in the right way, we can make Christ their Hero. However, not infrequently, this characteristic has manifestations which are not quite so healthy. Thus, for instance, we often find that girls tend to get what is usually called a " crush " on some person older than themselves. They try to copy them in everything they do, their mannerisms, way of walking and talking and so on. Now, this need not be a very serious problem in every case, because normally it tends to right itself owing to the very fluid character of the adolescent's affections and also because the person concerned is not always one of the domestic scene, but someone whom the adolescent does not meet very frequently. But when it is a question of someone whom they do meet frequently, whether of the same or the opposite sex, then there may be trouble. Such friendships are obviously unhealthy if they go too far, and your first difficulty is to know when they *are* going too far. Usually the very behaviour of the adolescents will give you your first clue. They become moody and very jealous if the person concerned shows any attentions to anyone except themselves, and in general, they show an exaggerated affection for that person. They are constantly talking about this person and making opportunities for meeting him or her. If the object of this adolescent affection is in any way sensible then it will be quite easy for them to deal with the situation. There is need for a good deal of bluntness and sometimes what almost amounts to cruelty, but it pays in the long run. If you think that the person is of this type, then have a word or two with him or her, because it is just possible that he or she is not alive to the situation as it stands. Then he or she will soon be able to put it right.

However, it does happen now and again—fortunately not too frequently—that the object of this adolescent affection is not at all a suitable person from your point of view. Perhaps he or she may be one of those people who actually like that sort of affection and tend to foster it rather than getting rid of it at the first opportunity. Then what are you to do? Your actions will, of course, depend very much on the gravity of the general situation, taking into account the person concerned as well as the character of your child. Perhaps a word or two to the child will be quite sufficient to meet the case, and if so, do not hesitate to speak out, but do make sure first of all that you are not doing so just out of a sense of jealousy because your child shows friendship for someone outside the family circle and a little older. It is quite easy to imagine wrong where there is nothing at all but pure friendship. Be open with yourself first of all, but once you are sure that the friendship is not a good one, then you must be prepared to act.

If a word in season has not put a stop to the whole thing then you may even have to go so far as to forbid the child to associate with that person altogether. At the same time, you should not be merely negative in your attitude to this sort of thing, but try to provide distractions by getting the child to associate with others of her own age. You will find that, usually, this is sufficient to finish the whole affair without more interference on your part. Keep in mind that the trouble usually comes from the adolescent, and not from the older person. There are, of course, exceptions to this, but, fortunately, they are few and far between.

Perhaps a more general word of warning about this kind of thing may not be out of place here, especially since it is a particular fault of the present generation. Some of you may have seen, and you will all have heard about, those absurd scenes which take place outside the stage-doors of theatres and at the hotels of visiting film stars. Indeed, a sane observer from another planet would have good reason for thinking that our generation was slightly unbalanced if he could witness some of the things which happen in this connection. There is no need for you to think that your children will be quite so silly as all that, because the Faith has a great influence on people so far as keeping them relatively sane is concerned, thank goodness! However, it is just as well to be on your guard against it and to kill anything like that as soon as it appears by the judicious use of ridicule. I know that we have said, as a general rule, that ridicule is not a weapon which should be used against the fancies and the foibles of the adolescents, but there are exceptions to that rule, and this is one of them. You are not attempting to ridicule the person, but the absurdity of the thing they are doing. Once let the children see that it is really absurd and at the same time keep them away from company where such things are the usual topic of conversation and you will have done a great deal to cure anything like this at the very outset. Where possible, do try to get them interested in some other kind of recreation apart from the films—outdoor recreation, if at all possible. Give them opportunities for meeting suitable friends, and always keep open house for them, even though it may cost you an effort at times. Join in their conversations and try to draw them out about things in general. Never rebuff them when they attempt to talk to you. One of the greatest virtues of parents is that of being good listeners. There should be no need for these warnings, but facts have proved that this is one of the common complaints that adolescents have against their parents, namely, that they will not listen to the adolescents' point of view and do not seem to want to discuss things with them.

Another adolescent problem is connected with clothes. These do not seem to fit for very long at this age, especially in the case of the boys, while the girls seem to suffer from a form of what may be termed " clothes-madness ". Both of these manifestations, however horrid they may be, are very natural. The boy cannot help the rate at which his body is growing, or the fact that his taste in clothes is not yet adult and mature. It is also a very natural thing that the girl should like to be well and smartly dressed, and in general one may say with truth that most parents are not sympathetic enough with their adolescent children in this respect. As in most other things in life, of course, there are the two extremes to be avoided. We do not want our children to be untidy, but at the same time we must not encourage a vanity which knows no bounds, and it has to be admitted that some girls do tend to go to extremes in this matter, and that in two ways. First of all, they love to dress beyond their age, thus giving the impression of being at least two years (or even more) older than they really are. This is an attempt to reach maturity before its time, and the mother can usually deal with it by pointing out that one of the greatest virtues in life is to take what comes in season. There is a right time for everything, and the girl will soon be unable to wear dresses and suits which become her present age and build. It is a great pity to cut out a whole " season " from our lives by anticipating things too much. On the other hand, some girls are extravagant in the number of clothes they seem to need, and this has to be put down, because they will get worse, not better, unless you take them in hand now. There are several ways in which this can be done. One way is to encourage them to make their own clothes. This has the advantage of cutting down the demand, because time is limited. Another very good way is to give them a dress allowance for the year, and then they know how much they have to spend on clothes and can make their plans accordingly. Don't think that this is a futile method, because it is based on the adolescent mind and attitude to these things. Look at it in this way. You know your average expenditure on clothes for your adolescent daughter in the course of one year. Now, you are going to have to spend this on her anyway, so why not let her administer this same amount of money over the course of the year ? You may object that she will not buy the right things and that therefore the money would be wasted. While there is something to be said for that objection, you should also think of the advantages. You still have the rôle of adviser on this matter of clothes, and can step in, if you feel that you must, when things are getting absurd. Your daughter will learn what it means to have to plan for a certain sum of money and to make it last, and this will have the added advantage of making her more careful and also of preparing her for the future when she has to do the planning in her own home. You will find that she does not complain so often about not having new clothes either, because she knows that she is to blame.

A girl of this age is naturally proud of her looks and likes to be smartly dressed, and we would not really have it otherwise because then there would be something wrong. At the same time you might point out that there are limits to such lawful vanity, and those limits should be observed.

If she is earning money, then things may be a little different, because, while it is right and proper that she should contribute something to the general funds of the home, it is not right—unless there is a very good reason—to deprive her of all that she earns. If you do that then you are only setting up a basis for a valid complaint that your action is unfair, and it is always a bad thing to make an adolescent feel resentful. Your general authority and power for good will weaken. Let her keep at least a part of what she earns in order to buy her own clothes. You are saving that much from the general funds in any case, and it does make her feel much more independent. The same, of course, is true in the case of the boy. If you have been careful not to give in to every whim and fancy during early childhood then you can be quite sure that your judgment on these matters will be respected and followed out to the letter. Nor will you have discontented children.

Now we come to the last in this series of adolescent problems, that which is sometimes described as the religious-indifference phase. Let us make it quite clear that certain writers have tended to over-emphasize this problem; according to them, all adolescents, without exception, have to go through this trial. That may be true of non-Catholic boys and girls, and probably is, but it is certainly not true of Catholics. However, even with us trouble does arise from time to time, and that in two forms, which are both worth noticing here. The first of these two forms is the more common. When the adolescent goes out to work, or perhaps even when he is still at school, he will come across companions who love to argue about religious matters. In the Army, for instance, it is one of the favourite topics of conversation and of argument. Perhaps he finds that he is not sufficiently well up in the truths of his religion to be able to answer all the difficulties which are put to him. This may give him a serious worry about his Faith and its truth.

This worry can be dealt with if parents themselves are well informed on such matters and also if they are always willing to listen to their children's conversations. There are several ways of dealing with this problem. You can find out the answers for yourselves and then bring them up in general conversation, which is a very good method indeed, because it also makes sure that you know your Faith and are able to give some at least of the answers to the difficulties which can be put up against it. Another solution is to seek advice from a priest, who will be able to advise you as to literature, etc., which will provide the necessary answers. Alternatively, you might suggest that the boy or girl should join the local parish study circle. This will only take up one or two nights a week, and is well worth it in any case, as we have pointed out in an earlier chapter. At the very least, you can always draw adolescents out in conversation and thus discover the problems and the difficulties which affect them most; then you can get hold of such things as C.T.S. pamphlets on the subject, which will give them enough information to set their minds at rest.

But it is by no means sufficient to set their minds at ease on these matters, you have to make use of these very difficulties to deepen their faith and their religion. You can do this, in the first place, by pointing out that such a state of affairs is not uncommon, because God does not intend to force anyone to give Him the love and the service which are His due from us as His creatures. He lays down the laws which have to be obeyed but He will neither force our minds nor our wills. That obedience must be our free gift to Him.

Because of this attitude God has towards the whole question of our free consent in matters of Faith, it follows that there are bound to be difficulties from time to time. If things were all plain and clear to the human reason then there would be nothing we could do but believe, and thus faith would no longer be a virtue; it would be an intellectual necessity. We have Christ's word for the truth of what we believe, but the truths themselves remain veiled in mystery.

Such arguments as these are very useful for the adolescent's peace of mind rather than for defence against the attacks of others, and they should always be supplied and repeated from time to time in various forms.

However, this religious indifference may take a much more serious form. Modern life has no time for religion, and it demonstrates this point of view by doing all it can to ridicule it as something which is only fit for women and hysterical girls! Many of the arguments which are hurled against our Faith by others are intended to have just this effect, i.e., to drive youth away from that Faith. Now and again this kind of thing succeeds in having some effect on the adolescent mind, especially since the influence of companions is very strong at this age, and no adolescent likes being ridiculed for something which he is told is for " old women ". It is altogether a nasty attack, and very dangerous in certain cases. It needs strong courage to persist in one's religious duties in the face of chaff and ridicule such as this from friends and companions at work.

It is important to realize that, should this problem ever arise in your case, it is by no means an easy one to solve satisfactorily. Especially you must not leave it alone in the hope that it will solve itself. Some people would have you believe that all adolescents have to go through this some time or other, and that there is nothing to worry about because it will all come right in the end. Your own parental common sense, however, will certainly tell you that something should be done about this situation, and you are quite right. The difficulty is to know exactly the best method of dealing with it, so as to restore fully the sense of balance and responsibility to the adolescent. You are not dealing with a child any longer, but with a boy or girl on the very threshold of maturity, and if you are at all careless in handling this situation then you may find that you have turned him or her away from religion altogether. Obviously, what we must do if we can is to use this situation in order to make their religious instinct even stronger than it was before the crisis came upon them. Pray about it frequently, because you have a right to the graces which are necessary to fulfil your obligation as parents, and those graces yield to prayer.

First of all, you should try to make an effort to discover the real cause behind this religious indifference. Until you know that then all your attempts to find a solution may easily be directed at the wrong point in the defence which the adolescent is sure to put up. Real success will only come when you are in a position to put forward the right motives to defeat the objection which lies at the root of this difficulty. Perhaps you may find this cause in their companions or in some moral problem which they feel unable to cope with and which has caused a kind of religious despair ; perhaps the root is in false arguments which they have heard and to which they have no ready answer—there are so many possibilities that it would never be possible to list them all here. Slowly—especially by winning their confidence, and by listening to their conversations carefully—you will get at what is behind this new attitude towards religion. Once you have managed to do that, then it will not be so difficult to provide the cure in the form of arguments which will tend to overcome the difficulty. If you do not feel very sure of yourselves go to see your parish priest and tell him what has happened. He will help you as far as he can. Remember that the Church has an answer to all our problems, but sometimes we have to seek hard before we find it.

Whether this particular difficulty develops or not, you should make sure, during this stage of development, to provide once again the general arguments for the need of religion which will already have been taught either by you or by the teachers or the priests in the school. For that reason we shall include here a very brief summary of these basic arguments just to refresh your memories.

Religion can be considered under at least three different aspects, all of them useful to remember, viz :—

(a) It is a direct result of the mere fact of creation, which necessarily implies a direct dependence on God for all that we are and for all that we have. In this sense it can be thought of as a debt which we are bound to pay to God and which includes such things as love, obedience, respect and adoration gratitude and worship, whether personal or social. It is moreover, a debt which must be paid, not in our own coin, bu in God's, since He has told us exactly how He wishes us to pay it.

You can compare the love we show God through religion an

the obedience we owe to Him to the love and the respect which we give to our parents. They both have the same cause, namely, the fact that, just as we depend on our parents in many things, so we depend on God for a great deal more. This is a strict duty, and duties are not always easy!

(b) The coming of Christ on this earth as Man, and the Redemption which He won for us by His death on the Cross give us the supreme cause for gratitude to God for His benefits and also a complete expression of our religious obligations, through a form of worship and also a code of precepts which have to be obeyed.

The fact that there is another life after death, and a life which is eternal and final would itself be enough to justify the necessity of religion for all men.

(c) Lastly, it is the perfect expression of all our inner and secret sentiments and longings. Man desires happiness, and his own bitter experience tells him that he cannot find that perfect happiness here on this earth. It does, however, await him in the next life provided that he is faithful to the commands of God, which are given to him in a simple fashion by Christ and the Church. To deny religion implies that there is nothing at all wrong in such things as murder, theft, adultery and so on, because without the eternal sanction of the next life such prohibitions would be useless. If there were only one end for us all then what would be the use of our keeping such laws, which are often hard and inconvenient?

This brief summary will help you to collect your arguments under clear headings and present them to the youth in ordinary conversation.

This chapter would not be complete without a word or two about that mental religious illness which we call scruples. First, let us deal with this from the point of view of the parents. Those parents who are themselves the victims of such religious scruples should be very careful indeed not to pass on this malady to their children. This is such a very easy thing to do that the warning is really necessary. Just as it is possible for nervous parents to infect the child with their fear, so it is very likely that a parent with scruples will cause them to appear in the children. The root of all, or at least nearly all, of the common adolescent disorders is fear—and scruples are a manifestation of fear mingled with pride. Such a combination is very dangerous, and such parents owe it to their children to overcome their scruples, not merely from the religious point of view, but mainly because of the bad effect these can have on their children.

In spite of all our care, however, scruples are fairly common at this period of the child's life, and if they are allowed to develop unchecked will be ever so much more difficult to cure later on. Naturally, the priest is the one to deal with the confessional angle of this question, but that does not mean to say that the parents are helpless, by any means, or free from all obligation to do what they can to help. Here are a few simple yet effective rules which will give you some idea of the line your action should take if you find that your boy or girl is beginning to be scrupulous.

First of all, realize the cause—a wrong attitude towards God, generally. Point out that God is a loving Father, not a policeman looking for our slightest fault in order to condemn us at once. The love and the service of God through our religion should be easy and a help to us, not a hindrance ; and once we allow scruples to develop in our dealings with Him then we are showing Him that we do not really trust Him sufficiently. True love casts out fear—and you can drive this point home with many stories from the Gospels. After all, Our Lord's favourite phrase to sinners was " Fear not."

Impress on them the need for strict obedience to their confessor, because so long as we do as we are told then we cannot go wrong. Our confessor takes God's place in our regard, and so we must obey him if we wish to serve God properly. If he should be wrong that does not make any difference, because the responsibility is his, not ours. This is the only really safe rule to follow in order to get rid of scruples completely—" Do as you are told."

We should never allow scruples to keep us away from God, because if we do then the devil has achieved his purpose. Especially we should never let them keep us from our regular confession and Holy Communion. This is a spiritual illness, which needs those powerful medicines to cure it. If the scruples are concerned with such matters as bad thoughts, then you should insist once more on the simple rules which have already been given for dealing with such things.

The frequent repetition of the act of Hope, said slowly and with deep attention, can do much to get rid of the wrong attitude towards God which is so frequently at the root of all scruples. Trust in God is the only thing for all of us on this earth if we wish to get to heaven—and we have plenty of motives for that trust. Point out the main ones several times until they go home to the adolescent.

Insist on a real devotion to the Mother of God. Your children should have learnt to have a deep love for Mary, Mother of God and Mother of men, before they reach manhood or womanhood. The family Rosary should be said every day, no matter how difficult it may be to arrange it at times. They should be accustomed to look on Mary as their Mother in heaven, and you should speak to them often about this theme, pointing out that she is all-powerful with her Son, as the marriage feast at Cana demonstrates for us quite clearly. He has given her charge over us, and we need never have any fear where she is concerned, because it is her delight to help us. We should tell her of our needs, our hopes and our fears, and she will give us the benefit not merely of her counsel and good advice but also of her effective assistance to draw us ever nearer to her Son.

Tell them the story of Our Lady's appearances to the children at Fatima, and then point out the real significance of this, namely, that the Mother of God was asking for our help to save the world from the dreadful consequences of its rejection of the Redemption won for us all by Christ. Our Lady came to warn us all, but also to ask for our help, too. This should be an inspiration to them to co-operate with her and with Christ in this great task. In this way you will teach them practical charity and consideration for others, and you will make sure that their religion really does mean effective participation in the Mystical Body of Christ—a thing which is demanded of us all.

Point out to them that there are many countries where the open profession of the Catholic Faith is now impossible. There, the faithful suffer from a dreadful persecution—and they are our brothers and sisters in Christ. We are very lucky, because we can practise our religion openly and without fear. Therefore we should often think of those who are so much less fortunate, and do what we can, by our prayers and good works, especially through the Sacrifice of the Mass, to help them. Charity demands that from us as fellow members of the Church of Christ.

CHAPTER TWENTY-ONE

VOCATION AND GUIDANCE

ONE OF THE CHARACTERISTICS OF CHILDHOOD IS THAT IT
does not worry very much about the future. The
present is all-important to the child, and the future
seems a very long way away ; but, as childhood passes into
adolescence, then the problem of the future intrudes itself little
by little into the picture until finally it overshadows everything
else and colours the whole period of later adolescence and early
manhood. The adolescent sees life before him, and in spite
of his ideals he knows almost instinctively that it is a hard life.
He realizes that, very soon now, he will have to go out into the
world without many of the safeguards which he has had up to
now, and will have to make his own living. That, in itself,
implies a new responsibility. Once again, it would not be
possible to discuss all the varied problems which can arise from
such a situation, because, for one thing, the individual characteristics and the family circumstances will play a great part
in the solution of those difficulties in individual cases. So only
some general principles can be suggested which may help
parents, and also the adolescents themselves, not merely in the
choice of a career, but also in the foundation of a sound mental
attitude towards this important factor in human life.

In spite of his youth the adolescent will have already given a
certain amount of thought to the general lines on which he
would like to plan his future. In this sense the choice before
him is limited. Usually he does not think in terms of celibacy
unless that implies either the priesthood or a religious life, since
for the single man or woman living in the world youth has
nothing but pity—a wrong attitude, perhaps, but one which is
natural to its age and experience. The choice is therefore

limited to either marriage or the religious life ; which does not necessarily mean that the adolescent has any very definite ideas about either state. Like most other problems of this age, this one begins in a vague fashion, since we are still dealing with the stage of formation.

There is, however, another and more definite aspect of this problem, namely, that of the choice of a career in the world, and that is nearly always more difficult of solution, since youth, in spite of its airs of superiority and confidence, is really very diffident as to its own capabilities. There is the ever-growing realization that the time is fast approaching when a definite step has to be taken and a choice made which may well determine the whole shape of the future. On the choice of a suitable career may easily depend the ability to make a decent home for a future wife and children. The actual choice may, in fact, be limited by family circumstances as well as by other individual factors, but it is still sufficiently varied to be bewildering to the adolescent. For this reason he relies very much on his parents for guidance, and consequently, as so often happens, the whole problem comes to rest on their shoulders. Therefore, the advice which is offered in this chapter is directed especially to the parents, in the hope that it may help them to see the general lines on which they should work in order to reach a satisfactory solution to this problem.

The need for their guidance is obvious. Youth cannot be expected to have the experience of age, nor can the adolescents see clearly all the advantages and the disadvantages of the different careers which are open to them. So often they are blinded by the very variety of the choice itself, or else they may be attracted by the atmosphere of glamour which appears to surround some careers, more than by a full understanding of what those careers imply. The parents, with their knowledge of the family circumstances and also of the capabilities of their children, should be the ones who can give the best advice to the adolescent who is confronted with this problem.

First of all, let us consider the question of a religious vocation, either to the priesthood or to a religious order of men or women.

It should not be necessary to point out that parents should not raise any objections if their sons or daughters show signs of a religious vocation ; and yet experience teaches us that not a few parents are really afraid of such a thing. Sometimes they go to the extent of speaking against the religious life as something rather useless, especially when compared with the married state. Needless to say, such an attitude is entirely wrong and un-Catholic, and it usually comes from a misconception of the meaning of the religious life. If it should be God's will that a boy or girl undertakes such a state of life then it would be very wrong for the parents to object. We have already pointed out that education should be directed primarily towards the salvation of the souls of the children and not to merely material ends. The sacrifice made by those who devote their lives to God is a very glorious one, and leads to the salvation of many souls who would otherwise be lost, not to mention the fact that it also brings great blessings down on the whole family. Catholic parents should understand that the very best gift they can give to God is this gift of their children. Far from opposing such a sacrifice they should encourage it, no matter what it may cost them.

On the other hand, parents should not go to the other extreme of forcing a vocation simply because they would like one of their sons to be a priest or one of their daughters a nun. Such an action would be equally wrong, and it should be remembered that it is the child who has to have the vocation— not the parents! Let us speak quite frankly with regard to this matter. Some parents are inclined to see only the glamour of the priesthood, thus losing sight of its sacrifices and hardships. Others think of it as the best possible career for their sons, with the added advantage that by means of it they can avoid certain of the hardships which fall on others, particularly military service. All such motives should be completely excluded from your mind, and you should never force a vocation where there is none.

This does not mean that parents should not do all they can to put the ideals of the priesthood and the religious life before their children. They should talk to them about it and let them see the glory of this sacrifice quite clearly ; they should encourage them to pray about it in order to see if God is calling them to such a state of life. Meanwhile they should foster a spirit of true piety in their children, encouraging them to go to Mass frequently and to the Sacraments ; they can leave the rest to Almighty God.

From the parents' point of view, a vocation to the priesthood or to the religious life usually means a good deal of material sacrifice, but this should be made cheerfully, safe in the knowledge that God is not to be outdone in generosity. Not the least of these sacrifices is the fact that their children will be separated from them, at least to a certain extent, and dedicated to the service of God ; but for a true Catholic that should not be a difficult cross to carry. Given a good Catholic home and education, good health, with a reasonable intelligence and, what is still more important, solid piety, there is every reason why parents should be proud if they see their children developing a religious vocation.

Consequently, when you begin to speak to your children about the future make sure that you put this element of the choice before them clearly, so that they have time to think and to pray about it. Your own personal inclinations may be against such a sacrifice, but that is no reason why you should neglect to lay the details of it before your children, and in the *first* place, which is the only place for the service of God.

Here are some of the ideas which you should put before them.

Everyone has a special vocation from God, no matter in what particular state of life it may be exercised. This is just as true of the married man or woman as it is of the priest or nun. First of all, we all have the great vocation of saving our souls, and that through and in our life in this world. Salvation will be attained by living a human life in a superhuman way through the grace which God gives us and in accordance with His will. Therefore the very first thing we all have to do is to find out in which particular state of life God wishes us to save our souls. He may call us to the life of the priesthood or to that of a religious order ; He may wish us to love and serve Him in the married state or even by a single life in the world, and it is of the greatest importance that we should make the correct choice, in accordance with the will of God. How is that to be done ?

There are several things we must do in order to make quite sure that we choose correctly. We must first of all ask God, through our prayers, to show us what He wishes us to do. That prayer will not go unheard, and He will give us His grace to enlighten our minds, especially if He has chosen us for the religious life or for the priesthood. The best time for such prayer is, of course, after Holy Communion, when Our Lord is with us in an intimate way.

Next, we must give the whole subject earnest thought. We should think about these three possibilities, with all they imply. We must also get to know ourselves, with our inclinations and desires ; because God will use those inclinations to indicate to us the way we should choose to serve Him. Then, too, we should get to know something about the priesthood and the religious life ; about the married state, with its obligations and its advantages, as well as the single life in the world. Then we shall see more clearly what is before us in those states, and so be able to choose with greater ease between them.

Lastly, since we cannot be expected to know all the advantages and the disadvantages of these various states by our own instincts, we should take advice about them from people who know what they are talking about, and also read some books on the subject. On the question of a religious vocation it is best to consult a priest both inside and outside the confessional. The priest who usually hears your confession will be able to give you some good advice which will come from his intimate knowledge of the state of your soul and your whole character. He will also be able to guide your reading on the whole subject of the religious vocation. Parents can help you with their knowledge of the other two states.

If you feel that God is calling you to a life of self-sacrifice for others in the religious state, then naturally the next step will be to discover *where* you are to fulfil that call. There are very many factors which influence this decision, and we cannot discuss them all here, although it is hoped that we shall be able to do so in another book in this series. In general, find out about the priesthood, about the various religious orders ; take advice on the matter, especially from your confessor—and don't forget your own temperament, which is also a gift from God and which will have to fit in to whatever life you lead in this world. Remember that this call is a very glorious thing, but that it implies much hard work and much sacrifice. See it from all sides, with its advantages and disadvantages; remember that it is God who chooses you for this state of life, and also remember that at times all our inclinations may be against making this sacrifice at first. The devil will naturally do all that he can to prevent you from giving your consent to it, because he knows well how much good will follow from it. Do not be surprised, therefore, if it is a difficult sacrifice to make or if others put difficulties in your way. If God wants you, then it is your duty to follow Him. Do it with all your heart.

After this deliberation, consultation with others and earnest prayer, you should be able to make your decision. If you think that God has called you to the life of a religious or of a priest then you should start at once to prepare your soul for that great grace. This means solid piety which will serve as a foundation for your future training. Learn now to make sacrifices for Him who has called you to this state, especially by going to Mass as frequently as you can and by reception of the Sacraments. Bend all your energies to the acquiring of solid virtue which will stand the test of time and which is not based on mere sentiment, but on the true love of God. Above all, be absolutely frank and open with the priest in confession and then he will be able to do much to guide your steps.

Once you know that God has *not* chosen you for the religious life then you can turn your attention to the other two states. Since we shall have more to say about these later on in this chapter we can leave this subject for the moment and return to our advice for parents.

It may seem very obvious and even trite to say that we should never force an adolescent into a job which does not suit him, but the remark is rendered necessary by the very frequency with which such a mistake is made. At the very outset, then, let us have a right attitude to this important question of a career in life. Once you know that your child has decided against a religious vocation then this matter of a suitable employment will become ever more pressing as time goes on and your own family circumstances may make it even more urgent. In spite of all this, never force a youth to take an employment to which he or she does not feel attracted. The reason for this is very simple.

Man's life on earth may not be a bed of roses, but that does not mean to say that he should choose deliberately to sleep on thorns—unless, of course, some higher spiritual motive should prompt that action! We are all called to a certain degree of spiritual perfection in our human lives, and a plumber can quite easily be a saint ; but one of the necessary conditions for that is almost sure to be that he should be a good plumber. That, in its turn, is going to depend to a great extent on his being a happy plumber! How many times we have seen people who were gloomy and irritable, fed up with everything—including their religion—simply because they were not happy and contented in their employment. Work is a necessary condition of human life after the Fall, and it is necessary for both material and spiritual happiness, and ultimately for our eternal salvation —but that does not mean to say that man should not attempt to find some type of work which he can do well and without too much complaint. To condemn a man whose whole inclination is towards farming, for example, to sit all day at an office desk is worse in many ways than the old-time sentence to the galleys.

Now, obviously, it is impossible for everyone to make his work and his hobby coincide, so to speak; but I do think that we can approach a good deal nearer to that ideal than we have done in the past, especially if we are careful to retain the right attitude to the whole problem. The knowledge of your responsibilities as parents, and the fact that the first choice of employment is very often a decisive one for the future wellbeing of your children, will make you think seriously about this matter of a suitable career for them from all angles, without rushing into a decision.

There are several factors which have to be taken into consideration. In the first place, there are the natural talents and dispositions of the child, which can give us a lead in determining which kind of job will suit him best. This is especially true if we can combine these natural inclinations with the school studies, so that the children gradually acquire the knowledge necessary as a background for that particular job. Nowadays this is made much easier for us than it ever was before and we should be prepared to take advantage of that fact. Have a talk with the school teachers about this aspect of the problem, because they should be able to give you some idea at least of the kind of employment for which your child is best suited, and they may be able to help you in the remote preparation for that career.

Nowadays we have another and a very important factor to take into consideration, namely, the question of military service. At the moment it seems to be a necessary evil, but it still remains an evil for all that, because, although it only lasts for a relatively short period, it does come at a most important stage in the adolescent's life, and forms, as it were, a complete break. However, it need not be completely useless from many points of view. Physically it can be a very good thing, because it implies a regular life with plenty of exercise and discipline, which never did anyone any harm. From the moral and the religious points of view things are not so satisfactory, but even there, provided your education has been carried through on the right lines, no real harm need result. Indeed, through coming into contact with all types the youth can acquire much valuable experience and a stability which would normally take a much longer time to develop as part of his character. There is also a possibility of continuing during military training the learning of a trade which will be useful in ordinary life—the Forces do their best to provide for that as far as it is possible. There will be time for reading and for study which need not be wasted. If you, as the parents, take care over such things and point out their importance, also helping the youth to make his plans before the period of military service begins, there is no reason why you should fear any evil development from that more than from any other type of employment.

Once you have decided between you what particular employment will suit your child best then you should bend all your efforts towards preparing him for that career as efficiently as possible. In your particular family circumstances you may think that there is very little you can do and that what is most urgently needed is that he or she should earn wages in order to help with the running expenses of the family. Be unselfish about this as far as you can, and realize that your children have to make their way in the world. They don't want dead-end jobs if they can avoid it. Consult your parish priest, because it is possible that he may know of just the very thing you are looking out for. Not infrequently Catholic employers do ask the priests to keep their eyes open for suitable boys and girls, and on some occasions they are even willing to take them on and train them at the same time for quite responsible positions. If all else fails you should at least try to find your children employment with a firm which has a good reputation for treating their employees well and also one which will be reasonably free from the danger of bad companions. Remember that the wages he or she earns at the moment are not the all-important factor ; look to the future rather than the present.

Perhaps it may be necessary for him to take a temporary job while he is training for the thing he really wants to do. In that case encourage him as much as possible, because youth is inclined to lose heart, and it is hard to have to go to school again after a day's work. However, a little effort and self-sacrifice now may mean a great deal in the future. The career he has chosen for himself may be one which you do not like for some reason or other. In that case make sure that you are not looking at the whole thing from the merely material point of view. He will be much better off later on in a job in which he is happy and contented than in one which may give him greater financial stability but less happiness.

Now, just a special word or two about your daughters—because although what we have been saying applies to both sexes, still there are special factors which have to be taken into consideration in the case of girls.

Once a girl has decided that she has no religious vocation then you may be reasonably sure that her ambition is the married state with a home and a family of her own. Keep this fact in mind all the time. It is a surprising thing that people will prepare for years for any other career, and yet very little time or effort is ever given to the remote preparation for that great vocation—to be a good Catholic wife and mother. This is not only a pity, but it is also a great mistake on the part of the parents, who are really to blame. Here are one or two guiding principles which you might think over very carefully.

It is quite true that most girls have to work for some years before they get married, and all too often they are allowed to drift into jobs which are bad for their future in some way or another, either because of the type of work, the hours, or the companions they have to mix with. When the time comes for them to get married they are liable to know a great many things which are completely useless, but are unable to cook properly, to sew, run a home or look after children. Often, indeed, such a girl comes to look on marriage as the easiest escape from a life of monotony. Try very hard not to let that happen in the case of your daughters. Few parents fall into this error deliberately, but facts and experience go to show that only too frequently they are liable to allow this situation to develop without any interference on their part.

Once again, look to the future! Your idea should be to prepare your daughters in every way to be good Catholic wives and mothers, while at the same time giving them every chance to meet suitable friends in the right atmosphere. Therefore you should try to persuade her to accept some employment which will be of use to her in the future. Again, personal inclinations and also ability have to be taken into consideration, but far too many girls find themselves in dead-end jobs when a little encouragement from the right quarter would have helped them to do much better. Do not be in too much of a hurry to find her a job once she leaves school nor allow her to rush into one just simply for " something to do." There is nothing quite so disastrous, either for the community or for the girl herself. There are plenty of things you can give her to do at home which will help to train her in the right way and keep her busy while you and she look around for something which will suit her.

The majority of elementary-school girls have about four types of job in mind when they leave school. Their choice is usually limited to shopwork, office work, domestic or factory employment. In all these careers they are very liable to fill the rôle of cheap labour if we are not careful, and most of them are, unfortunately, dead-end jobs from our point of view. The work is often routine and mechanical with little or no sense of personal responsibility attached to it. Factory employment especially tends to make the young girl mentally lazy, since it occupies the hands rather than the brain in most cases. Shopwork, where it can be found, is often more interesting to the girl herself and generally less mentally harmful. Domestic service has its advantages, because it does teach the girl things about a home which she might never learn in any other way ; but it also has certain disadvantages from the point of view of the adolescent, unless the employer is one who really cares for the servants. Many girls dislike domestic service because it brings them into contact with persons outside their own social class, and they feel humiliated by this at times. However unreasonable this feeling may be, it is not one that we can ignore altogether. Also, the free time is usually rather limited in comparison with certain other types of employment. If these two obstacles can be removed by the right mental attitude, then domestic service can be a good thing for a girl, and something which will help her later on in life.

Office work usually demands a higher standard of education, but there are possibilities in this class of employment if the girl is prepared to do a certain amount of study in her spare time, either through evening classes or in some other way.

A very useful job for the right type of girl is the nursing profession ; and it has added advantages today, because not only are nurses in great demand, but also their conditions of work and their wages are sure to be bettered as time goes on. This career is now open to the girl from the elementary school provided she has the requisite mental ability and is willing to work hard. In every way it is a career which will be of great use to her later on in her married life and the openings it provides are many and varied.

School teachers, especially Catholics, are in great demand. This work demands, as nursing does, a real vocation, and on the whole Catholics have not given as much thought to it as a possibility for their daughters as they might have done. Once again, it is a career which has its advantages later on in life.

Girls who have had a secondary-school education usually have a much wider range of choice before them than the others, and in their case there should be no reason why they are unable to find an employment in which they can be really happy and feel a sense of vocation. We have tried to stress this idea that work should always be undertaken with a sense of vocation where possible simply because it is the key to the Christian solution of the mystery of life together with Christ. If we all lived our human lives in this spirit of vocation, then it would be much easier for us to save our souls.

In the case of both boys and girls, what they do with their free time once they leave school and begin to earn their own living in the world is of great importance for their future well-being. We have already mentioned this subject in a general way when we discussed such things as the films, reading and dances. Once the adolescent begins to go to work he feels much more independent than before, and thinks that he can do more or less as he pleases with his free time. You will need all your tact to secure the right attitude on these matters. So many of the youth of today know nothing at all of the finer things of literature, art or music simply because they have not been encouraged to use their leisure hours in cultivating such tastes. This is particularly true of those who grow up in the larger cities. The parents can and should do a great deal to encourage such pursuits, especially by getting the youth interested in the Catholic Youth Movement in all its branches, including such things as clubs, study circles, etc. If a Catholic club is well run—and there is no reason why it should not be—then it will take care of a great deal of these leisure moments, and it will do so in a way which is pleasant. It will give the youth new and varied interests, friends, and also opportunities to learn things about art, literature and music which he would probably never have had the courage to tackle on his own. Good taste in these things helps to prevent the mind from being flooded with a mass of shoddy and useless material which will only serve to drag the mind down to the level of the senses. Material poverty does not prevent anyone from enjoying the better things of the mind.

Certain types of reading matter can be a great danger to these adolescents, because instead of the mind (which is now capable of excellent work) being trained in the good things of life, it can easily acquire the habit of wasting time in useless trivialities, if they are not worse than that! The trashy novel and the sentimental magazines which so many of our adolescents delight in reading give them a distorted picture of life which tends to standardize things at a relatively low level. There is nothing in such stories which can make any appeal to that great idealism of youth of which we have already spoken and which matters so much for their future. They acquire the habits of speech and action of these heroes and heroines about whom they read—and pretty poor stuff it is, too. Such stories only provide an unsatisfactory escape for young people from the drab monotony of their surroundings. Do try to educate your children's reading from an early age, and see to it that they get opportunities to read good literature which will satisfy their minds much more than any amount of trash.

With the girls the mother can have a great influence by giving them their basic training in such things as cooking, sewing, housekeeping in general, and the care of children. In this connection it is useful for you to know that the Young Christian Workers' movement has a " marriage training service " which is doing really fine work in educating Catholic youth to a sense of responsibility in marriage both from the spiritual and the material aspects. There are two kinds of service provided; the " immediate marriage service " for those who are already engaged or are over 20 years of age, and the " distant marriage service " for younger people between the ages of 17 and 20. If you get in touch with your local Y.C.W. organization you will soon be provided with all the information you need about these services and the courses. There is no doubt that they are very useful indeed. There are lectures on the spiritual, cultural, social and medical aspects of marriage, together with courses in such practical things as budgeting and the setting up of a home, hygiene in the home, child welfare, cookery, dressmaking, etc. In fact, if you can interest your children in these courses a good deal of the responsibility for their training will be taken off your shoulders.*

Now, this does not mean that you have no responsibility at all, because your position as parents gives you special graces to fulfil your obligations. It has been proved time and time again that no amount of training outside the home will have much effect if your example and watchful guidance are missing. During these later years of adolescence you have one special task, namely,

---

* The Y.C.W. girls' organization has a Head Office at 62 Offley Road, London, S.W.9, and from that address, information and literature can be obtained.

to see to it that you do all you can to secure a suitable partner in marriage for your children. The main emphasis here must be on the question of religion ; and your advice and your attitude to this question may easily have a decisive effect on your children's future.

You should put before them quite clearly those arguments against mixed marriages which have already been mentioned in one of the earlier chapters of this work, so that they can see quite clearly the great advantages of choosing a Catholic partner. The Church puts before us an ideal in marriage which may be difficult to attain but which is by no means impossible, given good will, namely, a marriage in which the partners are Catholics and are united by the Sacrament of Matrimony for life, not only physically, but also morally, intellectually and in their relationship with God. This religious unity is all-important if marriage is to be an influential factor in our eternal salvation. People do not get married in the same way that they choose a bridge partner ; nor is marriage a debating society. On the contrary, for Catholics, marriage is a means towards the salvation of our souls. The husband or wife who is not intensely interested in the spiritual welfare of the other partner has no real conception of those high ideals which Christ puts before all married people. In every one of its aspects this is a great and a wonderful vocation ; and for this reason the girl should ask herself if this boy is going to be a good husband and father to their children—one who will be interested in their home life together, and one with whom it will be relatively easy to reach eternal salvation. The boy should seek a good Catholic girl who will be a help to him spiritually as well as materially, and a good wife and mother.

You will have to keep these great ideals before the minds of your children so that, as time goes on, their own intimate convictions with regard to them will be strengthened, and they will see marriage for what it is—a most important step in their journey towards eternal salvation.

Do not be afraid to point out in detail the many disadvantages of mixed marriages—disadvantages which are undoubtedly felt by the non-Catholic party just as much as by the Catholic. The fact that sometimes these mixed marriages turn out quite well does not argue against the other undoubted fact, that, in the vast majority of cases, there are very many grave difficulties which do not exist in Catholic marriages. The difference in Faith makes itself felt in a lack of unity over the most essential thing in any marriage, and it affects not merely the attitude of the partners but also, later on, the whole religious life of the children. Nothing has such a great effect as the good example of the parents, and naturally, if the children have to accompany the Catholic partner to church while the other partner either goes elsewhere or stays at home, then this example will lose much of its force. Normal topics of conversation between two Catholics have to be either avoided altogether or at least dealt with very gently so as not to give offence or to stir up arguments. Then there are those delicate moral questions on which Catholics have unshakable principles, and in which they differ very much from most non-Catholics. There is the question of the children's education in their religion—only too often the non-Catholic will promise before marriage that all the children will be brought up Catholics, and then afterwards regrets that decision and tries to go back on it. For all these reasons, and for others which need not be mentioned here, Pope Pius XI did not hesitate to say : " . . . it is unlikely that the Catholic party will not suffer some detriment from such a marriage. Whence it comes about, not unfrequently, as experience shows, that deplorable defections from religion occur among the offspring, or at least a headlong descent into that religious indifference which is closely allied to impiety. . . . Assuredly, also, will there be wanting that close union of spirit which as it is the sign and the mark of the Church of Christ, so also should be the sign of Christian wedlock, its glory and adornment. For, where there exists diversity of mind, truth and feeling, the bond of union of mind and heart is wont to be broken, or at least weakened. From this comes the danger lest the love of man and wife grow cold and the peace and happiness of family life, resting as it does on the union of hearts, be destroyed."*

The day will come when your son or daughter becomes engaged to be married, and then you will have a great deal to do in immediate preparation for the wedding, and not very much time to do it in. In the hustle and flurry some of the most important

* Pope Pius XI, Encyclical on *Christian Marriage*, C.T.S. pp. 40-41.

things may easily be overlooked.   But first of all a word or two
about engagements.   In general this is a time when those who
are about to be married get to know each other even better
than they did before.   It is, in many cases, the deciding factor in
the future marriage.   Now, there are two extremes to be avoided.
Long engagements are useless things and only serve to bring
many dangers to both parties, because the waiting seems
interminable, both are liable to get bored with it and perhaps take
liberties with the moral law which they would never have thought
of doing otherwise.   Do not allow your children to become
engaged if there is no immediate prospect of marriage ;   advise
them to wait, and explain to them the reasons for this.   They
will understand your point of view and will see the wisdom of
it if you are sympathetic and understanding.

On the other hand, the very short engagement of two or three
weeks is worse than useless, because then the whole purpose of
this period, i.e., the increase in the knowledge of one another's
character, is frustrated.   Do not allow what some young people
call " unofficial " engagements, because they are liable to drag
on for years, and, as experience has shown, they have no real
meaning.

There is very little which need be said about the material
preparations for the wedding.   It might be useful to point out
that it is stupid to spend a great deal of money on a wedding
when it might have been put to better use in helping to set up
the married couple in their new home.   More important than
these material preparations, however, is the intellectual and the
spiritual preparation.   Now is the time for you to give to your
children all that immediate instruction they need in order to
be fully prepared for married life.   Do not think that they know
all there is to be known ;   because there are a great many things
which can only be learnt by experience, and a word from you
now on such matters will make all the difference.

Mention has already been made in the earlier chapters of
this book of the pre-marriage medical examination of both
parties, if possible, by a Catholic doctor.   This will prove to be
a very useful thing, especially if you prepare your children for
it by telling them that this is their chance to find out from a
medical source all those things they wish to know about marriage,

and which they may be afraid to bring up in ordinary conversation with you. They should tell the doctor the object of their visit, and he will then know just what to look for and what advice to give.

Sometimes you may be asked to recommend books on married life to your children. Remember that they should be Catholic books, and you will find a selection of such literature in any Catholic bookshop. To help you, some titles will be included at the end of this chapter. In any case, the book should not be allowed to take the place of your own personal advice and also that of the Catholic doctor.

The most important element in this immediate preparation for marriage has still to be mentioned, i.e., the spiritual preparation.

Marriage is a great Sacrament, expressing as it does the union which exists between Christ and His Church. Consequently, it requires a special spiritual preparation, in order to draw from it those great graces which are going to be so necessary for a good Catholic life as a husband and wife, a father and a mother. It is one of those Sacraments which we call "Sacraments of the living," which means that it must be received in a state of grace. Therefore the very minimum of preparation should be Confession and Holy Communion. It is a good thing to receive this Holy Communion at the Nuptial Mass itself, if possible ; but if that Mass should take place too late for the two parties to remain fasting then they should go to Communion together at an earlier Mass on the same morning.

It should not be too much to ask the future husband and wife to make a short retreat before their marriage. There are many convents which have retreats for three days, usually at week-ends, so this should be easy to arrange. That will give them both three days to think carefully over what they are about to do, to pray about it and to make the necessary resolutions which can secure them a happy and united married life together. The Psalmist says that unless the Lord build the house they labour in vain who build it, and this is particularly true of marriage.

Nor should it be necessary to remind Catholics of their great privilege of the Nuptial Mass ; yet it is not unknown for Catholics to be married without that Mass. This is a great pity, because a little effort could secure for them that great blessing of having their union sanctified by the Sacrifice of Calvary, the Source of all graces. During that Mass the Church calls down a special benediction on those who have just been married, praying for their material and spiritual prosperity, and she does so as the Bride of Christ, reminding Him all the time of the intimate union which exists between Him and Her, and asking Him to bless this Catholic Marriage because of it. There is no need for me to mention to the parents the fact that they should join their prayers with those of the Church for the happiness and the salvation of their children.

Suggested Book List

Happiness in Marriage, by a Priest and a Doctor. (Sands and Co. 3/6).

The Catholic Home, by Fr. Aloysius, O.F.M.Cap. (Mercier Press, Cork. 6/-).

Love, Marriage and Chastity, by Rev. Fr. E. Mersch, S.J. (Sheed and Ward. 2/6).

Wedlock, by Fr. C. C. Martindale, S.J. (Sheed and Ward. 3/-).

The following C.T.S. pamphlets will also be found very useful :

Marriage, by Mrs. Wilfrid Ward (No. Do.88).

The Holiness of Married Life, by Archbishop Godfrey (No. Do.207).

Courtship for Girls, and Practical Instructions for those about to be Married (No. S.129).

Training for Marriage, a book for Catholic parents (No. S.134).

The Pope Speaks to Mothers (No. S.168).

Preparing our Daughters for Life, by a Catholic Mother (No. S.165).

The Marriage Service and the Nuptial Mass (D.290).

CHAPTER TWENTY-TWO

THE FINISHED PRODUCT

ONCE YOUR SONS AND DAUGHTERS ARE MARRIED YOU MAY feel inclined to think that your work as parents has come to an end; and yet in your hearts you know that this is not so, because you will still be interested in them as your children and there is still a great deal you can do to help them.

The first few months of married life, especially when combined with the idealism of youth, may easily give rise to many problems to which you hold the key. Marriage, as you know from your own experience, implies a way of life which is very different from that of a single person in the world or even from that of a member of a family. On top of this there are the natural difficulties which come when two people who have been used to a certain degree of freedom and independence begin to live together. There will be no need for us to examine all these difficulties individually here ; it is hoped to do that in a later book in this series. We are concerned more with the difficulties in which your advice, as parents, will be particularly useful.

A girl may very easily feel a sense of loneliness during the first few months of married life ; her husband is away at his work all day and she feels that there is very little for her to do compared with the old days before she married. This may easily develop into slackness about her home duties or at least a search for distractions outside the home. Your visits during this period will help her to develop a sense of proportion. Remember that you can give good advice but that you must not be too critical or attempt to force on her your own private opinions as to the running of her home. Leave her free and yet guide her at the same time. There is nothing worse than the " music-hall mother-in-law " and you do not want to develop into anything like that, nor is there any reason why you should do so. Remember that yours is essentially a watching brief. They must make their own home, and all you can do is to be sympathetic in their difficulties and give them the advantage of your experience when your advice is sought.

A father can be of great use to his son in these early months of married life, again by giving quiet, sympathetic advice when it is needed, and especially by being a good listener! Let him talk his problems out with you and give him the benefit of your experience. Help him to understand his wife's difficulties and temperament as you have understood yours. Remember that he still has a great deal to learn and that he is sure to make some mistakes.

Do not be selfish, either of you. Christ said about marriage, " for this reason shall a man leave father and mother . . ." and that is very true. Often parents feel that, in some ways, they have lost their sons and daughters once they get married and that things are not as they were before between them. However natural this feeling may be it should be carefully concealed, because it has its root in jealousy. If you give way to it you will only succeed in estranging them from you still more. Once they are married they are out to establish their own life together on a firm basis and so you must expect them to be a little absorbed in that task and sometimes almost forgetful of their parents. If you have brought them up in the right way this will soon pass after a few months and then you will realize that, although things are not quite the same between you as they were before, still it is true to say that their love for you has not changed. If anything, it will have deepened and matured. That is, after all, the end and the purpose of your education of these children—to enable them to stand on their own feet and not to have need of others in every decision they have to make. All great tasks are achieved at the cost of some sacrifice, and this is yours.

Do not interfere in their domestic affairs too much, and above all, never take sides in their little domestic quarrels. There are nearly always two sides to every question in marriage, and your idea should be to bring about peace rather than to further the sense of strain and strife. Marriage, for a Catholic at least, is for life, and the only way that intimate unity can be effectively safeguarded is by a certain amount of give and take on both sides. You can do a great deal to preserve this unity, especially by warning them both in time if you see anything which is liable to lead to serious trouble.

Remember that you still have one very serious obligation with regard to your children—the duty of praying always for them. They will need very many graces if they are to fulfil their obligations in a fitting manner, and those graces may very easily be conditioned on your prayers.

When they have children of their own then you will see the perfect results of your own training, because they will know, almost by instinct, through their own memories, what to do and what to avoid in order to bring them up properly. Again, your advice will be of great help to them here, and you will soon see that, far from being out of the picture, you are a very real factor for good in their lives still. This is a great blessing and a consolation which God sends you in return for all your loyal efforts.

If you have done all you can to educate your children along Catholic lines, then you can be quite sure that you have fulfilled your obligations as parents and that your reward will be very great in heaven. Look at the finished product of your labours for a moment. Once they have left your hands these children should be children no longer, but adults, with a well-formed character of their own. They will know and love their Faith because they have learnt it in the best of all schools—that of your example. You have taught them good habits of prayer and of regularity in their religious duties. They have a definite standard of what is right and what is wrong, together with those moral habits which are necessary in order to live up to that standard. You have also given them the best material education which your financial circumstances allowed and even their present good health and strength is, in a large measure, due to your care of them. In every way you should be able to look with pride and joy on a task well done, and that will be your greatest consolation. There will be difficulties perhaps, and imperfections, but you have done your best. God, who sees the hearts of men, will reward your efforts.

INDEX

Adolescence: father's influence during, 114; sex instruction should be given before the advent of, 136, 140; general description of, 169; new sensations during, 170; physical changes during, 171; uncertainty the basic characteristic of, 171-2; general education during, 172; physical education during, 178sq. ; mental education during, 191sq.; influence of reading during, 200-1; friends during, 203-6.; longing for independence, 206; religious education during, 209 sq.; special problems of, 224; dangers of day dreaming, 235; religious indifference, 241-5; vocational guidance during, 249sq. *Cf.* Authority, Parents *and* Masturbation.

Anger: in infancy, 45-7; in parents, 50, 96; as sign of jealousy, 68; never punish in anger, 73.

Art: help in development of adolescents, 260; as hobby, 184.

Apologetics: for adolescents, 213-6.

Authority : use of by parents, 36 ; right attitude in those who have authority important, 47-8; unnecessary or useless commands tend to lessen it in children, 51, 71; use of in maintaining discipline, 79, 109; place of authority in early school years, 112; adolescent attitude towards, 175-6, 199; authority of the Church explained to the adolescent, 213-4; use of in breaking up unsuitable friendships during adolescence, 205. *Cf.* Parents.

Awkwardness: in adolescence, 190. *Cf.* Clumsiness.

Baptism: 20.

Bed time: for younger children, 55; for adolescents, 179.

Bed wetting: avoided by good habits acquired in childhood, 53-4 ; as a manifestation of fear in older children, its causes and remedies, 84-6:

Blemishes: skin, 189.

Blessing: of mother before child birth, 20; of children by parents, 58.

Blood condition: in adolescence, 189.

Books: influence on the growing child, 154, 183; on the life of Christ, 223; on sex instruction, 158; on married life and courtship, 266; danger of in adolescence, 182, 260-1. *Cf.* Reading.

Boys: serving on Sanctuary, 127; different approach to the sex problem, 135, 144; methods of sex instruction for, 148sq. ; approach to affection, 154: physical changes in adolescence, 171; question on difference between them and girls needs attention, 144. *Cf.* Father *and* Adolescence.

Career: choice of, 249sq. ; parents' attitude towards, 254-5; preparation for, 256-7 ; for girls, 258-60. *Cf.* Vocation.

Character: of parents, 12; instability of during adolescence, 169-70; observation necessary to determine its main outlines in adolescents, 173; exercise in the development of, 182-4; elements which influence its development in adolescence, 199sq.

Chilblains: in adolescence, 189.

Child: needs parental affection, 35; religious education of, 37-42, 58; has no real problems, 63; inhibiting factors in development of, 64; position in the family group, 67-9, 105; reasons for fear in, 81, 84-91; backward, 108; in pre-school years, 92sq. ; his social development, 97; reactions to school, 102; education during early school years, 104sq.; the only child, 105-6; ideals during childhood, 109; motives in education of, 109-10; friends, 111; his prayers, 118sq. *Cf.* Motives *and* Education.

Church: visits to, 126, 129. *Cf.* Authority.

Churching: 22.